GENDER MATTERS

GENDER MATTERS
CIVIL WAR, RECONSTRUCTION, AND THE MAKING OF THE NEW SOUTH

By LeeAnn Whites

First published in 2005 by
PALGRAVE MACMILLAN™
175 Fifth Avenue, New York, N.Y. 10010 and
Houndmills, Basingstoke, Hampshire, England RG21 6XS
Companies and representatives throughout the world.

PALGRAVE MACMILLAN is the global academic imprint of the Palgrave Macmillan division of St. Martin's Press, LLC and of Palgrave Macmillan Ltd. Macmillan® is a registered trademark in the United States, United Kingdom and other countries. Palgrave is a registered trademark in the European Union and other countries.

ISBN 1–4039–6311–8
ISBN 1–4039–6312–6

Library of Congress Cataloging-in-Publication Data

Whites, LeeAnn
    Gender matters : Civil War, Reconstruction, and the making of the new South / LeeAnn Whites.
        p. cm.
    Includes bibliographical references and index.
    ISBN 1–4039–6311–8 (alk. paper)—ISBN 1–4039–6312–6 (pbk.)
    1. Southern States—History—19th century. 2. Southern States—Social conditions—19th century. 3. Sex role—Southern States—History—19th century. 4. Women—Southern States—History—19th century. 5. United States—History—Civil War, 1861–1865—Women. 6. United States—History—Civil War, 1861–1865—Social aspects. 7. Reconstruction (U.S. history, 1865–1877). 8. Felton, Rebecca Latimer, 1835–1930. 9. Georgia—Politics and government—1865–1950. 10. Georgia—Social conditions—19th century. I. Title.

F215.W545 2005
975'.03—dc22   2004043152

A catalogue record for this book is available from the British Library.

Design by Newgen Imaging Systems (P) Ltd., Chennai, India.

First edition: May 2005

10 9 8 7 6 5 4 3 2 1

Printed in the United States of America.

For Sarah

CONTENTS

INTRODUCTION

The central proposition of this historical work is that gender matters. Gender matters in the lives of individuals. We experience our lives filtered through the lens of gender norms and gender roles. We understand ourselves as gendered beings. Gender matters in our relations to others—whether in our personal or public lives, as mothers, fathers, workers, or employers—and structures our place in relation to others. It provides one lens through which we experience, interpret, appreciate, and judge the nature, the character, and the meaning of our relations to others. While gender matters most obviously in relations between men and women, and many would in fact argue that relations between men and women create gender itself, it is a proposition of this study that gender matters as much across the racial and class lines of the social order as it does between men and women of the same race and class. Altogether, gender matters in the myriad ways that it constructs individual's sense of themselves and their place in the social order; in the way that it serves as one frame of social relations across the social landscape, from the most personal and intimate relations of the family to the most public and anonymous relations of the workplace or urban life. Gender matters in the way that society develops, is experienced, is transformed by individuals and groups acting out of their gendered identity, and social relations based on that identity.[1]

The location in time and place of this historical work is the nineteenth century. The nineteenth century was, for the country as a whole, a period of astonishing social transformation along virtually every axis of prior social ordering, as the rural became urban, the subsistence economy became market based, and the relatively independent male-headed household became the dependent and yet "separate" sphere of the family. In the South, this transformation of a traditional to a modern social order was experienced in a particularly extreme and wrenching fashion. Many would argue that it was so wrenching and so extreme that the South never made it to "modern" in the nineteenth century. There was, in the first place, the extremity of slavery, extreme in its existence and extreme in its abolition. There was the wrenching fashion in which slavery as a social form, and the South as the politically and economically dominant region, was taken down in the violence of war, both the formal war of 1861–1865, and the long and grinding economic and social war in the decades that followed. These three factors: slavery, war, and the poverty and violence of the "reconstruction" of the late-nineteenth-century South have largely absorbed the energies of nineteenth-century southern historians. In the face of the particularly deep scars of race, region, and class on the experience of southern modernization, gender has, at times, appeared not to matter much. It certainly hasn't mattered much in the "mainstream" telling of southern history, as any brief encounter with the indexes of surveys of southern history for the period will confirm.

It is, however, precisely because gender has apparently mattered so little in the nineteenth-century South that it does matter so much. While the nineteenth-century South was marked by the visibility of race, it was also formed by the very invisibility not only of gender, but of class as well. Gender, race, and class are, of course, not the same kinds of things—that is, while they are all constituent parts of the social order, they are also different in their formation, nature, and social implications. In discussing the question of the extreme visibility of race in the nineteenth-century South, Barbara Fields has suggested that despite its critical centrality in the nineteenth-century South, and in the nation as a whole, race itself did not actually exist. By this assertion, Fields means to suggest that there is no biological, that is, no "real" material basis for race. Race, according to Fields, was essentially in the eye of the beholder. Class on the other hand, one's relationship to the means of production, is "real." Race, according to Fields, cannot therefore carry the weight that many historians of the nineteenth-century South have attributed to it. This does not mean that race is not important, but rather that it is the very visibility of race that needs to be problematized, alongside the relative invisibility of class. Here, I take a leaf from Field's work. Like the overvisibility of race, the undervisibility of gender as a factor that matters in the telling of "mainstream" southern history needs to be problematized. We need to ask why gender has entered the historiography as some minor tributary read largely by, for, and about women. We need to question the usually unstated assumption that gender does not really matter in the larger processes of development of the southern social order—particularly as it was arguably the very invisibility of gender at the time that made its greatest contribution to the way the South developed during the period.[2]

One of the most important ways that historians of gender have attempted to make the invisible visible as a historical category of analysis that plays an important role in the construction of the social order is through the method of intersectionality. Much like Field's juxtapositioning of race and class, historians have attempted to make apparent the role of gender in historical development by discussing its relationship to other already visible, or relatively more visible, categories of social analysis. Fields does this through her discussion of the relationship between the visibility of race and the relative invisibility of class. Indeed, the very hypervisibility of race itself came at the expense of seeing class. We as historians, but perhaps more importantly, historical subjects at the time, have seen race, when we should at times more appropriately have seen class. For example, white southern sharecroppers in the late nineteenth century rarely saw in a black sharecropper another cropper like themselves. Too often, perhaps most often, the white sharecropper saw only race difference rather than seeing a person situated in similar fashion to themselves in class terms. Indeed, those moments when the white sharecropper saw another cropper—that is, recognized class—those were the moments of powerful social transformation, when events were moving so hard and so fast that they even overrode the "ideological," as Fields terms the hypervisibility of race. In nineteenth-century southern history, the decade of the 1890s was one such historical period when the visibility of class competed with race for the cultural and political center stage. The Civil War represents yet another break in the southern social order of such force that significant sectors of the white yeomanry came to see the war as a "rich man's war and a poor man's fight," and to view the newly freedman, not simply as a raced person, but also as a fellow Republican, an ally in what, for the moment, they experienced as a class conflict.[3]

If the problem in seeing class in the nineteenth-century South was that it was so overlaid by race, the problem with seeing gender was that it was so overlaid by both race and class. In the recent literature of intersectionality, this has at times become the reason why gender does not matter. A by now classic example of this "why not" approach to gender as a social category that matters would be the work of Elizabeth Fox-Genovese, in her pathbreaking work, *Within the Plantation Household*. Fox-Genovese suggests in this history of the antebellum South that precisely because gender was so overlaid by both race and class in the slaveholding household, only those women who were the most class and race privileged could hope to exercise it. Following this logic, enslaved men and women, who were rendered property rather than women or men, at least by the dominant social forms, were in no position to exercise their gendered interests. And even women of the planter class themselves, who did have the protection of familial and marital rights, were more inclined to act through their class and race interests, which secured those rights to them, than to identify across the social structural abyss that slavery created and see gender in the circumstances of an enslaved person. Indeed, Fox-Genovese suggests that in their position as the weak members of their race and class, planter-class women were even more committed to privileging their class and their race position in relation to their slaves or their yeoman neighbors, than planter-class men were themselves.[4]

If the white yeoman was rarely able to "see" class as a larger social factor in the workings of the nineteenth-century South, in no small part because his very lack of class position inclined him to see race instead, the class and raced privileged woman was arguably even less likely to be able to "see" gender, or so Fox-Genovese suggests. Why see the world through a lens that disempowers you? The problem with this approach is that we, the historians, at times appear to be caught in the vision of our historical subjects, caught, as Barbara Fields has suggested, at the ideological level of the vision of the individual. While planter-class women may have privileged their class or race position in the southern social order and may have stood stalwartly by as their men's first "lieutenants," as Fox-Genovese terms them, that still does not mean that gender did not matter in the manner in which southern society developed and southern history unfolded. In such historical circumstances of hyperinvisibility, we need to think even harder about the systematic construction of social categories, particularly across the lines of other constituent social factors such as race or class—rather than capitulating to the apparent invisibility of gender to particular individuals at the time.

So what would it mean to look at the nineteenth-century social order in systemic gender terms rather than weigh the significance of the ideological, as in this case of the elitism of planter-class women, as just one more sterile end to one more sad story? Perhaps David Roediger's work, *The Wages of Whiteness*, has most successfully negotiated this question for the nineteenth-century white working class. Rather than continuing to view race as the historical actors themselves saw it and thereby writing the history of the nineteenth-century white working class as the sterile end of yet another sad southern story, Roediger takes a step back onto the location of the system, to the level of the social order itself, as raced. This allows him to see white as well as black as a race, and the tragedy of southern history not only in the way that whites saw blacks, but also in the way that white people saw, or perhaps were unable to see, themselves. Roediger's key point here seems to be that while the burden of race, or for that matter, the burden of gender, may have fallen disproportionately upon the nondominant, those on the dominant side of the relationship, the wealthy, the white, and the male, were also defined by their participation in them, both as systemic social categories, as well as individual burdens to bear and to somehow negotiate and perhaps even overcome.[5]

Some historians of southern gender relations have taken a similar approach to articulating the role of gender identity and gender relations as a constituent player in the larger social order by expanding their understanding of gender to include men as well as women. By doing this, they have destabilized the relationship between gender as a constituent part of the larger social order and the individual experience of it at the time. By recognizing that just as all people are raced and classed, so too are they also gendered, they emancipate gender from the nineteenth-century understanding of women as "the" sex and open it to having a larger social and systemic significance. By locating men as gendered beings in the social order, they render gender a relational and not simply an individual experience. A good example of the contribution that this social structural approach can make to furthering our understanding of how gender mattered in the nineteenth-century South is Stephanie McCurry's work, *Masters of Small Worlds*, which considers how the secessionist politics of the white yeoman of the antebellum South Carolina Low Country were in fact grounded in gender relations and in male gender identity. By demonstrating how gender mattered to the white yeoman's very ability to establish and sustain his position as a free man in the larger social order of the low country, McCurry is able to offer a new answer to the question of why the yeomanry would ally with the planters to the extent that they did in the sectional crisis. While the yeomen may not have had the "rich man's slaves" to fight for, that is the privilege of slave ownership, they did have household dependents—their women and children—whose relationship to them secured their position as free men as surely as slave dependents undergirded the position of the planter. They were, indeed, masters, if only of the "small world" of familial dependents and, according to McCurry, they were willing to line up alongside the planters in the secession crisis to preserve what they saw as their common stake in the race and gender hierarchies of the southern household order.[6]

What was previously invisible when gender was understood as an individual matter that defined and limited women, suddenly matters when we open it to men, to a relational, material, and thus to a social structural approach. The nineteenth-century South is a very hard nut to crack when it comes to showing that gender mattered in the causality of historical events. This is precisely because, as Fox-Genovese has so powerfully argued, slavery literally turned some women into the owners of other women, and so rendered their common position as women null. Without some larger relational power, as in women as a social group that transcends other social categories, gender then becomes the private, class and race bounded identity that Fox-Genovese presents it as. Those historians who have moved on from this point to consider the role of men as gendered, are able to see how gender matters in the way important historical events unfold not only because gender interests are now located in the hands of those who hold formal political power, but more importantly, because they are able to invest gender with a constituent presence in the social order. Because it has again become a relational category, it can be shown as an active force in making history. Gender, defined as a relationship between men and their dependent women, mattered in the nineteenth-century South, even as the system of slaveholding fractured the possibility of a common relationship based on gender between women across race and class lines.[7]

If gender mattered in southern secession because it provided a basis for the alliance between planters and yeomen despite their class differences, it mattered even more in the conduct and outcome of the Civil War itself. Perhaps no single event in the nineteenth century so disrupted the normal functioning of the social order, so destabilized relations between classes, races, and genders than the Civil War. It quite literally turned the household inside out, as first the white men went to war to defend secession, but were shortly followed by their former household dependents, either in defense of their master's world, or in pursuit of turning the war toward the end of their own empowerment as free men and women. In doing so, the Civil War opened the door to the visibility of gender as a socially constructed and socially constructing part of the social order. Indeed, if gender mattered in secession, it became critical in the Civil War that emerged as a result. For what we see in secession, in the retreat to what Michael Johnson has termed a "patriarchal republic," is the way gender matters to dominant groups, in particular to yeomen, who may be class oppressed, but are gender dominant. But gender, like race or class, has transformative power in the social order when wielded by those who are nondominant in gendered terms. After all, dominant groups rarely choose to dislodge their own dominance, planters and yeomen left the Union in hopes of preserving theirs. And so, while the white men of the South led the movement out of the Union, in the name of preserving their location in the social order, the Civil War itself, in turning the household inside out, offered all the dependents the opportunity, even the necessity, of social structural visibility.[8]

Here, then, is where this work begins. Because the household was the core organizational structure of race, gender, and class relations in the nineteenth century, the Civil War, by turning the household inside out, laid bare to public view and public significance the role of gender in the social order. The first chapter of this book, "The Civil War as a Crisis in Gender," discusses the sectional crisis and the war that followed as quite literally a war of divided households, a war in which the particular form of gender relations in southern households was as much at issue and intertwined with the rise of sectional politics, as was race. In the essays that follow, I further discuss how gender mattered in the conduct and outcome of the war itself. Here I focus to a great extent on the experience of St. Louis and the state of Missouri, as border areas, where the divided nature of the population intensified the divisions between and amongst households, creating conditions of guerilla warfare, and thereby generating the most extreme experience of turning households inside out, as men not only left for war, leaving women to become the heads of their households, "men," for the duration, which both sides experienced, but also turned the household, and the household dependents, into active agents of war themselves. In "Strong Hearts and Strong Minds," I discuss how gender mattered in what became an intragender war, as loyal women organized as men, into political leagues, but did so in order to fight a domestic war that only they, as women, could fight. In "Home Guards and Home Traitors," I discuss the way gender mattered in the sexual practices of soldiers as the Union army struggled to maintain the reputation of the Union occupying forces as the true "Home Guard" while disarming the southern elites of their respectable reputation in the city and rendering them visible instead as "Home Traitors."

As much as the war destabilized the structure of the household based gender order, rendering gender visible, the reconstruction of the household in the war's aftermath was grounded in its return to invisibility. While women of "strong minds" continued to agitate for the visible role the war had given women, the politics of "strong hearts" won the day, as gender was written into the U.S. Constitution for the first time in the effort to assure the permanent reversal of the war-born racial transformation of the southern household order. The last two essays in this section consider the role of the hyperinvisibility of gender relations in the reconstruction of the southern social order. In "Stand by Your Man," I consider how the politics of strong hearts, so publicly visible during the war, could be rendered so invisible in the war's aftermath. In "You Can't Change History By Moving a Rock," I discuss how this politics of invisibility, pioneered by organizations like the Ladies Memorial Associations and the United Daughters of the Confederacy (UDC) in the war's aftermath, was finally dissolved in the civil rights era through the twentieth-century politics of the Women's Liberation and Black Power Movements.

While the first half of this book considers how gender mattered in the Civil War and Reconstruction, the second half of the book begins by considering how gender mattered in the industrialization of the postwar South. As with the Civil War, industrialization threatened to undermine the gender and racial hierarchies of the southern household order, this time on a more lasting basis, as industrialization threatened to invert the household order permanently, potentially empowering women to be like men, blacks to be like whites, and reducing white men to being like blacks or women in the process. In this destabilized terrain, in this effort to construct a New South, gender mattered a great deal. Here, I trace out the continuing legacy of the Civil War and Reconstruction in the intertwined persistence of racial hierarchies and the intense postwar commitment to female invisibility. As these essays discuss, we can see the continued and intertwined role of this particularly southern brand of invisible gender/hypervisible race politics in the labor struggles and class organization of the textile industry of the postwar South, as well as in the very form and emergence of progressive political reform in the region, particularly in the emergence of a "white only" movement for women's rights.

So why is gender, arguably so omnipresent in the nineteenth-century South, also so invisible? Is it because gender really didn't matter? Or, is it actually because in some ways gender has continued to matter too much; too much as an individually lived experience and too little as a recognized category of social and historical analysis. In the last section of this work, I consider the question of how gender mattered according to one of the late-nineteenth-century South's most prominent advocates of women's rights and racial reaction, Rebecca Latimer Felton, as an illustration of this very point. Considered as an individual alone, Rebecca Latimer Felton was one of the region's most prominent "why nots," that is an elite white woman arguably more intensely committed to the racial hierarchies of the nineteenth-century South than even the men of her own race and class. Why then is Felton useful for those concerned about how gender matters? Because as much as Rebecca Latimer Felton is a big "why not" on the individual level, she is a big "why yes" on the social structural level. Felton, for all her limits, saw gender as a systemic social construct. She saw that men had gender. She recognized intersectionality. She thought that gender mattered in all the pivotal events of nineteenth-century southern history, beginning with the Civil War, which she attributed to the overweening power of planter-class men. Arguably, her very racism was driven by the limited structures through which gender could matter in the making of the New South.

Throughout this collection of essays, some new and some reprinted here, I focus on critical moments in the development of the nineteenth-century southern social order. Through this tour of the antebellum South, the Civil War and Reconstruction, the process of industrialization and progressive reform, I hope to elicit a discussion of what gender's role in the nineteenth-century South "really" was. Since my main concern in these essays is to explore the ways in which gender mattered, I focus on the ways in which gender can be understood to have contributed to major social transformations of the nineteenth-century South. In the process, I explore the usefulness of various methods that I have discussed in this introduction: gender as male, the role of intersectionality, and the larger social and cultural significance of gender's invisibility in the nineteenth-century southern social order. In the end, I conclude that gender matters when it can be emancipated from the level of the ideological and the individual to the larger workings of the social structure, workings which are beyond us all as individuals, but which make up the very core of history and of historical study.

CIVIL WAR AND RECONSTRUCTION: TURNING THE HOUSEHOLD INSIDE OUT

CHAPTER I

THE CIVIL WAR AS A CRISIS IN GENDER

It was a cold winter's day and greenish ice flows clogged the turbulent river. Across its vast expanse, Eliza could see the far shore of Ohio and freedom. Behind her, coming ever closer, she could hear the baying dogs of the slavetrader, Haley. What could she do? On the one side was slavery and the certain loss of her child to the slavetrader. On the other was an impassable river and probable death. Looking down at her small son, Eliza only knew that she could not bear to lose him. And with one desperate burst of courage, she jumped onto the nearest ice flow. Scrambling and leaping from one teetering piece of ice to another, she struggled across the mighty Ohio and gained the far shore of freedom for herself and her child.

Laying down the collection of antislavery tracts she was reading, Harriet Beecher Stowe was deeply moved. In Eliza's desperate act of undaunted mother love, Stowe heard an almost irresistible call to action.[1] She would tell the world Eliza's story, for herein lay the true sin of slavery—the way in which it thwarted and repressed the maternal bond, separating mother and child, brother and sister, husband and wife, eroding the emotional fabric of the black family in the name of the vested property rights of white slaveowners. The emergence of the family as a separate sphere in the North, freed from the sordid economic concerns of men, had constituted the domestic realm of the mother as a sphere in its own right, allowing her older sister, Catharine Beecher, to claim a new and boldly autonomous role for women as the moral arbiters of social life.[2] Now Harriet Beecher Stowe would shine this newly emancipated light of the family and of the moral mother as the spokesperson of its interests upon what increasingly appeared to be a domestically retrograde southern slave system.[3]

The rest is history. *Uncle Tom's Cabin*, the novel that Harriet Beecher Stowe wrote as if driven to it, swept the nation by storm to become the most popular novel of the entire century.[4] Its claim for the domestic rights of slaves popularized the antislavery cause in the North in a manner that no abstract calls to the inherent equality of all mankind had ever succeeded in doing in the past. As Abraham Lincoln commented upon first meeting Harriet Beecher Stowe in the midst of the Civil War, "So you are the little woman who wrote the book that made this great war."[5]

If, however, popular antislavery sentiment in the North, and the war that followed from it, was grounded upon a new understanding of the domestic rights of the family, and in particular in the expansion of the private and public authority of the mother as the bearer and rearer of life, then we must ask, what did this war of domestic liberation mean for women of the South? How are we to understand the widespread support for the war among Confederate women, support for a war of southern independence that was understood by at least some of their northern sisters to be nothing less than the defense of the independence of Confederate men from the dictates of reproduction and the moral authority of motherhood? An independence that so subordinated the interests of reproduction and the family as a whole to the particular economic and productive interests of the individual planter that it gave him the right not only to own the child of some woman's heart and body but also to dispose of it as his material interests would dictate.

While the readership of *Uncle Tom's Cabin* in the South was not as widespread as in the North, those who did read it were undoubtedly at least equally consumed by the critique of the southern slave household structure that it presented. Mary Boykin Chesnut, daughter of a prominent planter-class family and wife of a member of Jefferson Davis's staff, was haunted by the novel and returned to it time and again in her Civil War diary.[6] She took particular umbrage at Stowe's claim for the moral superiority of northern women. "What self-denial," queried Chesnut, did northerners like Stowe practice while sitting in their "nice New England homes—clean, clear, sweet smelling?" She contrasted this picture of the northern household, pristine in its isolation, with the experience of her female relations, living in households enmeshed in the institution of slavery.[7] These women of the planter elite were, according to Chesnut, educated in the same northern schools as their abolitionist critics. They read the same Bible and had the "same ideas of right and wrong," yet they were not so fortunate as to be safely ensconced in a separate familiar sphere dedicated to the domestic interests of their families alone. Instead, they lived in "negro villages" where they struggled to "ameliorate the condition of these Africans in every particular."

> They set them the example of a perfect life—a life of utter self-abnegation . . . Think of these holy New Englanders, forced to have a negro village walk through their houses whenever they saw fit . . . [these women] have a swarm of blacks about them as children under their care—not as Mrs. Stowe paints them, but the hard, unpleasant, unromantic, undeveloped savage Africans. And they hate slavery worse than Mrs. Stowe.[8]

Here the ultimate figure of domestic self-sacrifice and thus *the* "true woman" was not those abolitionist spokeswomen for the "cult of domesticity" and the family as a separate sphere, but rather the planter-class woman, who precisely *because* of the presence of slavery within the southern household was placed in a position to act as the mother of not only her own children but of her slave dependents as well. Of course, in Harriet Beecher's account, the most militant defender of motherhood was not in fact the northern abolitionist woman like herself, who risked only her good reputation in taking a public stance against slavery. Domesticity at its most insurgent was represented by those slave mothers, like Eliza, who in the very act of mothering their children could be called upon to subvert the institution of slavery itself. Chesnut's defense of the motherhood of the plantation mistress, on the other hand, spoke from within the confines of the institution of slavery. For it was the very same slave system that worked to deny Eliza her motherhood that gave Chesnut the basis for claiming it as the slave mistresses' own. Ownership in slaves not only made the planters the wealthiest men in the country through their appropriation of the productive labor of their slaves, but it also served to make their women into "ladies" by virtue of their own ability not only to "mother" their slaves but also more fundamentally to appropriate their domestic labor. It was this ownership in slaves that empowered the white mistress, like Mary Boykin Chesnut, to define the slave woman not as a mother in her own right but as one of the many "children" under her own maternal care.[9]

As slavery was an organic part of the southern household, it became organic to the slaveowners' very conception of themselves as men and as women, as mothers and as fathers. It both served to expand their own domestic claims as *individual* mothers and fathers, while it served to subordinate, literally to enslave, the sphere of reproduction and of domestic life as a whole to the class interests of this same planter elite. Ultimately the extent to which motherhood was rendered unfree within the southern slave system served to undermine the domestic position of even those women of the planter class who benefited from it most in class terms. For whatever power they gained for their own domestic position by having slave dependents, they lost by the manner in which slaveownership further empowered their own men. So while women of the planter class could claim to "mother" their slaves, at least some of their husbands were literally fathers of slaves. The outcome, concluded Chesnut, was often far more devastating than even Harriet Beecher Stowe envisioned. She recorded the conversation among one group of elite Confederate women. ". . . I knew the dissolute half of Legree well," asserted one of these women,

> He was high and mighty. But the kindest creature to his slaves—and the unfortunate results of his bad ways were not sold, had not to jump over ice blocks. They were kept in full view and provided for handsomely in his will. His wife and daughters in the might of their purity and innocence are supposed never to dream of what is as plain before their eyes as the sunlight, and they play their parts of unsuspecting angels to the letter.[10]

"Southern women," wrote Ella Gertrude Clanton Thomas, in her antebellum journal, "are I believe all at heart abolitionists."[11] When she made this claim, she in fact meant that all women of her class and race were abolitionists. Had she actually meant to refer to all southern women, her case would have been a stronger one. For, to the extent that planter-class women were abolitionists, it was not in the first instance the consequence of their recognition of a common likeness among all women. It reflected instead their desire to be full-fledged members of their class, empowered like their men to dictate the cultural norms of their society.[12] Planter-class women burned, admittedly in private or in the company of other women, at the power that the ownership of slaves gave their men to create a double standard of sexual behavior within the planter class itself. As Rebecca Latimer Felton, a Georgia planter-class woman, wrote in her memoirs many years after the war, for the "abuses" that made "mulattoes as common as blackberries," the planters deserved to have their entire system collapse.

> In this one particular slavery doomed itself. When white men put their own offspring in the kitchen and the cornfield and allowed them to be sold into bondage as slaves and degraded them as another man's slave, the retribution of wrath was hanging over this country and the South paid penance in four years of bloody war.[13]

Hindsight is twenty–twenty, but where was this voice for the larger interests of southern motherhood in 1860? Jumping across ice flows? Not, certainly, coming from the likes of Rebecca Felton, who asserted in her memoirs that upon the outbreak of the Civil War, a war that she perceived to be a "battle to defend our rights in ownership of African slaves," there was "never a more loyal woman" than herself. "I could not," she wrote, "fight against my kindred." Besides, she concluded, she was "only a woman and nobody asked me for opinion."[14] The political voice of domesticity was silenced even among these most powerful of southern women, if only by the force of their own class interests. For at bottom was the undeniable fact that the slave plantation economy promoted their own material well-being. Therefore, no matter how frustrated they may have been in their own efforts to claim an enlarged sphere of authority in relation to the men of their class, they could not ignore the benefits that their own position as members of this class, however subordinated, gave them. If only out of their concern for their own children, women of the planter class were forced to recognize that the same planter who "defied the marriage law of the state by keeping up two households on the same plantation," as Rebecca Latimer Felton wrote, was also, as Mary Chesnut concluded, "the fountain from whom all blessings flow."[15]

In the face of mounting domestic criticism from the North, planter-class men and women, however, entered into an increasingly uneasy bargain.[16] Take for instance the courtship of Caroline Davis and Joseph Jones. In the spring of 1859, Caroline Davis made it clear in her correspondence with her suitor that marriage would in her estimation cost her her freedom as an individual, with which she was loathe to part. Joseph Jones replied by pointing to the benefits that her dependent position within his household would confer upon her. "Will the possession of a friend who will be your protector and defender when all friends and relatives fail, involve the loss of freedom?" he queried.[17] In exchange for her subordination, he promised that he would use his position to promote her own interests more effectively than she could ever hope to do in her own right. Caroline Davis did in fact accept Joseph Jones's suit, but while grudgingly relinquishing her own autonomy, she informed him that she would now be even more ambitious than ever for his success in life because, "*we poor women* have no name or existence of *our own*, we pass *silently* down the stream of time without leaving a single trace behind—we die unknown."[18] She would accept her subordinate status, but she would also expect him to maintain and enlarge his power to "protect and defend" her through his individual achievements in life.

The mid-nineteenth-century South presents the picture of a society teetering on the edge of a critical racial and gender imbalance, pushed to the brink by changes in the sectional social and economic structure. The incredible demand generated for cotton by the industrial revolution taking place in Britain and in the North made cotton the king of plantation staple crops and made the planter king as well—a king empowered by the profitability of this crop to buy the reproductive capacity of ever larger numbers of slave women as well as to turn the domestic voice of the women of his own class to his own self-empowerment. Almost perversely, however, the very same industrial revolution, which served to fuel the expansion of the patriarchal power of southern planter-class men, also created the basis for the emergence of the family as a separate sphere in the North. Therefore while reproduction remained enslaved within the plantation household economy and the voice of domestic politics was muted, it burst forth with equally dazzling clarity in the North.[19] Northern feminist and abolitionist women formed organizations and petitioned for fundamental changes within households and in the society at large. Some of these women even claimed the right to demand a single sexual standard of behavior from their men.[20]

While the emergence of a domestic critique of slavery served to popularize the cause of abolitionism in the North by sidestepping the unpopular issue of racial equality, it only served to enflame white southern men by simultaneously attacking their right to own slaves while threatening to empower their wives and daughters. The North intended nothing less than to "subjugate the South," as one southern newspaper editor wrote, "to a yoke more intolerable than the bondage of the African." It was therefore, he concluded, the duty of every liberty-loving man to "close the ranks, stand shoulder to shoulder as brothers animated by one pure, patriotic impulse . . . to fight this fight out, come what may . . . and never submit to the domination of a fanatic, puritan horde of agrarians, abolitionists and free lovers, while there is a dollar or a man among us."[21] After all, concluded one planter upon the outbreak of the war, "The fight had to come. We are men, not women."[22] For many southern men, as Bertram Wyatt-Brown has written, the Civil War constituted a "simple test of their manhood."[23]

Southern advocates for secession could actually argue that northern abolitionism threatened southern white men with "a yoke more intolerable than the bondage of the African," with no recognition of the irony of the statement, because they truly did not see their "African" slaves as having manhood to lose. Slavery constructed the white man as *the* head of the household, and in the process as the *only* legitimately independent, that is to say, "free," member of southern society. Just as it robbed the black woman of her motherhood, so it robbed the black man of his fatherhood.

So, as much as the Civil War constituted a test of white southern men's willingness to fight and die to protect their "manhood," it also presented a much more fundamental challenge to enslaved black men. For as much as white southern men saw in northern abolitionist criticism a fundamental threat to the extent of their patriarchal prerogatives, for their slaves, the war opened up the possibility that they might be able to acquire the material basis for manhood in their own right. They might hope to gain the position of heads of their own economically independent households—the widely rumored outcome of Union victory among the enslaved population—forty acres and a mule for every black family. On that basis they could look forward to the day when they would be equally empowered with white southern men to protect and support their families, to become "fathers" and "husbands" in their own right.[24]

The stakes were high. The conflict was fundamental. Either the black man in his capacity as slave to the white man would go on making his master a *man*, or the white man would lose his slaves and with them his concept of himself as a free man, while the black man achieved his own manhood. The possibility that the black man might be empowered like any other was such a threat to the southern social hierarchy that some white southerners were inclined to fear not only for their position as slaveowners but for the entire basis for their claim to patriarchal power. They feared for their power not only over their slaves but over their women as well. As one white southern minister painted the likely outcome of emancipation:

> Then every negro in South Carolina and every other southern state will be his own master; nay, more than that, will be the equal of you. If you are tame enough to submit, abolitionist preachers will be at hand to consummate the marriage of your daughters to black husbands.[25]

Ever since the outbreak of the Civil War, Americans have been arguing over its causes, but rarely has the conflict been discussed as a crisis in gender relations.[26] There were, however, two groups of Americans at the time who saw its gendered face clearly. One was northern feminists such as Harriet Beecher Stowe, and the other was black Americans, especially black American men. As Frederick Douglass argued before northern audiences as early as 1858:

> The "vital question" at stake in the great sectional crisis is not whether slavery shall be extended or limited, whether the South shall bear rule or not ... but ... whether the four million now held in bondage are *men* [emphasis added] and entitled to the rights and liberties of men.[27]

Of course, as Frederick Douglass was painfully aware, it was not just black slaves who were denied the "rights and liberties of men." Even in the antebellum North, black men, although free in the sense of owning their own labor, were denied the political and economic prerogatives that created the basis for the antebellum social construction of manhood. Economically discriminated against, northern black men were rarely in a position to employ themselves, to therefore be the heads of economically independent households. Politically, they were frequently denied the vote, and they were *universally* denied membership in state militias and in the regular military. So, the Civil War not only constituted a test of the southern black slaves' manhood, but it was also widely perceived by the northern black community as a test and an opportunity for the establishment of their own manhood as well. As one Philadelphia schoolteacher organizing black recruits told his audience:

> We have been denounced as cowards. Rise up and cast off the foul stigma. Shame on him who would hold back at the call of his country. Go with the view that you will return *free men*. And if you should never return, you will die with the satisfaction of knowing that you have struck a blow for freedom, and assisted in giving liberty to our race in the land of our birth.[28]

Surely, leaders of the northern black community reasoned, if the black man was to stand by the Union in this critical juncture, if he was to offer up his life for the well-being of the nation, surely he could no longer be denied full membership in society? Frederick Douglass was convinced that the war offered the black man a rare opportunity to establish himself as truly free. He believed that a rebirth of the nation was finally at hand. Out of the destruction of the war would emerge a new nation and the glory of its founding would be shared this time by *all* the fathers, and the inheritance would be enjoyed by *all* the sons.[29]

Upon secession and the outbreak of war, northern black men did seize their opportunity. They formed themselves into militia units and began to drill regularly. They petitioned their state governments to have the legislation removed that banned their active participation in the military. Their efforts on the drill fields were met by white mobs yelling: "We want you damned niggers to keep out of this; this is a white man's war." And according to the common northern perception of the war, the contest *was* a "white man's war."[30] It was a struggle between competing white men's visions of manhood, there was no room for the black man. Even in the face of northern military defeats and a critical shortage of Union manpower, the North refused to relent and allow black men to serve until late in 1862. They insisted, as Douglass put it, in "fighting with one arm tied behind their back." As he wrote:

> Our President, Governor, Generals and Secretaries are calling, with almost frantic vehemence, for men—Men, men! Send us men they scream, or the cause of the Union is gone . . . and yet these very officers . . . steadily and persistently refuse to receive that very class of men which have a deeper interest in the defeat and humiliation of the rebels than all other. . . . Why does the government reject the negro? Is he not a man? Can he not wield a sword, fire a gun, march and countermarch like any other?[31]

Of course, Douglass knew the answer to these questions. To take black men into the conflict was to acknowledge their manhood. The northern black community knew it and this is why they demanded the right to serve. The northern white community knew it as well, which is why they militantly claimed that it was a "white man's war." Ultimately northern white society was forced to choose—between recognizing their common manhood with black men or losing their own status as free men to the continued domination of white southern manhood, of the "slavepower," as they put it.[32] Finally, Lincoln issued the preliminary Emancipation Proclamation in September of 1862. The Union War Department declared all slaves within captured Union territory freed and opened the door to the formation of black regiments.

The Confederate government responded to this newest challenge to their effort to defend what they saw as their liberties by making it clear that although the North might have decided to treat black men as *men* for the purposes of conducting the war, as far as they were concerned, blacks were all escaped property, and treasonous property to boot. If they were captured in Union uniform, they could receive none of the normal courtesies of war, but would instead be summarily executed.

This was truly a struggle to the death. By recognizing the slaves for their manhood, the Union was empowered with the very lifeblood of the Confederate cause. For here was the *ultimate* test of the southern social order. Would the white men's "dependents" forgo their own emancipation and continue to subordinate themselves to his empowerment? For now the war constituted not only a test of the white man's courage on the battlefield, but also a test of his dependents' loyalty on which this courage was built. If his dependents failed to support him at this critical juncture, his cause was surely lost. The eager enlistment of ex-slaves in the northern military, the huge numbers that flocked behind Union lines whenever the opportunity to do so presented itself, was only the tip of the iceberg in the internal crumbling of the southern planter's world. Slaves who remained on the plantations slowed the work pace, and when the opportunity presented itself, they aided and abetted Union troops, leading them on back roads, supplying them with critical information.[33]

As the fiction of slave servility and childlike dependence upon the patriarchal planter dissolved in the crucible of war, it left only the subordination of southern white women—as the only dependents on whose loyalty the planter could continue to rely. As the racial and class basis for dependence slipped away, gender thus emerged as an ever more critical basis for the persistence of southern white men as "free men." Not surprisingly, Confederate men at the time and for years afterward have written in self-congratulatory tones of the loyalty that their women demonstrated during the conflict.[34] Confederate women, we are repeatedly told, constituted the "very soul of the war," offering up that which they did possess, their domestic attachments to those nearest and dearest to them, for that which they as individuals could never hope to obtain, the liberties of free men.[35] This was the discipline that the patriarchal slave system had reared them up to, to deny the interests of domesticity in the face of the interests of their class. Now, however, the necessity of placing class prerogatives over the interests of domestic life had come to their own families, rather than to those of their slaves. But they did not flinch. At least, not in public.[36]

After explaining at some length the reasons why his enlistment was necessary to defend "liberty and justice" and "true freedom," Joseph Jones closed his letter to his wife by saying, "I know my Dearest that you feel & appreciate all this, as a noble and true woman."[37] Joseph Jones relied on his wife's own sense of honor, the mirror of his own. And she did not, in fact, fail him in her reply, writing, "My beloved you are more to me than everything on earth, but I know & feel what you say is true that life would be valueless under such a rule as these miscreants would force upon us & that honor & feeling & everything else compels you to take part in this struggle."[38]

Some historians have gone so far as to argue that the women of the Confederacy were even more intensely committed to the war than were their men, packing the galleries of secessionist congresses, hissing at the delegates who opposed secession and cheering on its advocates.[39] One Selma belle was reputed to have broken off her engagement when her fiancé failed to enlist. She sent him a skirt and female undergarments with the message, "wear these or volunteer."[40] A letter of one young woman to her local newspaper upon the outbreak of war certainly reflected an intense identification with the cause:

> You will pardon the liberty I have taken to address you, when I tell you that my great inclination to do so assails me so constantly that I can only find relief in writing to you . . . My father and family have always been the strongest of Whigs, and of course not in favor of immediate secession; but as that has been the irrevocable act of the South I submit to it, and say "as goes Georgia, so go I." But at the same time I am conscious that that very

act has increased our responsibilities tenfold. We have outwardly assumed
the garb of independence and now let us walk in the path our state has
chosen. And shall man tread it alone? . . . no, no a thousand times no.[41]

Urging other Confederate women to join her in the cause, she suggested
that they "hurl the destructive novel in the fire and turn our poodles out of
doors, and convert our pianos into spinning wheels." Not only would this
return to home manufacturing make a critical contribution to their male
relation's pursuit of political autonomy, the drive for political independence would make Confederate women more independent as well. As she
concluded, "I feel a new life within me, and my ambition aims at nothing
higher than to become an ingenious, economical, industrious housekeeper,
and an independent southern woman."[42]

The demands of the war effort offered Confederate women a rare
opportunity. Through their contributions to the cause, they could enter
into the heart of the struggle and like their men define themselves as
"independent" southern women. Women who were independent because
their privatized domestic pursuits were now thrust onto the center stage
of southern life were not in violation of their subordinated domestic
status.[43] Confederate women in their role as mothers found themselves in
a particularly critical position. It was after all their children who were the
very stuff of the war machine. If men, especially young men, were to participate in the war effort, women, especially their mothers, would have to
acquiesce in their departure. As one newspaper noted, "The man who does
not love his mother and yield to her influence is not the right stuff to make
a patriot of, and has no business in a patriot army."[44]

With such influence came a newfound responsibility for southern
women. Letters in southern papers therefore urged women to consider
the long-range impact the war might have on their sons. "Let them not, in
future years . . . be forced in sadness of heart and reproaches of conscience, to say that in all this they took no part." Mothers should, according to this writer, consider with what "humiliation" sons would be forced
to recognize that they were "unworthy of the liberty and home secured for
them by the valor of others."[45] Motherhood should exert a public and
political presence.

Not only did the war serve to intensify the centrality of reproduction in
southern society, it also gave public, political significance to the domestic
manufacturing of women. For not only did the war demand the contribution of women's reproductive product, their children, but critical economic problems now revolved around essentially domestic questions of
how the troops were to be clothed, fed, and nursed. Cotton proved to be
virtually useless in this regard as it could not be eaten, made poor shoes,
coats, and blankets, and could hardly be shot. Local newspapers urged
planters to turn their production toward subsistence crops instead and
promoted the public organization of women into local Ladies Aid
Societies dedicated to organizing their previously privatized labor in order
to more efficiently clothe, feed, and nurse the troops.

From the perspective of Confederate women, patriotism took on a peculiarly domestic cast. After offering up their children, patriotism constituted a continued, and in fact, an intensified commitment to the domestic labors women normally carried out for them.[46] Upon receipt of uniforms from the Augusta Association in June of 1861, the Confederate Light Guards indicated that such sentiments were understood and reciprocated. "Nothing can be more cheering to the soldier's heart," wrote Sergeant Ells of the Corps, "than news from 'the loved ones at home,' but when the news comes accompanied by such substantial tokens of regard for him and his welfare . . . as have so recently reached the members of this corps from the ladies of Augusta, our duties are indeed lightened and our hearts made brave to battle for the firesides of our noble countrywomen."[47]

While Confederate men may have gone to war in defense of what they perceived to be their prerogatives as free men and in rejection of the threatened domination of a "horde of agrarians, abolitionists and free lovers,"[48] the actual demands of fighting the war made them increasingly conscious of their own dependence upon women's love and labor. As a result the southern soldier had to recognize, if only unconsciously, the extent to which his manhood and independence was relational—a social construction built upon the foundation of women's service and love, out of the fabric of his women's "dependence." For the more the war called forth women's domestic labor into the public arena, making public those "small gifts of service," the more the war itself was transformed from a struggle of men in defense of their individual prerogatives into a battle for the "firesides of our noble countrywomen." Confederate women seized this opportunity to lay claim to an increased reciprocity in gender relations. As one woman wrote to the newspaper, ". . . do impress upon the soldiers, that they are constantly in our thoughts, that we are *working* for them, while they are *fighting* for us—and that their wants shall be supplied, as long as there is a *woman* or a *dollar* in the 'southern Confederacy.' "[49]

Confederate women found that the war might support a newly independent stature on their part. As Rebecca Latimer Felton wrote, "Nobody chided me then as unwomanly, when I went into a crowd and waited on suffering men. No one said I was unladylike to climb into cattle cars and box cars to feed those who could not feed themselves."[50] Nor did the press find Amy Clark to be "unwomanly" when it was discovered that not only had she enlisted with her husband, but after he was killed she fought on alone in the ranks as a common soldier. She was described as "heroic *and* self-sacrificing" (emphasis added).[51] But then as Sarah Morgan recorded in her diary upon hiding a pistol and a carving knife on her person in order to defend herself against the invading Union soldiers in Baton Rouge, "Pshaw! There are *no* women here! We are *all* men."[52]

As their women became more independent and, hence, more "male," Confederate men increasingly had to recognize their own dependence upon women, whether in managing their households in their absence, outfitting them in the field, or nursing them when wounded. Such men, in fact, became increasingly feminized. The male world of the camps was enough in and of itself to make many men think longingly of their lost domestic comforts. As Will Deloney wrote home to his wife, "Don't imagine that I have forgotten you—for I think of nobody else—and if you could see the discomfort my life held now you would conclude I could never forget. . . ."[53] Deloney had lost his mess and was forced to scramble for meals as best he could until he could get new gear. As he described his situation to his wife, "Here I am away from all I love sleeping on the wet ground, my horse poor, nothing to do, nobody to see, nothing to eat and not a pot to cook it in . . . I smoke my pipe and think of home and try to bear it as best I may."[54]

William Deloney was shot from his horse while leading a cavalry charge in the fall of 1863. He died a hero to the cause, but he was lost to his family. He left his wife, Rosa, with four young children to carry on as best she might. In a letter written shortly after his death, a cousin urged Rosa to "take care of yourself for your dear children. Who can fill a *Mother's* place?"[55] Who indeed? Here was the expansion of the domestic autonomy of planter-class women with a vengeance, as impoverished widows.[56] For those Confederate men like Frank Coker, who were so fortunate as to survive the war and return to their homes, being a father and a husband was also at once more and less than it was before the war. For despite his wife's clever management and hard efforts at retrenchment during the war, the Cokers' finances were in great disarray.[57] The economy was devastated, their section was defeated, and their slaves were emancipated. Frank Coker was no longer the same "lord of creation" that he once was; no longer a veritable "fountain from whom all blessings flow."

The Cokers' economic loss was mirrored in their slaves' domestic gain. For the ultimate *structural* rebalancing of southern domestic relations began when the southern household was sheared apart with the emancipation of the slaves. As the freedmen departed en masse from the households of their ex-masters in search of members of their own families lost to them under slavery, they moved toward a new domestic integrity for *all* southern families. They established themselves as heads of their own households, fathers and husbands in their own right. As freedwomen turned their labor toward the needs of their own kin, withdrawing from the kitchens and the fields of the master class insofar as they were able, they laid claim to a common status with their white counterparts as wives and mothers.[58] In so doing they began to carve out what might have become a common ground for a future unity among southern women.

At the time, however, this newfound integrity of the southern family structure and the increased gender commonality of all women that it portended presented itself to planter-class women not as a victory for their gender interests but rather as the defeat of their men and of their class. For if the war served to intensify Confederate women's commitment to their men's class interests, their defeat served to set that commitment in concrete. "It was as though," in the words of one southern newspaper editor, "the mighty oak" was "hit by lightning" and only the "clinging vine" now kept it erect.[59] Planter-class women urged their men to take solace in their own family circle, a family circle that should be more valued for that which had been lost. "Your wives and children are around you," wrote one woman, "sharing your sorrows as well as your joys. Though you may not have as many luxuries as in former days, you still have enough to eat and wear and can repose in security."[60]

A retreat to familial life could make the sting of defeat more palatable, but it could not erase the necessity of subordination for defeated Confederate men. The "proud Southron" wrote one planter-class woman, Susan Cornwall, must now learn to "obey those laws which neither you nor yours had any hand in framing and those men who you fought four long years to be free from."[61] It was defeat at the hands of other men that would finally force these men to adopt a worldview more like that of their dependents. For as both slaves and women of the planter class had recognized before the war, the way to accept such subordination to another man's will and yet retain some sense of self-respect was to acknowledge a master above the master—to believe that subordination on this earth was but a prelude to some ultimate self-realization in another. "Teach us Oh, Father," wrote Cornwall, "those lessons of patience and resignation which hitherto we have refused to learn and grant that once more we may lift our hearts to thee and cry *Our* father."[62]

Years later, the presiding minister at the funeral of one Confederate veteran, John Francis Shaffner, indicated the role that such religious faith could take on in the war's aftermath. He noted that it was in the daily trials of his postwar life that veterans like Shaffner had discovered the true warfare, by comparison with which the "great civil struggle was but as child's play." Though defeated, John Shaffner did not enter this deeper struggle unarmed, for he found solace in his family and "in faith" where "he committed himself to the mercy of his Savior." Through his faith Shaffner was able to achieve "a higher and blessed victory" than he could hope to attain in his daily life as a vanquished Confederate. Whatever trials worldly existence offered, "God," the mourners were reminded by the minister, had "no provision for an Appomattox." "That is not his plan. There shall be, God tells us, only victory, blessed, happy victory, ahead for all who are faithful."[63]

This lesson of victory in defeat—the proper place and power of the virtuous sufferers—was the lesson that Harriet Beecher Stowe meant to convey in the closing scene of her novel, through the story of Uncle Tom's fateful struggle with his rapacious owner, Simon Legree. For Harriet Beecher Stowe, Simon Legree represented the potentially devastating consequences of a male domination untempered by a recognition of the domestic claims of either his own family or that of his slaves. Running away to sea as a young man and abandoning his poor mother to die of a broken heart, Legree had eventually ended up in the South. There he acquired a plantation and many slaves, but never a home and a loving wife. Living in domestic squalor, he sexually exploited his female slaves while he worked all his field hands to exhaustion. Uncle Tom in fact sacrificed his own life to protect one of the slave women on the plantation from Legree's sexual abuse.

In the character of Uncle Tom, Harriet Beecher Stowe presented what she considered to be the highest exemplar of moral social behavior among men; men who, motivated by a keen sense of their own humility, turned their energies to upholding the human rights of those who were even more subordinated in the world than themselves. From this feminized vantage point, the defeat of the Confederacy and the economic difficulties of the region that followed upon it were perhaps not an unmitigated loss. The possibility of some gain ensued from the expanded significance and integrity that domestic life achieved. By sacrificing his own life, Uncle Tom had succeeded in forcing Simon Legree to recognize some limits to his power to dominate others. For although Legree won the battle and killed Uncle Tom, he was forced to acknowledge that he had lost the war for his soul. Through the moral power of his ultimate sacrifice, Tom found a better home, one in which he would be freed from the defeats and oppression he had endured in this world. "I'm right in the door," he gasped with his final breath, "I've got the victory."[64]

For one brief moment in the course of the war itself, as advancing Union forces intensified the erosion of slavery that was already occurring from within, it had appeared that the defeat of the Confederate war effort would underwrite the earthly victory of the enslaved southern black population. The land would be redistributed and freedmen would acquire their forty acres and a mule and thereby their status as "free men" as it had been constructed in the antebellum social order. At the same time, it appeared that the subordinated status of motherhood would also be at least mitigated as the abolition of slavery promised to ratify the increased public status and significance that domestic concerns had gained during the war. The collapse of the slave plantation household in war and reconstruction did indeed fundamentally limit the extent to which some men could define their own status as free men by the measure of the limits of freedom on others. It did set certain structural limits to the subordination of reproduction and the family to the interests of the market. Families could no longer be bought or sold. It did not, however, create the basis for racial or gender equality in this country. For although the planter class was defeated, it was not vanquished. They lost their ownership in slaves, but not their control of the land. As a result, the war left white southern men feeling like less than men. It left black men with a manhood that frequently continued to cost them their lives. It left white southern women clinging to what was left of white southern men's ability to provide, and, all too often, it left black southern women with no alternative but to work in some white woman's kitchen. All men were not created equal and few women found themselves even comparatively free.

CHAPTER 2

STRONG MINDS AND STRONG HEARTS: THE LADIES NATIONAL LEAGUE AND THE CIVIL WAR AS AN INTRAGENDER WAR

By the spring of 1863, the prospects for Union victory were looking dim. On the military front, the Union had experienced a string of depressing defeats. It was, however, the "fire in the rear," the rising levels of disaffection and ever more active disloyalty among the northern citizenry that Lincoln most feared would bring down the Union war effort. In his 1858 campaign for the Illinois senate seat, Lincoln had correctly predicted that a nation half slave and half free, a "house divided" could not stand. No one could have predicted, however, the ferocity of the war that ensued over how, in what way, with what consequences the nation would be purged of slavery. In the South, the abolition of slavery threatened the very foundation of the most powerful households of the region, but Lincoln's issuance of the Emancipation Proclamation in the fall of 1863 also tested the depth of northern households' commitment to the liberties of free men. Would they continue to send their men to fight and die now that defeating the southern slavepower—the overweening power of slaveowners—meant that their slaves would be rendered free?[1]

Fortunately for the ultimate success of the northern war effort, the rising levels of disaffection and even disloyalty in the North in the second year of the war were matched by equally militant and rising levels of loyalty. As early as the summer of 1862, formally organized Loyal Leagues were formed in the Midwest. Dedicated to rallying loyal sentiment and to actively countering disloyalty there, these organizations were positioned to grow rapidly, and in the fall of 1862, they spread throughout the mid-Atlantic states, and in March of 1863, a national organizational meeting was held in Cooper Hall in New York City. At this mass meeting to form what would become the National Loyal League, the first speaker, James T. Brady, opened his speech before the assembled crowd with the critical question, "How is this thing to end?" In the face of calls for ever more northern men to serve, ever more horrendous casualty rates, ever more radical social policy to cut out the root of the rebellion, how would the war ever be brought to a successful close? Brady singled out two groups of men that he identified as being the most responsible for the mounting war weariness and disaffection among northern citizens. The first group, southern sympathizers in the North, especially powerfully placed southern sympathizing men in the Democratic Party, could have come as no surprise to his audience. It was, after all, the organized political threat of the Democratic Party in the North, particularly their ability to consolidate ever-increasing support based on opposition to the Emancipation Proclamation, that Lincoln had most in mind when he referred to the "fire in the rear." It was, however, the other "group of men" that Brady singled out that would have surprised his audience that night, if only because this group of men was actually not literally composed of men at all, but were rather, "the women of this country."[2]

Organized, public political loyalty to the state, like the military contest on the field to defend it, was on the face of it a male activity. Women might applaud men's speeches in state houses from the galleries or organize critical support for particular candidates or policies at their dinner tables or soirees, but it was men who held formal political power, who ran for office, who ran party journals, and who held the right to vote. In the antebellum order of things, women had the properly private and domestic power of "influence" over the men of their household, while their men, especially the male heads of their households, held the direct and formal political power. Brady, however, proposed that northern women were directly responsible as individual citizens for the crisis of political loyalty that the National League was organizing to defeat. As Brady noted, "If the women of the North had manifested that interest which the women of the South have, thousands more men would have been stimulated to take their position in the field." According to the National Loyal League, while the rising anti-abolitionist sentiment of southern sympathizing northern men was fueling the growing power of the Democratic Party and threatened the possibility of a negotiated peace, the failure of loyal women to match the alleged militancy of southern women threatened an equally devastating disaffection with the draft and demoralization in the ranks. Together these "two groups of men" threatened the North's very ability to put an army in the field and keep it there.[3]

While historians have recently come to attribute more significance to the role of women's influence to the course of formally organized politics in the antebellum period, the crisis in northern loyalty in the spring of 1863, two years into the war and at the belly of the North's fortunes, reveals with particular clarity the ways that gender mattered in the construction of an intensified allegiance to the Union and to the ultimate success of the northern war effort. The National Loyal League called for an unprecedented organization of women into their own political organizations in order to address the crisis in the northern war effort. Women across the North responded to this call forming organizations in the spring of 1863 variously named the Women's Loyal Leagues, Ladies Loyal Leagues or Ladies National Leagues. These Ladies National Leagues played a critical role in bridging the gap between Union military policy necessary to Union victory and flagging popular support for the war. Perhaps best known are the activities of the Women's National League that collected more than 100,000 signatures in support of emancipation on a petition that Charles Sumner presented to the U.S. Congress in the fall of 1864. At least equally significant, however, were the local Ladies Leagues that worked to reinforce the morale of their men in the field and in their communities at home. Together those two approaches to the war served to present a reformed domesticity, as one wing of the women's loyal movement came out in militant public support for cutting slavery out of the structure of the household, while the other turned their energies toward publicly reinforcing the domestic ties that could make it happen, the loyalty of fathers, brothers, and sons to the military defense of the Union war effort.[4]

One way to understand the basis for this unprecedented politicization of women is to consider the ways that the demands of fighting the war had already shifted and altered the relationship between women's private, domestic "influence" in relation to their men and the formal, public and political nature of men's loyalty to their state and their nation by the time of the northern loyalty crisis in the second year of the war. The Civil War was, after all, a war of divided households, a war that pitted the resources of those households against each other, turning them inside out, emptying their human and material resources onto the formal and informal fields of public battle. The unprecedented call for the organization of Ladies National Leagues indicates that in this process of rendering public and political so much of the privatized relations of the household, whether that be making sons and fathers into soldiers or slaves into free men, this war of the household had now also reached to the most privatized depths of the household and demanded that women's very influence itself be formally organized and recognized as a political form. Southern women, as Brady indicated in his National Loyal League speech, experienced this inversion of their households much more immediately and initially than northern women did. From the outset, the Confederate cause was envisioned by some southern women to be a matter bearing directly upon the very structure of their households. Certainly the abolitionists of the North threatened to cut the material flooring, slavery, out from under the world of slaveholding women. Beyond that, the fact that the war was experienced as a war of invasion, was fought on southern soil, meant that Confederate women directly encountered Union troops as they marched through their fields, confiscated their household goods, and certainly by 1863, liberated their slaves.[5]

Although spared the ideological threat or the actual invasion of their households, by 1863 many northern women also saw the war cut to the quick of their households. By that time, northern fathers and sons had given their lives to the cause, mothers and daughters had sent them off and made up for their absence. If only to compensate for the loss from their households, some women took up what were normally considered to be male roles and responsibilities within them, making critical decisions regarding the running of the household, doing actual labor normally the work of absent fathers and sons, or going outside their households altogether in order to earn sufficient wages to support them in their men's absence. By the spring of 1863, many northern women had also felt called upon to contribute to the war effort through their public benevolent work. The initial demands of outfitting the troops, especially the provision of uniforms, caused many women to either expand and reorganize their preexisting antebellum charitable organizations or to form entirely new Soldier's Aid Societies to assist their men in the field.[6]

Unlike their transformation into heads of household, however, the actual activities of these soldiers aid organizations were gender role appropriate, that is sewing, nursing, or feeding the returning troops was work women customarily did for the members of their own households. Even before the war, the public organization of this kind of work for the less fortunate members of the community was not viewed as inappropriate for respectable women. The call, however, for the formation of Ladies Loyal Leagues in the spring of 1863, dedicated to the independent organization of women to explicitly political ends, was arguably gender inappropriate in both role and location. That is, as with their substitution for their men's absence in the household, the National Loyal League proposed that women violate their appropriate gender roles by entering into what was arguably the highest form of directive male behavior, politics. Men were appropriately the heads of their own households as they were the heads of the larger household of the state. In entering the political realm, women essentially proposed to enter politics, to carry their private assumption of the role of head of household into the direction of public affairs. As with their benevolent associations, they proposed to violate their appropriately private location, but now they also proposed to do so in a role inappropriate fashion. They arguably did propose to behave, as Brady indicated, like "men."[7]

Perhaps not surprisingly, Elizabeth Cady Stanton, who had for many years publicly agitated for the rights of women, including the political rights of women, responded a week after Brady and National Loyal Leagues' call for the increased presence of loyal women in the northern war effort. In an address published in the *New York Tribune* on March 30, 1863, and addressed to the "Women of the Republic," Stanton noted that, "when our leading journals, orators and brave men from the battlefield complain that northern women feel no enthusiasm in the war, the time has come for us to speak—to pledge ourselves loyal to freedom and our country." Stanton acknowledged that there was some veracity in the charges that southern women were more devoted to their cause than northern women were. After all, Stanton noted, southern women, "see and feel the horrors of war, the foe is at their firesides." If northern women lacked the enthusiasm for the Union struggle to preserve the liberties of free men, however, Stanton suggested that it was also because the nation's commitment to liberty had never truly included them. Stanton argued that from its very founding the nation was characterized by fatal inconsistency, caught between a theory that proposed liberty for all and an actual political practice that excluded both slaves and women from equal rights. Here, Stanton concluded, was the Achilles heel of the Union war effort. No wonder the commitment to the war effort flagged. Northern women could not be expected to support a war for the rights of free men, when the war was grounded in exactly that, white men's freedoms. Certainly, Stanton concluded, the issuance of the Emancipation Proclamation was a hopeful sign that the northern war effort was finally to be grounded in a more expansive vision of liberty. Loyal women should now support the Union with a renewed conviction as a result, and Stanton called for a national meeting of local Ladies Leagues to consolidate women's newly energized and politicized contribution to the war effort.[8]

More than 1,200 women delegates responded to this call for the formation of a National Women's Loyal League. Meeting in New York City on May 14, 1863, the assembled representatives attempted to determine on what basis their newly formed Local Ladies Leagues might join together as a national organization. They were united in their conviction that northern women had a critical role to play in staunching the rising tide of war weariness. As Elizabeth Cady Stanton put it in her opening speech, "to exalt the purpose for which our grand army now bleeds and dies" was the reason for their having assembled at all. "Inasmuch as woman, by her common consent, is assigned the moral and religious sphere of action" it was therefore, "ever her duty to urge the national mind up to eternal principles."[9]

While unified in their conviction that the moral influence of women could inspire their men on to victory, some delegates balked at what they saw as the effort on the part of Stanton and Anthony to hitch the moral and domestic contribution of loyal women to the band wagon of antislavery and women's rights. Representatives from the West were particularly outspoken in their opposition to this approach. They opposed qualifying women's support for the war effort with a commitment to other, as they saw it, "extraneous" issues. "We have a great many flourishing Ladies Loyal Leagues throughout the West," one delegate asserted, "and we have kept them sacred from antislavery, Women's Rights, temperance, and everything else, good as they may be. We have kept them for the one purpose of uniting and strengthening the loyal sentiment of the people."[10]

This delegate went on to outline the activities of her own league. Women in her organization stood squarely within the domestic sphere and turned their resources from that location to the war effort. They worked, the delegate pointed out, to retrench household expenses, "so as to increase the government resources to fight the war." They used their domestic influence to "strengthen loyal sentiment of the people at home." Finally, they wrote to the soldiers in the field, indeed they had reached nearly every private in the army from their district. In so doing, they had reached out from their homes to the soldier far from home, serving to "encourage and stimulate" him in a way that only "ladies know how to do."[11]

What emerged at this national meeting then were two apparently opposing visions. Should women stand by their men, their nation, and their "place," as some of the delegates from the Western Leagues insisted, or should they jump the gender tracks, as Stanton proposed, and take up the antislavery standard so tentatively waved in the Emancipation Proclamation, and push it gallantly forward? Was it critical to go to the root of the cause of the war, as the antislavery agitators like Stanton argued, and insist that the war be grounded in a commitment to liberty for all citizens? Or was it important for women to line up behind the northern government and the northern war effort, as the Western delegates suggested, regardless of what policies the government might embrace with regard to women or slaves?

After some sharp infighting, Stanton and Anthony were able to turn the strategy of the Women's National League toward the vision of universal liberty. Taking up the only political right that women possessed at the time, the right to petition, the Women's National League organized a huge drive in the summer of 1863, an effort that culminated in the fall of 1864 with the presentation of a 100,000 signature antislavery petition by Charles Sumner to the U.S. Congress. By striking this blow against slavery, Stanton and Anthony believed that the League also revealed the importance of women's direct political contribution to the war effort. They saw the petition as striking a dual blow, on the one hand going to what they believed was the root of the rebellion, slavery, and on the other hand, politically empowering women in the process of striking it down.[12]

While this twin strategy of emancipating the slaves and empowering northern women, arguably making them both into free "men," was adopted by the Women's National League, it was nonetheless not taken up by all the local organizations of the Ladies National League. This was particularly the case in the border areas where the divided loyalties of the citizenry made the question of political disloyalty a particularly immediate and pressing problem. In fact a consideration of the Women's National League's petition calling for the immediate emancipation of the slaves reveals that while 17,706 signatures in support of the petition came from New York State alone, and more than 40 percent of the total came from New York, Massachusetts, and Illinois, only a scattering, less than 200 signatures, came from the border states of Kentucky and Maryland. Indeed in the case of Missouri, the most contested border state, there was not a single signature.[13]

The lack of signatures from the border areas did not, however, reflect a lack of Ladies National Leagues, but rather the persistence of locals that worked according to their original call as Loyal Leagues, dedicated in the first instance to securing the support of the local population for the Union. While New York state, the home of Stanton and Anthony and the center of the Women's National League strength, certainly had its share of southern sympathizing citizens, the threat of disloyalty there paled before the experience of a slaveholding border state like Missouri, where southern sympathizers were so widespread and powerfully placed at the outbreak of the war that the Union was forced to institute martial law to even minimally contain the disloyal elements of the population. And while the Women's National League certainly made an important contribution to rallying popular sentiment in the North in opposition to slavery, they did so, of necessity, by abandoning the traditional place of women. As the western delegates who opposed the radical politics of Stanton and Anthony pointed out, loyal women already carried out activities vital to the war effort, as women. According to these delegates, only women could reinforce the sacrifice of their men as men on the battlefield. And perhaps even more importantly, only women could effectively counter the poisonously demoralizing impact disloyal women had on otherwise loyal Union men, either at home or while in military service.[14]

Early calls for the formation of a Ladies National League in St. Louis in the spring of 1863 indicate the way this domestic influence of loyal women was called out into the public and political realm as a sort of antidote to the seeds of demoralization cast by southern sympathizing women in the city. In one such call, addressed to "Loyal Women" and published on March 23, 1863 in the leading Republican newspaper, the root of southern sympathizing women's support for the Confederate cause was actually located in the machinations of Satan himself. According to this article, Satan was the original copperhead, introducing treason and rebellion into the world by first corrupting woman. Jefferson Davis, as President of the Confederacy, was only, "imitating the strategy of the arch fiend." Southern sympathizing women had forged yet another "unholy alliance," now with the leadership of the rebellion, all calculated to create a "second fall of man." Southern sympathizing women in St. Louis were simply once again using their power over men to the ends of the Devil. By "lavishing their favors upon the disloyal" and by applauding "rebel assassins as heroes," while denouncing loyal Union men as "murderous hirelings," they worked with all the "blandishments and witcheries" of female beauty to corrupt the loyalty of northern men. Indeed, the "fair Copperheads" of St. Louis and elsewhere were "malignantly striving to bury their poisonous fangs in the heart of the Union."[15]

Fortunately for the Union cause, loyal women held it within their power to counter this satanic influence of disloyal women through the public display of their own domestic loyalties. "The malady," editorial suggested, "shall bring forth its own cure. The loyal women of the North, blowing with fervid enthusiasm of a holy patriotism, must surpass the zeal of their wayward sisters." The impact of this public organization of northern women's domestic loyalty, normally reserved for their husbands, brothers, and sons, would be to "kindle the hearts" of Union soldiers with an "inextinguishable flame of loyalty and courage." While the current organizational efforts of loyal women to clothe and supply the soldiers were admirable in their way, they could not directly address the "syron charms" exercised by Confederate women. "Our army needs less the aid of the industrious needle than it does the incentives to dauntless valor which the applause and benedictions of mother, wives; sisters and lovers furnish."[16]

Other calls urging the formation of a Ladies National League in St. Louis expanded upon the extent of disloyal women's sway over otherwise loyal men of the city. In an article published in April of 1863, the author went so far as to claim that "hundreds and thousands" of young men "have literally been driven into rebellion against the Government . . . by the influence of women and girls." And the impact of these women on men who remained loyal to the Union was even more damaging. Indeed the list of their abusive behavior was almost endless: "the cutting and clamorous detraction, the hissing vituperation, the scandalous vilification, the taunts, the sneers, the sarcasm, the abuse, the railings, the revilings, scoldings, defamings and odious insinuations which Rebel women have let loose. . . ." Perhaps the most heart wrenching was the stories from the front where Union soldiers far from home and their own loyal women were presented with the picture of their gaunt and tired men, valiantly fighting on through every hardship, finally reaching some Union occupied town only to be taunted and humiliated with epithets of "dirty," "lousy," "filthy," and "stinking" from jeering women who lined the streets.[17]

Certainly the loyal women of St. Louis had themselves witnessed this sort of behavior on the part of southern sympathizing women in their own city since the outset of the war. As early as August of 1861, southern sympathizing women had literally lined the streets to spit at the funeral courage of Nathaniel Lyon, the commanding Union General killed at the Battle of Wilson's Creek in the southwestern part of the state. They paraded in front of the prisons holding southern sympathizing men, waving Confederate flags and donning Confederate colors. In February of 1862, as soon as wounded Confederate prisoners arrived in many numbers in St. Louis, they formed nursing contingents, and refusing to assist any Union men, they lavished every favor upon the Confederate wounded. Driven to distraction, the Union military issued order after order in an effort to cut off this sort of behavior on the part of these women in the city, banning the waving of Confederate flags, outlawing, strolling or driving their carriages near the prisons where southern sympathizers were detained, and even, in March of 1862, banning their work as nurses of wounded soldiers altogether.[18]

It was not that these expressions of loyalty to the Confederate cause were not matched by some Union women from the outset of the war in St. Louis. Women loyal to the Union cause organized the Ladies Union Aid Society to assist the wounded from early battles in the state as early as July of 1861. They played a critical role in the activities of the Western Sanitary Commission, which was centered in St. Louis. By the second year of the war, however, these women activists themselves realized that these public activities based on sewing and nursing for the Union soldiers was insufficient to the challenge presented by southern sympathizing women in St. Louis, not to mention Confederate women further to the South. Indeed, the call for the first meeting to organize a Ladies National League in St. Louis in April of 1863 and was itself prominently endorsed by many leading Union women, beginning with the wife of the mayor, and followed by the wives of other Republican politicians, ministers, and professionals.[19]

Some of these women would play a critical role in founding the first women's rights organization in St. Louis after the war and some would even identify strongly with Stanton and Anthony's wing of the postwar movement, however, in the spring of 1863, they not only publicly endorsed the initial call for the Ladies Loyal League, they, unlike Stanton and Anthony and the New York based Women's National League, never took issue with its central focus on disloyalty. For the St. Louis League, the first challenge of membership in the Ladies National League was not so much the opportunity to emancipate women from their status as household dependents by making a critical contribution to the politics of antislavery. To the women of the St. Louis Ladies National League, the more pressing question was how to address a war that presented as a crisis in domestic loyalty itself—an issue that they had been called upon to address and which they themselves felt that women were in a critical position to secure.[20]

Perhaps not surprisingly, the organizers of the Ladies Loyal League downplayed the extent to which the formation of Women's Loyal Leagues was a radical departure for women, that is antithetical to their proper domestic place in the antebellum household order, and emphasized instead the ways in which Loyal League activity was an appropriate extension of the work that women had already taken up in support of the war effort. As one of the League organizers noted, the Ladies Loyal League was like the heart of the war effort, pumping new vitality and organization into the hands, that is the "working" organizations of women, such as the Ladies Union Aid Society. "The heart does not the same work as the hands, eyes or brain; but it does that work whereby hands, eyes and brain are vitalized and invigorated for their functions. So this organization invigorates and vitalizes every loyal association. It is the heart to the whole."[21]

Indeed, the more public and political these women became in fact, the tighter and more intense their domestic rhetoric and focus became in theory. Authors of the initial organizational appeal even went so far as to claim that the Civil War itself was primarily a "social" struggle. From this perspective, the war itself while fought out on the formally organized battlefield, was actually grounded in the battle for the hearts and minds of the citizens at home. Loyalty to the war effort was from these women's perspective the critical lifeblood of the war effort and the battle at home, on the social front was telling. In a war such as the Civil War, "materially waged and sustained by social influences," it was loyal women who naturally carried the necessary weapons to combat it. After all, "to ladies especially belong the forces of social influence, the arbitrament of social usage, fashion, conversation and opinion." In their League pledge, these loyal women now promised to "declaratively" contribute their "social influence" to the war effort. In St. Louis, loyal citizens had certainly already seen the power of this "social influence" when wielded by disloyal women. As one supporter of the league noted, "Why, what has been and is the most pernicious influence in the city and state, but exactly this woman's influence, perverted to the cause of disloyalty and rebellion! It is not the armed brother, but the wayward sister that is hardest to overcome." Now, according to the Loyal League's organizers, northern women needed to fight fire with fire and "declaratively" organize to cut it out. For, ". . . if the community is ever to become thoroughly loyal, it must be by the power of female influence."[22]

While Stanton and Anthony saw in the formation of the Ladies National Leagues the possibility of gaining public recognition for the critical role strong minded women could play in striking down slavery, the root of the rebellion as they saw it, the leadership of the St. Louis League saw in the public organization of women's "social influence," in the recognition of the role of women as "strong hearts," an equally critical key to winning the war for the Union. For these advocates of "strong hearts," the problem they confronted was how they could in fact respond to the calls from loyal men to come out and "declaratively" be counted for the Union war effort, while simultaneously counter charges that the organization was really dedicated to promoting women's rights, a charge that the Women's National League certainly reinforced. Indeed as soon as the St. Louis League was formed the organization confronted widespread charges of this nature. Some citizens undoubtedly opposed the organization because they were genuinely opposed to political organization on the part of women, but as the League counter charged, others opposed the organization because they were in fact southern sympathizers determined to use the specter of women's rights to undermine the potential effectiveness of the organization in promoting the Union war effort in St. Louis.[23]

At root, the critics of the organization did appear to have a point, how could the members of the newly formed Ladies National League take up public political activity, arguably the highest male activity, while simultaneously tying it to the enlargement of women's "social influence," their traditional domestic place? In a tract entitled, "A Few Words on Behalf of the Loyal Women of the United States by One of Themselves," published in May of 1863 by the Loyal Publication Society, an anonymous female author attempted to chart a domestic course between and against competing visions of the appropriate role for northern women in the war. While northern women were currently being held up to southern women and found lacking, the critical contribution that the Ladies National League could make to the war effort was to actually reverse the ground of the discussion itself and to indicate the ways in which Union women's approach to the war was actually the appropriate approach, even as loyal men and some women themselves clamored for a more "radical" action on the part of northern women as the solution to the northern crisis in support for the Union war effort.[24]

The Ladies National League needed, in their own way, to fight their own war, to take on what they envisioned to be the "real" enemy, not, as some northern men imagined, faint hearted northern women or southern sympathizing northern men, nor the institution of slavery as abolitionist women argued, but the rebels themselves, especially rebel women. She did this by focusing on rebel women as the root of the war itself. While noting that it was currently the fashion to attribute the success of the southern military effort to the "courage and energy" of southern women, and to attribute the North's failure to the lack of a "similar zeal" on the part of northern women, she noted that it was a mistake for northern women to try to match the unsexed behavior of rebel women, to meet their gender corrosive fire with an equal and opposite gender corrosive action. The key lay in keeping their focus on the real root of their war, the war as a war of social influence, and to take on the their real enemy, the enemy that only strong-hearted women like themselves could hope to disarm, mean-hearted women, those southern sympathizing and rebel women of the South who were so bedeviling their men.

According to this Loyal National League author, while it was certainly critical that northern women form Ladies National Leagues, it was even more critical that these Leagues should be constructed upon the domestic values of northern women, not upon the distorted values of the women of the South. There certainly was a difference between the women of the North and South but it was not so much about who was most supportive of their men as it was about southern women's ability to loathe their enemies, not so much about loyalty, that is, as about disloyalty. "We do not," as she put it, "hate and despise as southern women do." Unlike southern women, northern women were not inclined to flaunt their most intimate feelings in public. They were aware of their appropriately private and domestic place. This author suggested that what passed for the coldness of northern women was simply the consequence of their "sense of propriety, of restraint." This restraint was unfortunately being read by some Union men as a lack of love and attachment, really of loyalty to their men, when in fact it was actually the manifestation of an appropriately private and intimate expression of affection.[25]

Rather than criticizing northern women for their lack of commitment to the cause, loyal northern men should themselves reconsider the social significance of the bizarre levels and intensity of southern women's hatred for the Union soldiers and the extent to which they were both willing and able to unsex themselves to manifest it. According to this author, the extremity of this hatefulness was almost beyond belief, verging upon the genocidal. Not only did southern women fire "hideous grins, or insulting gestures or unspeakable outrages on the nerves of blushing soldiers," but they also went so far as to make jewelry out of their bones and flaunt them as ornaments. They were even willing to prepare Union soldiers skulls for "detestable orgies" of human blood drinking. With perhaps some under-statement, given the nature of her allegations, the anonymous author concluded, "this species of patriotism could not, even in barbarous times, have been considered appropriate to our sex."[26]

How could things have become so twisted that the first fire that northern women were compelled to take on in the formation of their Loyal Leagues was not that of the enemy, but rather the fire they experienced from loyal men who held them up to such women and found them lacking? How could these most disloyal and most degraded of women have come to be a model for the behavior of the most respectable and the most loyal? One answer was that the vision of northern men was apparently clearer when it came to southern men than when it came to southern women. Southern men did not, after all, have the power the make northern men blush simply by wielding a "hideous grin" or an "insulting gesture" in their direction. When it came to southern women, northern men were vulnerable in ways that northern women were not. And so while the northern men who orga-nized the National Loyal League were wrong to blame the state of the war effort on the coldness of northern women, they were right to think that they needed the organized "declarative" presence of loyal women to win the war. As it was, the vision of northern men, especially Union soldiers, only appeared able to read the behavior of southern men with any accuracy. They fell wounded before the expression of southern women's political commitments.[27]

What northern men needed was the normally privatized domestic vision of northern women organized and recognized as a political vision in order to gender their own political critique of the southern social order. They needed the heart made visible. Once they did this, once they could see southern women as a vile and distorted form of femininity then they would find the answer to their loyalty crisis. It was in no small part the consequence of the Republican Party's brilliant success in placing a condemning read upon southern slaveholders that the party rose to power in the North in the first place. This idea of the slavepower, that is, that southern men's ownership of slaves was a social, economic, and political threat to the liberties of free men, was gendered as male, however. It was the overweening power that slavery gave southern men that posed the threat, and the threat was also gendered male, as the Republican Party found its most steadfast adherents in small property owners of all stripes, who increasingly feared for their continued independence in the rapidly industrializing North. The leadership of the Republican Party fed their fears of proletarianization by pointing to the greater threat posed by the ownership of slaves, that is the slavepower. This slavepower according to Republican political advocates not only caused slaveholding men to lord it over their chattel slaves, it empowered them to exert inappropriate dominance over the rest of southern society as well, whether that was their wives and children or their yeoman-class neighbors. Ultimately this usurpation of power even led to the slavepower controlling the highest levels of state and national politics.[28]

While Republican men had no trouble characterizing southern slave-holding men in this fashion, the "slavepower" appeared to have little bearing on women of the slaveowning class. Indeed, in so far as southern women found any place at all in this critique of southern society, it was as victims of the slavepower, not as active agents in its generation. The picture of the antebellum southern lady as the long suffering victim of her husband's tyrannical slavepower was in fact perhaps most widely and successfully promoted by the female antislavery and women's rights advocates of the northern abolitionist movement. Surely the Grimké sisters, two of the most prominent members of the antislavery movement, and themselves originally of the South Carolina planter class, testified to the experience of southern women in this vein. Sarah Grimké declined to marry in a social order, not to mention a household structure that empowered slaveholding men to treat slave women as they saw fit. Instead of identifying with the men of her class, she and her sister, Angelina, claimed allegiance with the other household dependents, that is the slaves, in southern households. Leaving the South altogether before the war, the two sisters moved to the North and joined other abolitionist activists there, using their own personal story as a vehicle to call for women in particular to form antislavery organizations and take a stand against slavery and for their rights as women. They even went so far in their conviction of the oppressed position of women of the southern slaveowning class as to write tracts addressed specifically to follow their lead and rise up against the tyrannies and the abuse of power by slaveholding men, the worst sort of "lords of creation," as they were not uncommonly called.[29]

No wonder Union troops were shocked that southern women, who arguably should have welcomed the arrival of the Union army as their liberators from the abuse of the slavepower, instead turned a cold shoulder upon them or openly insulted them to their face. They, after all, were the good men—the good men who were risking their lives to put down a rebellion of power hungry and tyrannical men. It was, however, this scornful treatment that needed the reenvisioning, according to the Ladies National League writers. Union men needed a new lens, the lens of strong-hearted northern women through which to understand the behavior of southern women. They needed to see that it was southern women, even more than southern men, who stood at the cultural center of the southern slavepower. In order to do this, however, they needed to reevaluate the significance they themselves attributed to women's domestic place in society. They needed to recognize the ways that the public political system of men was itself grounded in the domestic order of women. They needed to see the traditional domestic place of women as inherently political.

As corrupting and evil as slaveholding was for men, turning potentially decent individuals into power hungry tyrants, power hungry tyrants who had organized a rebellion against the democracy as surely as they had lorded over their households and communities at home, its impact on slaveholding women was arguably worse. Indeed publications of the Ladies

Loyal League even went so far as to claim that it was the lack of moral compass on the part of southern women played a critical role in "the climax of unreason"—that is, secession. Raised up in a slaveholding society, exposed to the licentiousness and greed generated by the degraded power that slaveowning conferred upon the slaveholding class, it was not surprising that southern women grew to maturity, the "unresisting prey of degraded passions." The presence of slavery within southern households meant that every relationship, whether that be between mother and child, husband and wife, or brother and sister was shot through with distortion and degradation. The relationship between husband and wife was particularly compromised because of the way in which slaveholding men were empowered to sexually abuse slave women within their households at will. No loyalty could exist between southern men and women as a result and it was in this core failure of loyalty that the seed of national disloyalty was initially planted and grew.[30]

While northern abolitionist women and even some women of the planter class themselves had railed against the sexual license that slave-owning conferred upon some southern men before the war, it was only the context of secession and war that its consequences rose to the level of a national and political crisis in the public behavior of southern women. Before the war, northern antislavery advocates had assumed that women of the slaveholding class were themselves victims of the slavepower. As much as they believed that southern women had a powerful role to play as public and even political advocates in opposition to the slavepower, they saw women in the domestic role as victims. And while they were dedicated to empowering both women and slaves, they envisioned doing so by liberating the household dependents from their "place," as subordinates in slaveholding households. Southern women who manifested agency and loyalty out of this apparently victimized domestic location, could not be read through this lens.[31]

Indeed, before the war, abolitionist women assumed that women of the North and the South formed a single group. Thus Sarah Grimké could call upon the women of the South to unite with the women of the North, "in the bonds" of womanhood and in opposition to the patriarchal slaveholding system. But now, in the context of Civil War, southern women had revealed themselves to be the enemy, and it became necessary to see them as the enemy—that is to "unsex" them, and to claim the category of "woman" for northern women alone. According to one Loyal League author, northern women would never behave in the degraded fashion southern women, with one critical exception. No northern woman would behave in such a degraded fashion, unless she was a whore. As she noted, "no woman within our borders, however low on the social scale, unless belonging to the unhappy class which is not nor can be loyal to God or man, to sex or nation, has brought reproach upon her country, or furnished matter of triumph to the enemy, by mistaking ferocity or vulgarity for patriotism." From this gendered location, slavery reduced all women to whores, both enslaved women, whose bodies were at the use and discretion of the owners, and the women of the slaveholding class, who were forced to participate in a system where no fidelity or loyalty could securely exist between husband and wife. The only comparable women in the North were women who also engaged in the buying and selling of women's bodies, prostitutes.[32]

General Butler was, in his infamous General Order #28, more accurate than even he imagined in characterizing southern women as whores. On the face of it, while he was concerned with the unladylike public behavior of Confederate women and its demoralizing impact on the occupying Union forces in New Orleans, this unladylike behavior was actually the manifestation of a more fundamental distortion, the distortion that slavery had wrought in their ability to manifest any kind of loyal behavior. Here was the generative core of the secessionist movement itself, "the climax of unreason," according to Loyal League writers, the true basis of political disloyalty lodged in the core of the southern household itself. Since all this seems obvious, why would northern women need to dispel the image of the southern women as patriot extraordinaire? Why could men see so clearly when it came to other men and be so misled when it came to women? The fact was that northern troops manifested a kind of vulnerability to southern women. They could be wounded by them as surely as they could be wounded by southern men on the battlefield. And while Butler could attempt to mark disloyal southern women as degraded and therefore not worth the concern of Union soldiers, he could not make soldiers experience them that way.[33]

According to the Ladies National League, this was the point at which the northern social order itself was in need of repair. The Union soldier's inability to recognize a degraded, unsexed, disloyal female, as something other than a woman, and their desire instead to acquire the admiration, allegiance, or even the possession of these women, was symptomatic of a more general lack of virtue in the northern population at large. Indeed, by the spring of 1863, it was clear that the flagging war effort was not the consequence of a lack of northern resources. "The only question, as to whether this war shall be conducted to a shameful or an honorable close, is not of men or money or material resource. In this our superiority is unquestioned." Instead, the real question that would determine the outcome of the war was, "whether this people shall have virtue to endure to the end."[34]

And just as southern women stood at the center of disloyal and wicked behavior of the rebels, some Loyal League writers suggested that in some ways northern women themselves stood at the core of this failure of loyal and virtuous northern behavior. If virtue was lacking in the North it was partly because northern women themselves had fallen away from the socially democratic commitments of their mothers and their grandmothers, whose values underwrote the establishment of the nation in the first place. By way of illustration of northern women's faltering virtue, this Ladies League author offered the story of one Union soldier who had fought valiantly on many battlefields in defense of the Union cause, but finally was so seriously wounded that he was forced to return home to die. None of the members of his local ladies aid society were willing to contribute to this poor soldier's comfort in his last days because his family was considered to be too low in the social order of their local community to be recognized. Only one virtuous and democratic soul was willing to visit him and be with him to the end. He was deeply grateful for any recognition at all and his dying words to her were, "I am glad somebody noticed me."[35]

The point of this story was to indicate the ways in which the common soldier really had been forgotten. Women's democratic domestic energy was being filtered through public considerations of class position, and even of personal self-aggrandizement, not unlike the way that the energy of southern women was distorted by the social nexus of slaveholding. Of course this author was quick to point out that the elitist behavior of some northern women paled before the extremity of class difference manifested in the system of slaveholding, nonetheless the women of the North were themselves laboring under a distortion of their core democratic values that was in some ways similar. Indeed, not only did class hierarchy weaken northern women's relationships with the common soldier, it distanced them from the experience of most northern women of the North as well. Public power and attention had been lavished upon the contributions of a few elite women to the Union war effort, but these contributions paled by comparison to what was lost in the creation of even more class difference between these now "public" women and mass of northern women still largely contained within their own individual households and struggling to provide even for them. "It is not Mrs. Stowe, or Mrs. Howe, or Miss Stevenson or Miss Dix, alone, who is to save the country, but the thousands who are at this moment darning stockings, tending babies, sweeping floors. It is to them I speak."[36]

The problem was that the common man thought that his contribution to the war effort was not truly valued by the women of the North, and at the same time, the common northern women thought that she had no significant contribution to make to the war effort. The domestic nexus of loyalty was lost. Enter the Ladies National League. By reaching deep into the domestic influence of women and activating their democratic potential, such women could revitalize the entire war effort. Women would redouble their efforts to aid the troops; they would encourage enlistments; they would honor those men who served and their families; and they would cut off all traitors and those who sympathized with them. Such women would, "tolerate no coward voice or pen or eye. Wherever the serpents head is raised, (they would) strike it down." This vision of an activist domestic politics was necessary to win the northern war for Union loyalty. It would serve both to encourage the Union soldier to fight on, as well as create the ground to cut disloyal women out of the military equation. Northern women sensible of the activist charge and political significance of their location within the household could even follow the soldier to the battlefield itself. Indeed, "the great army of letters that marches southward with every morning sun is a power engine of war."[37]

The military significance of the activation of the domestic nexus of political loyalty can be seen in the role that the Ladies National League played in the Union war effort in St. Louis. On April 20, 1863, after considerable discussion for the need for a Ladies Loyal League in St. Louis in previous weeks, the first call for an organizing meeting was published in the local press. While the leading loyal ladies of St. Louis affixed their names to this call, it was actually General Curtis, the Commanding Union Officer in St. Louis, who presided over the initial meeting held in the Mercantile Hall on May 2, 1863. General Curtis had particular reason to sponsor this meeting. In just the previous month of March, an entire ring of women running the Confederate mail was uncovered in the city. The house of one of the ringleaders, Mrs. McLure, was converted into a Female Military Prison to house these women, but the question of what to do with them hung heavily upon the Union military and particularly upon General Curtis, as the Commanding Officer. They were clearly disloyal, but they were also clearly ladies. Their class connections and their gender immunity as women fused to make them a virtually impregnable target.[38]

Indeed, the Union military had, since almost the beginning of the war, attempted to root out the influence of these southern sympathizers in St. Louis. As early as December of 1862, they assessed their estates to pay the costs of Union refugees in the city and by the following spring, they proscribed their wearing of Confederate colors or their practice of parading by the prisons where southern sympathizers were being held. For that matter, in the spring of 1862, they even restricted southern sympathizing women from nursing the Confederate wounded, or any wounded soldier. Nonetheless, the military was never successful in dislodging these women from their deeply imbedded position of respect and influence in the city's social order. The discovery of the Confederate mail-running ring in the spring of 1863, revealed once against just how deep, potent, and actively disloyal some southern sympathizing women remained in the city despite their best efforts to strip them of a public presence in the city.[39]

Indeed, on April 28, only a little over a week after the call for the formation of a Ladies National League was published, General Curtis published an announcement of his own in the local press, General Order #28. Perhaps the public announcement of leading loyal ladies' commitment to the formation of the League encouraged him to do so. The order increased the punishment for disloyal activity to banishment behind Confederate lines and included new forms of disloyal activities, particularly running the Confederate mail, in the list of reasons for such banishment. The order was clearly prompted by the discovery of the ladies' mail-running ring, a discovery that forced the military to address the issue of disloyal women, as it also offered them increased grounds to finally simply cut the most respected southern sympathizing women from the community entirely. Nonetheless, having issued the order that would make their banishment possible, General Curtis hesitated, assessing the public response, hoping to acquire the social approval he needed to fight the influence of these women, the public counter of loyal Union women. As General Curtis told the assembled ladies at the first meeting of the Ladies National League, "the sword of government has put down this spirit (of disloyalty) among us so far as it assumed the form of military power, but that power will rise again if it can. The monster writhes, but it is not dead. It is your mission, ladies, to put it down socially . . . to live and labor to establish a pure, wholesome, loyal public sentiment in this city."[40]

Other speakers at the meeting reinforced the call of General Curtis to the loyal women of St. Louis to come out and reinforce his newly militant stance against southern sympathizing women in the city. Referring to southern sympathizing women variously as "fiends . . . in woman's dress" and "the first family of vipers," these speakers argued for the critical role that loyal women's public political influence could make in the Union war effort in St. Louis. The 1,200 ladies who signed the pledge that day certainly walked out of the Mercantile Hall with a renewed conviction that their organized public presence offered a critical counter to the influence of southern sympathizing women in St. Louis. They were armed and ready to take on the intragender war. As southern sympathizing women had done until banned by the Union military, loyal ladies now publicly donned the Union colors, wearing with pride their League pin, a blue star, with Ladies National League, written in the center and on the five points of the star, the letters spelling out, "Union." Now it would be Union women who controlled the streets and the waysides of the city. As one speaker put it, "now your children will not hurrah for Jeff Davis in the streets, nor raise the rebel flags in the backyard, nor trample on the red, white and blue in the school room. . . . Your sons will not flee into the army of traitors, nor your daughters send letters in the rebel mail bags."[41]

Not only was the public presence of politically marked loyal women an effective counter to the social influence of disloyal women, it also served to encourage a "sweeter bond of sympathy" across class lines among Union women themselves. Women who stood divided by differences in class circumstances now realized that beneath their varied dress, whether, "morning robes," "old fashions," or "purple and fine linen" they all "have always worn in their true hearts the surpassing glory of the red white and blue." Not only did these badges identify Union women as being of one heart, across class lines, it also identified these loyal women, otherwise strangers to each other, wherever the chance encounter might bring them together, whether at "church, hospital or place of amusement." It also made publicly visible the love and appreciation loyal women felt for the many convalescing Union soldier who walked the city streets. Such men would now know upon seeing the badge, if at no other time, that their contribution to the Union cause was, "neither despised nor forgotten, and that the children of these women would rise up and revere and cherish and call him blessed in his old age."[42]

Perhaps the most significant impact of the public presence of these strong-hearted women, however, was the way in which they served to legitimize the efforts of the Union military in purging the city of disloyal women's influence through their public "rebuke to secession women." Certainly General Curtis must have felt affirmed by the response of the 2,000 ladies in attendance at the Mercantile Hall on that day, as the press reported that he was frequently, "interrupted by the enthusiasm of the ladies, visiting itself in their rapping upon the floor with their parasols, and a continuous fluttering of handkerchiefs and miniature flags." General Curtis responded in kind, assuring the assembled women that he would, "transmit to my command the inspiration received from your fair faces and patriotic hearts." True to his word, on May 7, some five days after the formation of the League, General Order #28 was finally put into effect. The first boatload of disloyal women was banished behind Confederate lines. The newspaper coverage of the banished women divided them into two groups, the wives of Confederate officers—that is, southern sympathizing women of the greatest social influence in the city, that is, members of the "first family of vipers,"—and women who were banished for being "fiends in female dress," that is, the spies, most importantly the female mail-runners. Even with the aggressive organization of Union women, removing these powerfully placed southern sympathizing women was not easy. As the local press noted with regard to this first boatload of banished southern sympathizing women, many more remained in Union military custody in St. Louis because "efforts made on their behalf have led to the postponement of their cases." Indeed, the war against southern sympathizers in St. Louis would continue to the end of the war. Boatloads of women would continue to leave the city throughout the summer of 1863 and the Ladies Loyal League would continue to play an important role in this process of cutting the disloyal influence of these women out of the social order. If nothing else, the influential friends of these women could no longer defend them simply by claiming special immunity for them because of their gender. The Ladies Loyal League, by rendering their domestic selves, their strong hearts, overtly and publicly political, took that domestic ground of defense from them.[43]

While women of strong minds, like Stanton and Anthony and the Women's National League saw in the strategy of jumping the gender tracks, the possibility of empowering household dependents and the war effort at the same time, members of the Ladies National Leagues saw a vehicle for the empowerment of women and the very success of the war effort itself in the possibility of increasing the respect attributed to women's domestic role, through the public recognition and organization of the politics of strong hearts. According to the Ladies National Leagues, women had an important role to play in the northern war effort, arguably a critical role, not only assisting in the gendering of loyal men's thinking and of thereby arming northern men against the fire of southern women, but in encouraging, promoting a more active agency on the part of the masses of northern women who themselves did not necessarily see the political significance and power of their domestic place, a place, however, that had according to the Ladies Loyal League been revealed as the critical core of loyalty, the generative center of the Union war effort itself.

This politics of domestic loyalty presents a powerful claim for the political and military significance of the domestic place of women, a claim we miss if we focus only on the ways in which the war generated possibilities for women to emancipate themselves from this very domestic location. For while the war certainly empowered women's claim to an equal public status by rendering their previously private domestic place so public, it did so by unleashing a structural shifting in the relationship between the social and the political, which underwrote greater claims for the significance of women's influence at the same time as it generated greater power for women's claims to direct political rights. Indeed, we can see both these strands of women's strategy for empowerment in the origins, history, and practices of the Ladies Loyal League. As surely as the war called out women to be "men," it called out women to be women. And while they may have fought each other, together these northern women of strong minds and strong hearts represented a deadly duo, a one-two punch, against the slaveholding southern household order, working to abolish slavery and to secure rights for women on the one hand and to expand the domestic authority of women on the other. Neither position was generated by the inclinations of these women alone, but was drawn out by the war and the structural changes and instabilities that it created.

CHAPTER 3

"A REBEL THOUGH SHE BE": GENDER AND MISSOURI'S WAR OF THE HOUSEHOLDS

In June of 1863, Anne Ewing Lane boarded a horse car with her young niece in order to visit a friend who lived in another neighborhood in St. Louis. As she began to read the local newspaper, a woman sitting nearby on the car interrupted her, asking if there was any news of the war. Anne Lane replied that there was not, but the woman continued to ply her with questions. Was Richmond not taken? Did she think General Price, commander of the Missouri Confederate forces, was in nearby Jefferson County? If not, did she think he was coming? To each question, Anne Lane indicated that she knew nothing, or that the persistent and rather invasive stranger certainly knew as much as she did. Finally, as she wrote to her sister, Sarah Lane Glasgow, ". . . thinking the catechism had gone far enough, I began to talk to Baby and turned a deaf ear to my inquisitive friend." Anne Lane was no fool, after all, she wasn't simply being rude, she was sure that she knew a spy when she saw one. As she continued in her letter, "they have a Ladies Loyal League here, the members of which are sworn to visit suspected sympathizers and report anything they may be induced to say . . . A nice state of affairs, don't you think?"[1]

In the spring and summer of 1863, the Unionist women of St. Louis were busy forming the Ladies Loyal League in order to promote loyal sentiment in the city. As a direct consequence, southern sympathizing women, like Anne Lane and her sister, found themselves and their families ever more publicly singled out and marked as disloyal. By the spring of 1863, women of the Loyal League were convinced that southern sympathizing women brought this discipline upon themselves. They, after all, stood at the root of southern secession. According to loyalist publications, it was southern sympathizing women who used their influence to urge their men into war in the first place and continued to press them on in battle. They were the ones eager to collect signs of Union defeat—some poor Union soldier's hair, now a bracelet, another's bones, now a pair of earrings. Union women who had never belonged to any organization beyond the local women's church auxiliary were now willing to stand up and be publicly and politically counted in what had become a war of women's influence. They were willing to take the pledge, wear the Union flag, board the horse cars, and make war on disloyalty.[2]

The objects of the Ladies Loyal League's war, women like Anne Lane, were appalled and frightened at what they experienced as the latest invasion of their private lives and personal convictions since the war commenced. Just the week before climbing aboard the horse car with her young niece, a friend of Anne Lane's, Mrs. McRee, had stopped by her house to tell of her experience of being called in and questioned by the Provost Marshal. Mrs. McRee was charged with making disloyal speeches some two years earlier in the spring and summer of 1861, when the allegiance of Missouri, a slaveholding border state, was still unclear. Mrs. McRee, a widow living at a boardinghouse at the time, expressed her southern sympathies with some vehemence to her fellow boarders at the dinner table, never imagining that her words would be pelted back at her verbatim by the Union military authorities some two years later. "Did you ever say that you would walk barefoot to Springfield to give Price any information you could offer him?" "Did you say that Mr. Bates was a hoary headed old traitor for accepting a position in Lincoln's cabinet?" "Did you say that the cortege of an athiest like Lyon through the streets of St. Louis was an outrage to a Christian Community?"[3]

Although caught off guard by this detailed knowledge of what she assumed was private conversation, Mrs. McRee told Anne Lane that she simply refused to respond to the line of questioning and remarked instead that "at *that* time Americans thought they had a right to say what they thought about everything." Obviously, by June of 1863, that was no longer the case. Southern sympathizers not only had to watch their casual conversations on the public transportation, but they also had to be concerned about their dinner table conversations, even when, or perhaps particularly when, these conversations had occurred years before. Anne Lane was left to consider her own circumstances. How had she managed to escape the increasingly long arm of the loyal forces in St. Louis? She too, like Mrs. McRee, had held forth "at that time" when Americans still thought they had a right to say what they thought about everything. She certainly had talked secession with her friends and family. When the Union forces took over the state in the spring and fall of 1861, she was, along with other members of her family, outspoken in her condemnation of martial law as a violation of the southern sympathizing population's civil rights. She not only committed herself verbally, but she also wrote numerous letters expressing her opinions to her sister overseas and watched with some combination of fear and outrage as those letters were increasingly subject to inspection by Union authorities, opened, read, and censored.[4]

So how was it that she managed to continue to fly below the disciplinary apparatus of martial law? By the summer of 1863, Anne Lane and her family, although prominent citizens, and known to be southern sympathizers, had managed to escape the fate of many members of the southern sympathizing elite in St. Louis. They had not been called in to be questioned by the Union authorities, asked to take the loyalty oath, assessed for war costs, or worse, imprisoned or even banished. When Anne tried to explain to her sister, Sarah, who was overseas with her husband and her older children, how she and their parents were managing to avoid the fate of so many of their friends and acquaintances, her thinking was twofold. There was her father's case and then there was her own. Although they shared the common experience of becoming increasingly cut out of the larger community, the timing and basis for their exclusion differed based on their gender. While William Carr Lane's public and political influence as an adult man flared initially and then waned, Anne Lane, like Mrs. McRee and southern sympathizing women more generally in St. Louis, found her own gendered location as an adult woman and substitute mother for her sister's children, rendered public and political in ways unimagined at the outset of the conflict.[5]

As the city's first mayor and later the regional governor of the New Mexico Territory, William Carr Lane held more political power than the average southern sympathizing citizen at the war's outbreak. He was politically well connected on the national as well as the local level. He turned to those political connections as he saw the Union forces enter the state, take over the St. Louis arsenal in May, and proceed to fight the Missouri State Guard down the Missouri River and south, literally pushing them out of the state and into the Confederacy. By August of 1861, martial law was imposed in St. Louis in order to control the large, now "disloyal" southern sympathizing population of which Lane was a prominent member. Throughout this struggle for the initial control of the state, Lane turned to his political connections, like Edward Bates, himself of St. Louis and recently appointed as Lincoln's attorney general, to protest what he viewed as the forcible Union occupation of the state. To others he raged at what he saw as the stupidity of men like Bates, who believed that the war was only about maintaining the Union and not about stripping southern white men of what he viewed as their right to own slave property. As Carr wrote to John Law, a U.S. Congressman, in July of 1861, "Stripped of all disguise, this war is John Brownism . . . A mighty abolition raid. All Republicans do not intend it . . . But you will see that I am right."[6]

Lane was convinced that Missouri, and St. Louis in particular, was too wedded to the southern slave economy to be economically viable as a "northern" state in the Union. He continued to believe in this underlying "southerness" of his state despite the military defeat of the state guard and the subsequent establishment of martial law. Once the Union military firmly established its control, however, the very extent of Carr's political connections, which prior to the war had empowered him as a male citizen, began to threaten his security. He watched as his very southernness became the basic ground of his disloyalty rather than the larger context of his social distinction and public political power. Under these new circumstances of martial law, Lane was fortunate that other factors, which before the war had limited the extent of his public influence, now actually served to protect him. As Anne Lane explained to her sister in 1862, "Everyone says that Pa will not be molested, some give one reason, some another, the true one is what the Democrat said, his influence is small. He has warm friends many who really like him but he belongs to an older generation."[7]

Lane's advanced age at the outbreak of the conflict meant that he was more of a "retired" politician than an active officeholder. Currently active officeholders, even city and county administrators, were required to take the loyalty oath by the state secessionist convention in 1861. Southern sympathizing men, especially prominent men like W. C. Lane, lived in growing fear that the Provost Marshal would demand such an oath from them as well. If asked, Lane probably would have taken the same course as P. B. Garesche, the City Administrator, who, when required to take the oath, chose instead to resign from his position in local government. His resignation was not, however, the end of his story. He was advised that as a consequence of his militant refusal to take the oath, he was in imminent danger of arrest by the military authorities. His decision to resign rather than take the oath really opened up yet another decision for him, whether he would leave the Union or go to prison. He chose to leave the state for the Confederacy.[8]

As William Carr Lane began to see the very real costs of the war to more vulnerable southern sympathizing men than himself, he stepped back and reassessed his altered circumstances under martial law. Lane began to realize that he was in no position to actively resist Union authorities himself, much less urge his friends and colleagues to do so. While he was potentially liable to the consequences of the loyalty oath because of his past political prominence, he was spared by his age the immediate consequences of southern sympathies that current officeholders, like Garesche, confronted. And both Garesche and Lane were spared the consequences that younger men faced in the expectation of military service as a responsibility of all adult white men in St. Louis. As his daughter noted, "Having no son and being too old to go himself he hesitates to urge others to incur risks he cannot share." Instead, William Carr Lane grew ever more publicly silent and withdrawn into the confines of his own household. By the summer of 1862, the Lanes even decided to leave St. Louis altogether and move to their farm outside of the city. This retreat into the private and the domestic did not mean that W. C. Lane accepted easily the loss of his public and political self. He continued to rail privately in his home against what he perceived as the violation of his own individual civil rights as well as the political autonomy of his state. Indeed in the last three weeks of his life as he drifted in and out of consciousness, he muttered endlessly about "Rebels" and "Yankees." When he died in the winter of 1863, his daughter concluded that it was not so much the consequence of old age, as it was a matter of "nervous debility."[9]

Anne Lane's story was in some ways similar to that of her father. She was, after all, a member of the same household. Like her father, she was outspoken in her southern sympathies at the outset of the war. Like her father her audience was also that of her peers, in her own case other women of the southern sympathizing elite in St. Louis. While her father was shooting off letters to his political associates, Anne Lane was expressing her opinions in correspondence with her sister or holding forth at the family dinner table. The difference between them was the significance that they and society more generally initially attributed to their opinions. Quite naturally, William Carr Lane assumed that his opinion held public and political weight, why else write those letters to his friends in public office? Anne Lane, on the other hand, never considered that she should take care in what she wrote to her sister in the spring and summer of 1861, much less that she should watch what she said in conversation with her family and friends in the privacy of their homes.

For Anne Lane, the war was not so much a matter of the folding of her political tents before they folded on her, her own ability to fly below the Union disciplinary forces rested upon the fact that as a woman, she had no such tents to fold. That is Anne Lane was not politically empowered as a man, on the one hand, and she was "protected" as a woman and a household dependent, on the other. The core of women's private and protected domestic status in the household was assumed to lie in their role as mothers. So when Anne Lane attempted to explain why she, unlike her friend, Mrs. McRee, was spared arrest and banishment, she noted her position as a substitute mother to her absent sister's young children. "As to myself," she wrote to her sister, "I suppose I owe it to your little ones that I escaped for I had said much more than Mrs. McRee had. And talking was all she was ever accused of." When she broke off her conversation with the strangely inquisitive woman on the streetcar that day in June of 1863 and turned instead to "entertaining Baby," her young niece, she did so in a calculating fashion. She hoped that her position as substitute mother to her sister's young children would continue to provide her with domestic immunity.[10]

By the summer of 1863, however, when Anne Lane boarded that streetcar, she knew that the domestic immunity that she and other southern sympathizing women had simply assumed to be a natural aspect of their world when the war commenced, was seriously eroded. There was, for instance, the experience of Juliette Garesche. When her husband, P. B. Garesche, the City Administrator, was informed that his resignation from public office rather than taking the oath would most certainly lead to his arrest, he left the city for points South. He left behind his wife, Juliette, with "minimally sufficient funds" and the task of somehow getting their household through the war in his absence. Juliette Garesche discovered that the Union military would cut her no quarter early in the war, when on December 12, 1861, she found herself on a list of 64 prominent southern sympathizers assessed for Union war costs. Rather than exempting Julliette Garesche based on her gender or even her role as mother and sole parent present to care for her children, the Union authorities considered her to be the representative of her household, a disloyal southern household, doubly marked by her husband's departure to the Confederacy. Whatever regard the Union authorities might have had for antebellum gender conventions, in particular the protected domestic status of women and children, fell quickly in the case of the Garesches. Juliette Garesche attempted to appeal to the domestic sympathies of the Union authorities in a letter she wrote to the Provost Marshal on December 23, 1861. She explained her straightened economic circumstances in her husband's absence and asked, "Can it (the $300 assessment) be done by taking some property for this purpose—a lot—and not strip me and my children of our only bread?"[11]

In the case of the Garesches we can see how the experience of southern sympathizing men, that of being stripped of their public political position was directly connected to the wartime experience of many southern sympathizing women, that is, the decline of their domestic immunity. P. B. Garesche had little choice but to leave his household exposed to the workings of martial law and his wife, Juliette Garesche, had little choice but to take up the task of publicly defending her household. The Union assessment of the Garesche household appeared doubly illegitimate to Juliette Garesche, in the first place for singling out southern sympathizers simply for their sentiments and in the second place for being aimed directly at dependents of the households like her own where there was no male household head to absorb the shock. Juliette Garesche's use of the word "stripped"—that the Union authorities should not "strip" her and her children—indicates the depth of violation that she experienced with the transgression of what she had previously assumed was simply a natural state of domestic immunity and protection of household dependents that presumably all honorable men recognized and respected.[12]

Anne Lane commented on this initial assessment against prominent southern sympathizing households with some contempt in her correspondence to her sister in January of 1862. "Instead of an abolition raid, the stereotyped phrase, I should rather call it a war upon women and men incapable from age or otherwise of defending themselves." Although her father, William Carr Lane, and presumably other southern sympathizing men of her acquaintance, had railed from the outset of the war about how the real underlying motive of the North was to strip southern white men of their ownership of slaves, it apparently did not occur to these men that the war would entail more than that, not only an "abolitionist" raid, but also a domestic raid more generally. As such, southern sympathizing men like William Carr Lane or P. B. Garesche were not only confronted with the potential loss of their slave property, but the loss of their ability to protect and thus render "domestic" their women and children, as well. In their defense, the process of stripping southern sympathizing men of their public position or even of their slaveholdings did not necessarily mean that the Union forces would proceed to strip the women, children, and elderly of their households. When Juliette Garesche appealed to the Union authorities to spare her and her children, she did so because she knew that public authorities routinely continued to protect women and children when male heads of household failed. That, after all, was the basis for much of the charitable aid that was distributed in the city.[13]

As taken aback as southern sympathizers were that the Union military would actually violate the privacy of domestic life and the code of protection for dependents in households even to the point of directly assessing women and children, to the Union military authorities the assessment of prominent southern sympathizers in St. Louis seemed like a necessary response to the circumstances of war in Missouri. Guerilla warfare raged out of control in Missouri, in the fall of 1861, and nowhere was this more the case than in the southwest corner of the state. By November of 1861, hundreds of destitute loyal households, driven from their homes by rebel raids, flooded into St. Louis. According to Commanding General Halleck, as the rebels overrunning the southern part of the state were responsible for causing the refugee crisis in St. Louis, it was appropriate that the Union military respond to this rebel guerilla war by attacking its supporters in St. Louis itself, southern sympathizers. So on December 12, 1861, Commanding General Halleck issued General Order #24, levying an assesment on the 64 leading disloyal households in St. Louis. As the Order read: "the suffering families driven by rebels from south western Missouri which have already arrived here have been supplied by voluntary contributions made by Union men. Others are on the way to arrive in a few days. They must be supplied by the charity of men known to be hostile to the Union."[14]

In levying this initial assessment against what the Union military considered to be the 64 most prominent southern sympathizing men in St. Louis, Halleck revealed the basic ground of the war in Missouri. For while the Union authorities had established nominal military and political control over the state, they actually had only succeeded in driving the conflict backward, off the formal public field of men's empowerment, that is, out of the statehouse and off the battlefield, back onto a more individualized and informal level of the household and the bush. This guerilla war that raged so out of control in much of the state presented itself to the St. Louis military authorities in the very concrete form of wounded Union households. Indeed the Republican press in St. Louis described the suffering of the loyal men who poured into the city in these terms. "Everything that gave 'home' its meaning has been polluted and destroyed . . . and the quiet, unoffending man whose only crime was that he would not take up arms against the government . . . has been compelled to turn his back on home, field, cattle and all his property, and leaving behind him all the hopes and the associations of home, to march to the wail of children calling for shelter, and the plaints of wife and children for food, toward the regions of loyalty and liberty . . . He finds himself houseless, homeless and friendless in our streets, with no means of giving the helpless ones dependent on him even the bread to keep body and soul together."[15]

Not only had these men lost their public and political place in their communities, they had, by virtue of these very political loyalties, been cut out of their private domestic position as well. Southern sympathizing men may have suffered the loss of their publicly empowered position with the Union occupation of the state, but in the thinking of the Union military their loss paled before the loss of these loyal Union men who not only lost their public place in their communities, but in the process lost their domestic position in their households as well. Reduced to being unable to even protect their dependents, much less publicly avow their politics, the loyalist refugee men that poured into the city had essentially been stripped of both the private and public face of their manhood. Fortunately for them, St. Louis citizens, most particularly loyal Union ladies of the Refugee Aid Society, took up their cause. Renting an old three-story mansion, the ladies furnished it with beds and bedding sufficient to house 60 persons at a time. The ladies converted the top floor of the mansion into a workroom where they sorted, repaired, and remodeled the donated clothing that poured in from the concerned citizens of St. Louis. By early December, some 600 refugees had already been provided with food, warm clothing, and shelter in their process of relocation.[16]

While the military authorities appreciated the efforts by loyal citizens in St. Louis to assist the southwest refugees, they knew that the initial 600 refugees were only a small fraction of the thousands of destitute and dislocated citizens that were expected to descend upon St. Louis throughout the winter. General Halleck's order addressed the situation by placing the responsibility where he thought it should more properly rest. In what had become a war carried out at the level of the household, it appeared reasonable to the military authorities that the 64 most prominent southern sympathizing households in the city should, out of the resources of their own households, compensate these loyal men and their families for their loss. Initially the military authorities expected a direct compensation from disloyal citizens, a total of $10,000 in clothing, provisions, quarters, or money. The Republican press described this policy as being a simple matter of an "eye for an eye." After all, as one editorial pointed out, these southern sympathizing men in St. Louis still had, "roofs over their heads . . . Can still spend money on gew gaws of fashion and finery for their wives and daughters, supplying them with the means of flaunting their colors in the faces of loyal ladies." Surely these disloyal men should not be able to provide so lavishly for their households, while loyal men were reduced to standing helplessly by while their women shivered, houseless and homeless, in the winter cold? As the editorial concluded somewhat ominously, "There are yet many rooms to be swept and floors to be sprinkled, and many that will need to be well smoked before they will be clean."[17]

Although the Union military policy of assessment was framed by the Republican press as being a simple matter of an eye for an eye, a loyal household for a disloyal household, the policy was inevitably complicated by the way that the very structure of households and the place of individual households in the larger social order was fused to gender identity. In driving loyal households out of the southwest area of the state, rebel forces not only weakened the Union cause and wreaked hardship on loyal citizens, they undermined loyal men's ability to act as men to their households, and they stripped dependent and loyal women and children of their "natural" protectors and their domestic immunity. When the Union military took this position to justify assessment, they were on safe ground. That is the dictates of war, defending loyal households, stood hand in hand with preserving the gender order, rendering male heads of loyal households once again fully empowered to protect and defend their own. From the perspective of male gender identity, even the loyal Union ladies generous efforts to clothe and house the destitute refugees was problematic. Better to kill two birds with one stone, and rather than have well placed loyal women of St. Louis cover for the weakened men of the southwest, clip instead the wings of the southern sympathizing men of St. Louis, while empowering loyal men as heads of their own households, rather than Union ladies, however generous their intentions.

Even more than justifying assessment in terms of a man's right to stand as protector to his household, the right of the dependents of the household to protection put Union authorities on the right side of antebellum gender conventions. Thus, according to the language of the assessment order, the victims of the war in the southwest were not even presented as being the loyal male heads of household, but rather they were described as being "suffering families." The assessed, on the other hand, were in the official language of the Union military pronouncement, southern sympathizing *men*, never women, like Juliette Garesche, and certainly not "suffering families." In this way, the Union military presented assessment in a way that reinforced both gender conventions *and* the Union war effort. The reality, however, was that the antebellum gender order did not necessarily fit the dictates of war, particularly the dictates of a war framed at the level of the informal war of the bush and the household as was the case in Missouri. So, while the overwhelming majority of the assessed were indeed male heads of household, not all of them were. And the presence of women on the list of the assessed, women like Juliette Garesche, who had already lost the male head of her household to the demands of Union loyalty, raised the question of how far the military would actually violate the domestic immunity of household dependents, indeed would be forced to do so, if only in order to protect or reconstruct the domestic immunity lost by loyal households in their support for the Union war effort.

Although the Union military attempted to frame Missouri's war of the households in a way that placed all the honorable gender policy on the side of the Union, they actually could not at one and the same time pursue the military interest of the Union war effort and protect "suffering families" in general. Their support for the household order was an intensely partisan one. What they did in the name of suffering households, what they did in the name of reinforcing manhood, they did to advance *Union* households and *Union* manhood in order to win the war. And they could win the war, that is, reinforce the loyal Union household, but not without attacking the southern household and the gender order of southern sympathizing households. It was this attack on the domestic order that opened the door for protest and wider public sympathy for the assessed in St. Louis. Citizens who did not necessarily agree with their southern sympathies might well take issue with the violation of their households, particularly in so far as it compromised the gender order.

Thirty-one of the 64 assessed southern sympathizers set out to test this public sympathy when they published a signed protest to the Union authorities on December 26, 1861, indicating their intention to resist assessment. They opened their protest by posing a question, and that question was, "why are we accused of nothing we have done, but because of acts alleged to have been committed by persons to us unknown, remote from the locality in which we move, and over whose acts we have exercised no control?" Here they took up the politics of the household in a serious way. Each household, they suggested, was discrete unto itself, a southern sympathizing household in St. Louis was not simply interchangeable with a "rebel" household in some other part of the state. Assessed southern sympathizers went on to suggest that if they were themselves guilty of disloyal activities, as citizens they should be given a, "speedy and public trial by an impartial jury." Instead, the Union military was treating them as military combatants, rendering judgment against them by secret conference of two or three military officers. As they suggested in their protest to the assessment, "If two or three military officers of the U.S., or other persons designated for such purpose, may meet in secret, and, without notice, single out such citizens as they may choose . . . What man who may perchance hold political opinions not altogether acceptable to the tribunal, can consider himself secure in his right to liberty and property?"[18]

From the perspective of the Union military authorities, assessment was just a reasonable military response to the nature of the conflict, a war fought literally from household to household, in Missouri. The assessed, however, attempted to resist this militarization of the household by clinging to the household as a civilian location. They asserted that General Halleck himself was given his military command of the region some 11 months earlier in order to put an end to the arbitrary treatment of civilians by the military authorities. They even went so far as to quote back to General Halleck his own orders. He was put in command in order to put an end to the "numerous cases of alleged seizure and destruction of private property in this department." His charge was not to protect only the property of known *loyal* households, much less to directly make war on households of suspected disloyalty. Indeed, according to the assessed, the Union military's policy of direct war against law abiding households, "shows an outrageous abuse of power and violation of the laws of war."[19]

By December of 1861, southern sympathizing men may have lost their public political place in the governance of the state, they may have been defeated on the formal field of battle as well, but what their resistance to assessment indicated was that at least 31 of the most prominent of them in St. Louis would retreat no more. They would stand on the ground of their own households, upon their own rights as heads of those households and as law-abiding citizens, and they would resist. Not only did they assert their right to due process at law and security of their right to their own property, but they also asserted their right to direct their own charitable giving. That is the Union military policy of assessment proposed both to *take*, without due process, the property of southern sympathizing men and they then proposed to *give* that property to the "suffering families of Union men." As the assessment order read, "They must be supplied by the charity of men known to be hostile to the Union." Southern sympathizers opposed assessment on both grounds, that is, on the ground of their right to the secure control of their property and also upon the right to determine who the recipients of their charitable giving of the surplus of their households would be. [20]

Although the assessed were militant in opposition to what they viewed as an illegitimate attack on their households, in the end, they were forced to acknowledge that they were in no position to militantly resist General Order #24. "You," they wrote in their published protest, "have the armed hand to enforce your orders and decree." They would, therefore, "respectfully protest and decline to pay." They would resist, that is, not as actively empowered public men, the Union military had that, but as passive domestic resisters. While the Provost Marshal might have arrested them for this passive resistance, instead he proceeded to confiscate portions of their households and to sell them at auction to pay the assessed costs. This confiscation generally entailed taking entire rooms of furniture, or perhaps the entire law office, books, furniture, or the stock of the merchant. In some cases it was the stock of men's businesses, such as 16 pieces of velvet carpet, 9 pieces of Brussels carpet, 40 rugs from John Kennard, 29 boxes of Adamantine Candles, and 51 boxes of star candles from Samuel Engler. In the case of D. Robert Barclay, an attorney, one can imagine his entire business being carried out the door by the military authorities: 1 iron safe, 2 book cases and assorted library, 1 office table, and 3 chairs. Perhaps the businessmen who had only their household effects to be auctioned off suffered less than others. In this case the assessment cut deeper into the working of the household itself, as in the case of David H. Armstrong where the authorities auctioned off 3 sofas, 6 chairs, 2 reception chairs, 2 arm chairs, 1 what not, 1 carpet, 2 rugs, 1 rosewood center table, marble top, and 1 oak sideboard. That is, the military auctioned off his living room, dining room, and entry hall. In some cases, the military took the horses, carriage, and harness, which was the transportation of the household. Perhaps the hardest hit was Alexander Kayser, who made a point of signing the protest at the very end with an individual note attached. He was assessed the maximum amount and lost all his living room furniture, including his piano along with his transportation, as his carriage, horse, and harness were auctioned off.[21]

The newspapers published detailed lists of the seized items, serving as an advertisement for those interested in acquiring items at good price as well as a warning of what could be lost in continued sympathy with the rebel cause. As the Republican press concluded, "The assessed citizens appear to have declined payment, in the hope that the military authorities would not proceed to the extremities, and in expectation that secession sympathy would be created by any attempt to force liquidation. That the property of these gentlemen is taken and at great sacrifice of its actual value to them is plainly their own fault." Nonetheless, the stripping of these households elicited sympathy on the part of their neighbors. One editorial to the Republican press suggested that those citizens who were "so afraid of irritating their secession neighbors, and cannot look upon a furniture wagon carrying the property of a rabid secession family without running across the street to console the victims . . . are 10 to 1 themselves actually connected to secessionists in some fashion". All the "cant" about "disturbing the amenities of social life" was just so much "execreable weakness and cowardice," according to this author.[22]

Union assessment policy can be seen as a sort of motor, driving through the civilian population, cutting out the disloyal, but perhaps more importantly, disciplining, really creating, the "loyal." The extent to which the population would support the domestic violation of the disloyal literally became the fabric upon which loyal citizens were counted, constructed, and viewed as committed to the Union cause. The Union military seized the moment to issue a whole new spate of requirements for citizens of questionable loyalty. Whole new groups of men were now required to take the loyalty oath. On January 26, 1861, officers of the Mercantile Library and the Chamber of Commerce were required to take the oath. Under this order, those men who failed to take the oath would be assumed to have resigned and those who continued in office without the oath would be arrested. In this fashion, the Union authorities moved from control of politics into control of the economic life of the city. They followed this order with one on March 3, which required all attorneys to take the oath, and one on March 14, which required the oath of all jurors. By demanding the oath of practicing attorneys and jurors, the military authorities seriously limited the extent to which southern sympathizers might look to the civilian court system for representation, much less redress.[23]

William McPheeters, a physician in St. Louis, was one southern sympathizer who was at this point caught in the net of the expanded scope of loyalty politics. He first came to public prominence as a disloyal citizen when he was listed as one of the 64 citizens assessed under General Order #24 in December of 1861. He undoubtedly made himself even more visible when he along with 30 other of the assessed signed the published protest to the order on December 26 of 1861. By the time the Union officials arrived at his home, McPheeters had already "sold" much of his assessed property including his horse to his liveryman, infuriating Union authorities. Union officers stripped his household of much of what remained and shortly thereafter began to seriously pressure McPheeters to take the loyalty oath. According to his account, "an arbitrary military order was issued requiring all persons to take an oath which honor and conscience alike forbid my taking, and police officers were put on my track to enforce taking this odious oath." At this juncture, McPheeters "chose" to leave the city, and in June of 1863, he joined the Confederate war effort as a surgeon in the Missouri Brigade under Sterling Price's command.[24]

In July of 1865, shortly after returning to St. Louis at the close of the war, William McPheeters sat down to write an explanation for his decision to leave St. Louis and join the Confederate war effort. In this account, which he labeled "private" and placed in his personal papers, he described the "amazement" with which he witnessed the rise of "deep animosity" and "diabolical hatred" against southern sympathizers in St. Louis. "The press, the pulpit and all classes of society breathed out threatenings of the fiercest and most malignant character, and with savage ferocity and fiendish malignity seemed to thirst for their blood and their annihilation." Despite his best efforts to "keep any opinions to myself" and to "put a guard on my tongue," he found himself singled out by the Union military authorities. "I certainly," he wrote in 1865, "had violated no law, civil or military, but was quietly practicing my profession, when by order of Maj. General Halleck, my house was entered in broad daylight by U.S. police officers and robbed of over 2,000 worth of furniture, and this too at a time when one of my children was lying at the point of death in the house, and did die a few days thereafter."[25]

In McPheeters's account his experience as a southern sympathizer was that of an innocent victim, who was systematically stripped of his standing as a free man, first denied his public rights of free speech and of political representation and then "robbed" of the domestic face of his manhood, his ability to protect his dependents. Certainly, the culminating image of the confiscation of his household effects even down to his dying infant's crib, the most vulnerable of his dependents in the most vulnerable of conditions, was presented to explain the extent of the violation of his own position in the community. Nonetheless, as he explained in his own account of the events, he hesitated to leave, in fact, he considered it, "his duty to remain at home and take care of my family and attend my business . . . ." As with the earlier cases of P. B. Garesche or W. C. Lane, William McPheeters found himself squeezed between his position as a known southern sympathizer on the one hand and his desire to protect his family on the other. The irony was that the deeper the politics of loyalty cut into southern sympathizing households, the more it created both the need to leave in order to protect one's honor and to stay in order to protect one's dependents, and, again, one's honor. There was a point at which, however, such men could be smoked out. For McPheeters, this point came in the summer of 1863 when, as he somewhat sarcastically put it, the "best government on earth" having not only reduced him to the position of being unable to protect his household from "robbery" (as he termed assessment), but also went so far as to insist that he pledge allegiance to the very government that authorized the policy itself.[26]

Three days after recording his own story, on July 27, 1865, William McPheeters once again sat down to write another account, this one being the story of his wife's banishment in January of 1865. According to McPheeters, after he left St. Louis for the Confederacy in the summer of 1863, his wife, Sally McPheeters, began writing to him, sending her mail South through the Union lines under a flag of truce. She was able to do this because the Union officer in charge of the mail was an acquaintance of William McPheeters's from before the war and he kindly agreed to send her mail through the enemy lines. When the Union officer in charge changed in December 1864, Sally McPheeters attached a note to the new officer, General Reynolds, requesting that he continue the favor of forwarding her mail to her husband, now on General Price's staff. She indicated in her letter that she hoped that the new officer in charge would continue to extend her the courtesy of moving her mail and that, "like some others had not changed from a gentleman to a fiend." As William McPheeters later explained, rather than taking this comment as it was intended, "a complimentary piece of pleasantry," Reynolds took it as an insult and as "an indignity through him to his government." Instead of forwarding Sally McPheeters's mail on to her husband, Reynolds forwarded it to his superior officer with the order, "Send Mrs. Sally McPheeters down and put her through the lines at once." Sally McPheeters was immediately arrested, thrown in Gratiot Prison, and two days later, on January 17, 1865, banished South, down the Mississippi River in what turned out to be a long and harrowing trip through embattled territory in the dead of winter with two young children.[27]

In his account, William McPheeters explained his reason for recording his wife's wartime treatment. He offered it as evidence of that way in which, "the best government in the world waged war on women and children." Sally McPheeters's only mistake, according to her husband was to assume that officers of the Union military were indeed "gentlemen." Men, that is, who would continue to respect the domestic position of household dependents even in the face of the absence of the household head. Men who could be expected to continue to assist a woman like Sally McPheeters in her simple desire to maintain contact with her absent husband. Instead, in banishing Sally McPheeters and her young children from St. Louis in the dead of winter, these Union officials indicated that they had indeed been rendered "fiends" by their wartime experience. Of course in laying the responsibility for his family's suffering upon on the doorstep of the government and the behavior of Union military officers of St. Louis in particular, McPheeters reduced his own responsibility for his family's wartime suffering. He certainly knew that in choosing to leave St. Louis for the Confederacy, rather than taking the despised loyalty oath, that he was leaving his wife and children vulnerable to such treatment. Indeed, it was his very leaving that opened his household up, if only by the necessity of attempting to maintain contact with him across what was now enemy lines. In writing these accounts of his own and his wife's wartime experience, William McPheeters remembered events in a manner that served to reconstruct his fragmented wartime self, especially his fragmented experience of manhood. In doing so he minimized the difficulty of his own position at the time, when he was forced to choose between his public political self, that is, taking the much despised loyalty oath and his continued ability to remain at St. Louis and protect his wife and children. By holding the Union military responsible for the continued protection of his wife and children, he absolved himself of the responsibility for the difficulties his wife and children encountered, particularly for their banishment from the Union in the winter of 1865.[28]

Southern sympathizing men, like Garesche, Lane, or McPheeters, were outraged at the violation of their position as free men, particularly when Union policy not only violated their public rights, but even went so far as to violate their domestic position and thereby "make war on women and children." Union officials, the Republican press, and certainly the refugees from the southwest part of the state, viewed the behavior of southern sympathizing men in much the same light. It was, after all, the rebels of the southwest who attacked those refugees for nothing more than their political opinions, their loyalty to the Union, and showed no mercy toward their dependent women and children who were reduced to penury and want in the process. On each side men clung to the belief that they were honorable men, even as they engaged in the violation of enemy men and their households in order to be so. Indeed, the abuse of innocent dependents was repeatedly trotted out—whether the victims were the "suffering families" that drove the assessment of southern sympathizers, or the assessed or even banished southern sympathizing women like J. Garesche, S. McPheeters, or Mrs. McRee.

The deeper this war of the household cut into the gender order of society, the more important it became to locate the responsibility for the abuse of household dependents with the enemy. In this pitched battle over which side could lay claim to honorable behavior, women and children were presented as the innocent victims, the field upon which men's contest over who could claim the position of honorable manhood was waged. Take for example, the story of Sally McPheeters. In William McPheeters's recollection, his wife's only error was to assume that Union military men were still "gentlemen," men, that is, like her own husband. But was Sally McPheeters simply the loyal wife, appealing to the Union authorities for the apparently small favor of some continued connection with her husband? Was she struck down by odious Union "fiends" intent upon totally destroying the households of southern sympathizers even to the point of once again violating dependent women and children? William McPheeters's presentation of the contents of Sally's letter is revealing when compared with the Union military's own file on her. While the Union officers did, indeed, take issue with being referred to as "fiends," as

McPheeters's claimed, they also took issue with another passage of Sally McPheeters's letter, a passage that William McPheeters never mentioned. They took offense at what they read as a militant statement of disloyalty on the part of Sally McPheeters's herself. As she wrote, "send a letter by southern flag of truce . . . And you will have the thanks of a Rebel though she be." The official complaint filed against Sally McPheeters was not simply that she referred to persons representing the U.S. government as "fiends," as her husband indicated in his account, but also that she signed her letter by "defiantly declar(ing) herself a Rebel."[29]

And so, why did William McPheeters omit his wife's militant declaration of southern sympathy, "a Rebel though she be?" After all, in his telling of his own story, the consequence of his commitment to his southern sympathies was the central pivot of the entire account. It was the reason for his household's assessment, for his refusal to take the loyalty oath, and for his decision to join the Confederacy. Why wasn't William McPheeters equally concerned to record the depth of his wife's commitment to the southern cause? Why doesn't her story appear as his does and her own banishment told as the moment when she, like him, could no longer continue to compromise her honor for the continued security of her dependent children? This was literally the way her letter read, the way the Union military read it, as a woman who was first a Rebel, a Rebel who would nonetheless lower herself to appreciate a domestic concession from the Union authorities, as she herself wrote, "send a letter . . . and you will have the thanks of a Rebel though she be."[30]

This would be the ultimate violation of southern sympathizing men, the ultimate collapse from within, not just that southern sympathizing men were rendered domestic, forced themselves to "choose" to expose their women, and were thus made less than men. What would go beyond that would be if in same process their women became more than women, not victims in a man's war, but agents of war, "rebels" in their own right. And as the war of the household pushed their men back onto domestic ground, and as their men took up the fight on the level of the household and lost even there, it did become increasingly difficult for the other household dependents, especially the adult women of southern sympathizing households, to remain politically inert and passive victims. Politics, that is, agency, in the conflict came to them whether they wanted it or not. It came to them structurally in the course of the war as the status of dependent was politicized as much by the actions of their own men as by the Union military authorities. Women responded in a variety of ways to the increased political significance they found attributed to their position in the household. Sally McPheeters apparently chose to take up the rebel flag, dropped by her husband as he left the state. Julliette Garesche attempted to continue to play the appropriately needy and dependent woman in her appeal to the Union authorities. Even so, in the very act of begging for mercy, Garesche was called upon to stand up for herself and her household, to take up what, in the context of a war of the households, had become a position of public political protest.

War for southern sympathizers was an experience of turning their households inside out. As the position of being a father was rendered domestic, the position of being a mother and a wife was rendered public and political. For southern sympathizing women this lead to the experience of apparently private conversations and familial correspondence in 1861 becoming suspect and even traitorous by 1863, as the very position of dependents was politicized and became charged in ways no one could have foretold at the outbreak of war in the spring of 1861. Take the case of Mrs. McRee, who was banished by the Provost Marshal for her disloyal sentiments in the summer of 1863. How did the Union authorities come to have a word-by-word account of her dinner table conversation of two years previous and why did he care? Her dinner table speeches of 1861, critical of the Union invasion of her state, became the grounds for her banishment in 1863 because by 1863 the war of the household had rendered the mother as mother itself political. The very first question asked of her when she was called before the Provost Marshal was very revealing in this regard, "Have you any relations in the rebel army?' Followed by, "Have you ever sent or received from the rebel army any letters?" For southern sympathizing women, these questions might just as well have been, are you a southern sympathizing wife, mother, or daughter? Do you maintain your relationship to your husband, son, or father? For the Union military, these questions were all about their concern over southern sympathizing women's ability to influence and even recruit St. Louis men into the rebel forces. For southern sympathizing women, they were all about a political and military struggle that had worked its way to the core of domestic life itself.[31]

Mrs. McRee was particularly precariously placed in this regard. She did indeed have a son in the Confederacy, which marked her as a confirmed disloyal mother. She was a widow and her home was a boardinghouse. She was therefore structurally more "public" than other southern sympathizing women, both because she had no husband or father to afford her whatever public protection he might be able to muster and because she had domestic influence over more than her own biological sons by virtue of her boardinghouse connections. Indeed, Mrs. McRee's dinner companions in 1861 included a number of young men of military age and the only testimony garnered against her was the written testimony of one of these young men, Harrison Glenn. Glenn was actually the brother of the boardinghouse keeper, who was herself a southern sympathizer. By the spring of 1863, however, when Glenn penned two lengthy letters to the St. Louis Provost Marshal detailing Mrs. McRee's traitorous speeches, he had come to reconsider his own early enthusiasm for the southern cause. By that time, he was himself a soldier in service of the Provost Marshal, stationed at Warrensburg, Missouri. Glenn made a point of indicating to the Provost Marshal that he now refused to set foot in his sister's house and had refused to cross her threshold for months at a time, even when he passed his previous home on an almost daily basis. As he wrote on May 13, 1863, "My dear sir there is scarcely a man in St. Louis less able to aid you in your glorious work than myself. My course has been plain and consistent as my intimacy with the rebel crew thank god has been growing beautifully less ever since those heartrending days."[32]

The problem for Glenn was to explain his own extensive knowledge of southern sympathizers, his obviously intimate connection with women like McRee, without tainting himself with the same disloyal brush. Obviously, he was now a loyal man, but what could explain his initial disloyal sympathies and connections? Eager to distance himself from his southern sympathizing connections, Glenn supplied the blow-by-blow account of Mrs. McRee's dinner table talk. According to his account, Mrs. McRee and the other southern sympathizing women at their common board, including his own sister, emerge as powerful and seductive traitors. "They are the most able women I have any knowledge of . . .They are informed upon all subjects. Treason especially to a degree that would be wonderful if they were not so sinful and wicked." So persuasive were these veritable "Lucretia Borgias," according to Glenn, that "they should be made to answer for the crime of others particularly the young. They left nothing undone to poison young minds against all that is holy in devotion to our country."[33]

According to Glenn, the answer to this question resided in the character of southern sympathizing women like McRee herself. ". . . to furnish a catalogue of Mrs. McRee's guilt would fill a volume. I regard those women Mrs. McRee and Mrs. Reyburn as the archfiends of treason in St. Louis." In such circumstances, what was a southern sympathizing woman, intent upon remaining apolitical to do? Like her father before her, Anne Lane attempted to retreat ever more deeply into her household. By 1862, her letters to her sister no longer carried any news of the course of the war in St. Louis or the state more generally. Instead, she focused ever more entirely upon family matters. Even so, she could not resist at one point prefacing her letter with a defiant note to the Union censors she was sure were reading her mail, "Whoever may open this letter may spare themselves the trouble of reading it. There will be nothing in it that will repay the task of deciphering it to anyone except the invalid mother away from her home and pining for news of her infant children."[34]

Anne Lane could never feel entirely secure. Was her role as guardian to her sister's young children enough to gainsay her known status as a southern sympathizer? Even worse, was her very position as substitute mother itself perhaps now itself the problem? Her young nephews were in fact outspoken to their classmates with regard to their Confederate sympathies. Anne Lane was fortunate to have sufficient wealth and personal connections to allow her to leave the country altogether. In the spring of 1864, she joined her sister and other southern expatriates in Europe. There she was once again able to reconstruct a safe, southern sympathizing domestic world. As she wrote to her niece, who was still residing in St. Louis, "went to a party at Mrs. H. on Friday. It was almost like home. None there but rebels. We had a real American supper, turkey, ham and chicken salad."[35]

For most southern sympathizing women in St. Louis, however, expatriation was not a viable antidote to the politicization of their domestic world. They could not escape their daily lives, and their daily lives, their social circles, their social relations with those nearest and dearest, were ever more the stuff of improper influence, disloyal intrigue, and political consequences. Indeed, by 1863, the streetcars in St. Louis were dangerous for southern sympathizing women attempting, nonetheless, to remain apolitical from both sides of the conflict. For every account like Anne Lane's of being accosted by loyal Union women increasingly aware of the political significance of their domestic influence, there were stories of southern sympathizing women who encountered the Sallie McPheeters, the "Rebels though she be," from both sides of the line. Take the story of Mrs. Elizabeth Concannon, who was riding on the Franklin Avenue car in January of 1863 with a friend when she was confronted by a strange woman, but in her case, the strangely inquisitive stranger was not a member of the Ladies Loyal League, but rather a member of a southern mail smuggling ring. According to Mrs. Concannon, her role, like Anne Lane's was essentially innocent. She was simply telling her friend about how she had not heard from her son who was in the South for so long that she thought she would go down there and bring him home. Suddenly a woman sitting nearby, a stranger to her who had been listening to her conversation, interjected, saying, "You would not counsel your son to desert?" This woman then suggested that if Elizabeth remained faithful to the cause she would have the opportunity to send a letter to her son. A few days later, a note was left on her doorstep. The note indicated that "knowing and feeling all that you suffer, for I have a son there I write to say that if you will send a letter to him ... I will try to send it through for you ... You wish to get him back; that can't be done, but you can hear from him ... I sympathize with you deeply."[36]

The strange woman on the bus and the writer of the note was Mrs. McLure, a woman that Elizabeth Concannon later described for the Provost Marshal as being "a stout handsome lady with short grey curls with a large wart on the side of her nose." Mrs. McLure was a widow, like Mrs. McRee, and herself ran a boardinghouse. She also had a son in the Confederate Army that she had received no word from until a card was left at her door in November of 1862 and another in February with these words written in pencil. "January 22 This is my birthday dear mother. I greet you." Offered the opportunity to send some items to her son, Mrs. McLure accepted. As she explained to the Provost Marshal upon her arrest in March of 1863, "The destitution ... Of the rebel army would induce a mother to accept such an offer, without asking any questions. I did not ask the man's name. I left the bundle tied up ... and I am told the man called and got it while I was at market. I never heard whether my son got the things. There were several other small articles besides the blanket, boot toothbrush etc."[37]

After her own experience, Mrs. McClure apparently herself became a militant worker in the southern mail connection. Was she a good mother?

Or a veritable Lucretia Borgia? What was the difference? To the Union military, she was a spy who deserved her imprisonment and eventual banishment, to southern sympathizers, she was a loyal mother. Each side experienced the other as the aggressor and themselves as the innocent victims. In fact, what they were experiencing was actually two sides of the same coin, the turning of the household inside out. No one, certainly not the women themselves, were about giving up domesticity. They did what they did because domesticity itself demanded it of them. What the Loyalty League itself saw as the politicization of influence when it came to Union women was indeed no different when it came to southern women. The only real difference was, who would win in the war between the women and what would both sides win, or lose, in the emergence of women as agents of war?

CHAPTER 4

HOME GUARDS AND HOME TRAITORS: LOYALTY AND PROSTITUTION IN CIVIL WAR ST. LOUIS

On the morning of August 29, 1861, a captain of the U.S. Infantry decided to take a stroll down Fourth Street, a major thoroughfare of St. Louis, with his new bride on his arm. According to a letter of complaint written that very day to the Provost Marshal, Major McKinistry, the hundreds of citizens who witnessed this act found it "exceedingly disgusting." It was especially humiliating to the Union men in the crowd. The author of the complaint, who preferred to remain anonymous, suggested that officers or soldiers in the Union forces, like McKinistry himself, must surely be even more concerned by such behavior on the part of a uniformed officer. The alleged bride was, after all, a notorious woman around the town. For years, she had kept a public house in St. Louis and was rumored to have amassed considerable wealth through her "iniquitous" calling. Indeed, it was rumored that the reason why the officer had so besmirched the honor of his uniform was in order to acquire the brothel keepers' ill-gotten wealth. According to the outraged citizen, "not another man could be found in St. Louis who would be seen with her (publicly) under any circumstances."[1]

The Provost Marshal of St. Louis passed this anonymous complaint on to his commanding officer that same day, noting that, "the matter is reported to this office as having caused considerable discussion in the city, and it is said that a large portion of the money made by the woman as a keeper of houses of ill repute has been transferred to the officer who is to claim her for his wife." Although the couple was rumored to have been married a few days earlier, the Provost Marshal indicated that he was unable to confirm that fact, nor was he able to name either the author of the complaining letter or the offending officer. He was, however, able to provide the name of the "woman of notorious character," or as he put it, "at least one of her names—Jennie A. Atwood." The commanding general took no action on the complaint, simply writing, "file" across the case. This was not the end of the matter, however, at least it was not the end of it for Jennie A. Atwood. For on September 23, 1861, some four weeks later,

Provost Marshal McKinistry ordered the first women to be banished from the city under martial law. According to the official order, the reason for their arrest and banishment was that they had been charged and proven guilty of "vagrancy, lewdness, disorderly conduct and keeping brothels and houses of ill fame." One name on this list was no other than Jennie A. Atwood.[2]

The story of Jennie Atwood and her army captain husband presents many of the dilemmas that the Union military faced in attempting to secure a major border state city like St. Louis for the Union. While the most pressing problem might appear to be the threat of powerfully placed southern sympathizers in the city, what one loyal Union citizen described as "Home Traitors," the Union authorities also had to be concerned about the thousands of Union men, like the army captain, who moved through the city on their way to or from the front. These men were indeed in a position, as the anonymous letter writer suggested, to particularly humiliate the Union war effort. As fighting men, they represented the highest sacrifice, the greatest valor, and the most loyal bearers of the Union cause. As men on leave or stationed more permanently in St. Louis, their behavior along a domestic axis of loyalty, when for example they squandered their pay in low saloons, in gambling dens, or even worse, in brothels, threatened to undercut their position as loyal Union men, as the Home Guard.[3]

When the Provost Marshal took up power in St. Louis, then, he actually faced two forms of disloyalty, two wars to fight. While he was intent upon rooting out the southern sympathizing citizens he found himself confronted with another form of disloyalty, domestic disloyalty, the worst of it arguably being manifest in a case like that of Jennie A. Atwood. It literally was not possible, however much the Provost Marshal might desire it, to simply come into St. Louis and fight a war against political disloyalty, to lop off the head of the old southern sympathizing elite in the town, and take over the reins of the power. In order to gain the loyalty of the population, to enlist them in the war for the Union, it was also necessary to maintain and expand the respect that the Union forces and Union men more generally held in the city. Winning the war for the Union in St. Louis, then, was both a matter of making southern sympathizers visible as "Home Traitors," while also ensuring that Union soldiers in St. Louis would behave like the loyal "Home Guards" they purported to be.

When Major McKinistry took up power as Provost Marshal of St. Louis in August of 1861, he faced a tough job on both fronts. Southern sympathizers were still firmly entrenched in positions of formal political and social power; that is, they were far from being publicly defined as "Home" Traitors. Even after some six months under martial law in St. Louis, one avid support of the Union cause in the city, S. T. Glover, wrote an impassioned letter to the Provost Marshal expressing his concern that the Provost Marshal was proving incapable of holding the line against what he perceived as the overwhelming "moral influence" of the southern sympathizers in St. Louis. As he put it, "We have many sorts of enemies to deal with in this war. Among these here in Missouri those in the field with arms in their hands are in my poor judgment the least formidable, *by far the least formidable*." The real key to winning the war in Missouri, according to this loyal citizen, was to continue rooting out the southern sympathizing civilian with a vengeance. As he put it in plea to the Provost Marshal:

> Cut off from the miserable vagabond devils who are in the field the sympathy of our home traitors. Cut them off from the information they constantly receive from our home traitors, cut them off from the aid and comfort of kindly speeches and enthusiastic admiration and encouragement of our home traitors cut them off from the potent advantages they derive from the preaching and recruiting of our home traitors . . . and how long would the armed enemy keep the field? Not a month.[4]

From this perspective, the southern sympathizing elite of St. Louis were the real key to winning the war, especially the war as it was fought in a divided area like Missouri. The problem, however, was that the "moral influence" of the elite was so entrenched that no effective policy could be carried out against them without a horrified hue and cry from their neighbors. In order to effectively route out their influence, the Provost Marshal needed to convince a sufficient portion of the citizenry that southern sympathizers were not in fact the respectable citizens they had always been held to be, but were indeed much more like the persons of greatest "ill fame" in the city, like the madam, Jennie Atwood, whose very public presence defiled its streets. Political "Home Traitors" were really whores, one might say, for the traitorous rebel cause. They really were, as Glover's letter claimed, like those "miserable vagabond devils . . . in the field."[5]

Unfortunately for the Provost Marshal, not only was the old southern sympathizing elite firmly entrenched in the city at the onset of martial law in August of 1861, but the Union troops also seemed, if anything, to be winning the war for the title of Home Traitor. And so while the task of rendering the old southern sympathizing elite of the city as disrespectable was obviously going to be a hard sell for the Provost Marshal, the same could not be said for Union soldiers like the army captain. For the citizens who lined the walk on that August morning when he and his wife, Jennie Atwood, promenaded by it was obvious who was the disloyal citizen. Respectable citizens, regardless of regional loyalty, could agree that prostitution and its associated "disorderly houses," the madams, and the common whores, were traitors to respectable homes. Of course, only the offending bawd was legally defined as the domestic traitor, and as such under antebellum city law, a vagrant, subject to imprisonment and hard labor at the rock pile in St. Louis or worse, banishment from the city. Still, many who lined the street that day, probably more of the women than the men, also thought men who spent their families hard earned money at houses of ill fame, men who violated their marriage vows with women of low repute, men who brought home loathsome diseases to their wives and passed them on to their children, also perpetuated an act of treason against the home.[6]

Indeed, in the face of the burgeoning business of the houses of ill fame, in the summer of 1861, at least some of the female citizens of St. Louis were willing to do more than simply write anonymous letters to the public authorities. They were willing to take direct action, as when a crowd of women shut down the "notorious residence" of Mrs. Knox on 7th St. on July 31. Armed with whatever they could find on hand, they marched on the offending residence, throwing rocks and "cracking heads" with their house-hold weapons. "Everything that could be smashed was," according to the newspaper account, "and what couldn't was thrown out the window." As a final blow, the outraged women chased the prostitutes out of the house and down the street, beating them around the head with sticks and throwing stones. They were only restrained by the rather tardy arrival of the local police force. At that point, the destruction was so thorough that the press account could only conclude, "they won't be opening again soon."[7]

The offense of this particular madam that pushed the neighborhood women over the line into direct action was the particularly rude and aggressive fashion in which the business of her disorderly house was cut-ting into the good management of their own respectable households. An uneasy peace existed between the respectable households and these houses of "ill fame" in St. Louis, even without the added pressure of large numbers of transient military men like the army captain. In the 1850s, the huge influx of immigrants into the city, which meant the addition of large numbers of unattached men and women, had already fueled the expansion of brothels and heightened conflict in neighborhoods over their presence. The attack on Mrs. Knox's brothel began when one woman in the neighborhood went to the madam upon learning that her husband had squandered his last fifty dollars at her house the night before. She appealed to the madam to return the money as her children were hungry and the money was rightfully theirs. Mrs. Knox simply scoffed at this suggestion and must have been shocked when neighborhood women appeared shortly thereafter to shut down her house by force.[8]

In the case of this neighborhood riot, the women were moved to attack the brothel because the husband overstepped the boundary of respectabil-ity when he bankrupted the running of his legitimate household. The case of the unnamed army captain was of a similar nature in that he also stepped over the line when he paraded the whore down the street in broad daylight. His act of actually legally marrying the whore, however, of using his position to actually render her disreputable house reputable, went even further than the wayward husband's expenditure of funds that properly belonged to his own household. The disloyal behavior of the army captain did not just drain resources from respectable households, his traitorship subverted its very core, the institution of marriage itself. No wonder the concerned loyal citizen was moved to write to the Provost Marshal after witnessing the new couple parading the street. No wonder Union men were "particularly humiliated" by the officer's behavior. How was the Union military, and Union citizens more generally, going to establish themselves as the new controlling elite, if the Union military forces behaved in such a disreputable fashion? Even if the Provost Marshal could lop off the head off the old social elite, even if local supporters of the Union war effort in the city could redefine them as "Home Traitors," how were they to establish themselves as the new elite, the "Home Guard," that they literally claimed to be?

The circumstances of soldiers in St. Louis only seemed to contribute to the likelihood that they would fall away from whatever commitment to respectable behavior they brought with them from their home communities. They were, after all, structurally anonymous. While everyone knew the "notorious" Jennie Atwood, no one knew the army captain. St. Louis wasn't his hometown, and he wouldn't be staying long in any case. He was, for the moment, the cock of the walk, an officer of the occupying forces. Domestic disloyalty came cheap under the circumstances. Far from friends and family, such soldiers found themselves exposed to the attractions of a big city, many for the first time, with time on their hands and money in their pockets. One soldier wrote a letter of dismay to his younger brother when he heard of his enlistment in the Union forces, a letter that was published on the front page of the St. Louis newspapers. "A young person might almost as well be placed in a drinking and gambling saloon, and remain there, as to go into the army," he wrote. "That is the great reason I was so sorry to hear of your enlisting . . . .The greatest temptations with which you will have to contend are intemperance, gambling and profanity."[9]

Indeed, by August 15, 1861, when Governor Fremont formally established martial law in the state of Missouri, and appointed Major McKinistry in charge of its administration in St. Louis, the city had already experienced serious levels of disorderly behavior on the part of Union soldiers. The strategic location of St. Louis on the Mississippi River meant that throughout the war, thousands of troops would march through its streets on their way to and from the Mississippi River and the military front. The location of two major barracks, Benton Barracks within the city and Jefferson Barracks on the city's outskirts, ensured that the city would also serve as a major recruiting and training center for Union soldiers. Benton Barracks alone could accommodate 20,000 soldiers. With the first outbreak of fighting within the state at Wilson's Creek on August 10, the city also became a major hospital center with the capacity of some 5,000 beds. With so many men stationed or passing through the city, only a small number of fractious soldiers could create social chaos.[10]

By the time McKinistry took charge of the city in August of 1861, local citizens had already been confronted with thousands of such transient men, some under direct military control and others not. The *Missouri Republican* described one scene of military embarkment shortly before the declaration of martial law, as an event that, "presented scenes that have seldom been witnessed in any city on this continent, and never before in

St. Louis." Soldiers crowded into the levee saloons and jammed the sidewalks, intent upon spending their pay before shipping out. Their officers were equally intent upon loading their men upon the waiting boats. The outcome was a veritable melee among officers, rowdy troops, and local citizens.

> The most notable trouble was the levee retailers of eatables, who might be seen eagerly picking up the contents of jars that had been smashed, or chasing soldiers towards the boat, to recover articles of food, taken but not paid for, the outcries of the owners, and the angry remonstrances of the soldiers, as portions of cheese or other eatables were snatched from their grasp, made a scene of confusion that at times drowned the noise of the bells kept ringing to draw the soldiers to their boats. Occasionally the sound of a musket, fired off by some reckless reveler, would cause a momentary silence in the vicinity, as people crowded around to discover whether the contents of the weapon had been discharged into the body of a human being. Scattered at intervals might be seen officers and guards struggling to drive the soldiers on board of their boats, or carrying someone who had forgotten his duties by a rest on a pavement. Nearer the river, wagons with their loads of baggage and soldiers, rushing with the articles through the crowd to the vessels caused a confusion almost equally as great as that further back near the saloons. In some instances the attempt to drive stragglers to their commands resulted in their resisting and a fight ensuing and so the scene continued until, through exhaustion and force, the soldiers were driven to the boat.[11]

While the difficulties of moving large numbers of troops through the city was challenging for the officers, at least the troops on the levee were under direct military control. More problematic was the control of troops when they were not under direct military supervision. St. Louis was a large city in 1861 of more than 100,000 citizens, much larger than the soldiers, most recruits from small towns or rural areas, had ever encountered before. With pay in their pockets and no family or community to restrain them, these men found themselves presented with a whole urban world of low saloons, brothels and gambling dens. Only two days after the riotous incident at the levee, on August 3, 1861, Union soldiers were once again in the news. This time the story was one of riot and property destruction in one of the low districts of the city.

> Last evening some drunken soldiers got into a difficulty at a low house on Almond Street, which speedily increased to a riot. . . . The soldiers in the city having been lately paid off, have in some instances, squandered their earnings as fast as possible, in dissipation. When the police arrived, the streets in the vicinity were filled with a drunken and reckless crowd, who were counseling an attack on all the buildings of like description near. With a good deal of difficulty they were dispersed, and the streets cleared.[12]

In this case, someone at one of the brothels on the street had "Hurrahed for Jeff Davis" and the Union soldiers, well aware of the southern sympathies of many of the citizens of St. Louis, decided to demolish the place. When the police arrived, they were in the process of moving on from the initial brothel to attack the other low houses on the street.

From legitimate grocers on the levee to brothel keepers in the low quarters of the city, business proprietors had reason to be seriously concerned about theft, riot, and property destruction in the summer of 1861. Along with the security of their property, citizens had to be concerned about the security of their very persons. In May of 1861, the Union forces were successful in securing a critical arsenal located on the outskirts of St. Louis for the Union. When the triumphant Union troops, mostly the inexperienced Home Guard, marched back through the city they encountered heckling from southern sympathizing citizens who lined the walks. Some of the troops opened fire on the crowd, wounding many and killing several bystanders. The possibility of a repeat of such an incident was always a possibility in a border city like St. Louis, only tenuously held by the Union forces. Indeed, on August x another potentially similar incident was nipped in the bud when a bystander took aim at a group of transient troops. Fortunately, the bystander missed and though some of the soldiers chased after the offending individual, the officer in charge was able to restrain his men from firing into the crowd in return.[13]

This sort of heckling from the curb continued as a sort of political statement, even after martial law was established. One young southern sympathizing Washington University student described the continued resistance to Union forces in this fashion shortly after martial law was established in the city. "Whenever regiments return from battles, as from Carthage and Springfield, they are looked at by the people but not a cheer, not a kind word, this shows the spirit of the people of St. Louis, and it is keenly felt by the worn out soldiers . . . notwithstanding the newspaper lies, which say they were enthusiastically received and all that sort of stuff." The student's description reveals a sort of stiff-necked pride in the unwillingness of some citizens to show anything but disdain for the tired and battle worn Union troops. The kind of explosive rage that fueled the brothel riot by soldiers in response to an anonymous "Hurrah for Jeff Davis," reveals the level of hostility between the troops and many of the local citizens. The consumption of alcohol only served to intensify hostilities and a drunken "Hurrah for Jeff Davis" remained a common reason not only for arrest, but also for imprisonment by the Union authorities throughout the war. As with heckling passing troops, "Hurrahing for Jeff Davis," was a sort of war cry of the local community, both sides heard it for it was.[14]

When McKinistry announced the establishment of martial law in St. Louis on August 14 then there was some reason for citizens, whatever their position on the war, to welcome it if only for the way that it promised to bring some order to the behavior of Union troops while in the city. McKinistry's formal explanation of the nature and intent of his office, which was published in the daily press, appeared to address this common concern of St. Louis citizens. The purpose of the establishment of martial law was, according to McKinistry, to "insure the preservation of public peace." He promised the citizens of the city that martial law would only step in when civil law was "inadequate to maintain public peace and safety." From respectable shopkeepers on the levee to more questionable brothel keepers on Almond Street, merchants could agree that martial law was desirable if it promised to restrain theft and property damage. Ordinary citizens, whether southern sympathizing citizens lining the walks as Union soldiers passed through or loyal Union citizens out for an innocent morning stroll, could agree that no one wanted to see another Camp Jackson Massacre, as the local population referred to the bloody conflict between Union troops and southern sympathizing civilians of the previous spring, and certainly few respectable citizens welcomed the public embrace of the city's low life by the Union soldiers.[15]

Given McKinistry's stated commitment to insuring public peace, which was widely published in the city's leading newspapers, one might reasonably expect that his first orders in office would concern improving the behavior of Union troops in St. Louis. While the good discipline and respectable behavior of Union troops was undoubtedly of concern to him, judging from his course of action, it was apparently not his most pressing concern. McKinistry's very first order as Provost Marshal on August 14, 1861 was to shut down the southern sympathizing newspaper, the *War Bulletin*, followed by an order to arrest the President of the Board of Police Commissioners, John A. Brownlee. The Provost Marshal proceeded to replace Brownlee with a man known to be a loyal Union man and to order Brownlee transported to Cairo, making him the first person ordered banished from the city under martial law. McKinistry then turned his energies toward the suppression of two more southern sympathizing newspapers, *The True Missourian* and the *Morning Herald* and ordered the arrest of the editor of the *War Bulletin*. Having done what he could in an opening salvo to secure the loyalty of the police and the press, McKinistry then turned the power of martial law on the raid of southern sympathizing households suspected of hiding caches of arms. He issued orders directed at controlling the possession of arms by disloyal citizens, the most important being orders that proscribed gun sellers from selling or even giving away arms to citizens known for their disloyal political sympathies.[16]

It was not until the third day of martial law and a slew of orders had been carried out against high placed southern sympathizers that Major McKinistry turned the power of his position in the direction of addressing the problem of social disorder among the troops and citizenry more generally. He ordered the sale of liquor restricted between the hours of midnight Saturday and Monday morning, offering local citizens some relief from riotous drunken behavior on Sunday. He also limited the late hours of places of public amusement, such as the theatre, concert halls, dance houses, and Negro minstrels and closed them entirely on Sundays. While many of the citizens of St. Louis undoubtedly appreciated the limits martial law placed on the late night drunken revelries that had culminated in events like the brothel riot, these initial efforts to secure respectable behavior seem fairly insignificant compared with the attack on powerfully placed southern sympathizers. Indeed the removal of the Chief of Police, Brownlee, while undoubtedly critical to the pursuit of a successful war against the political "Home Traitors," arguably undercut the ability of the city police to preserve good domestic order. Not only did the new chief of police proceed to remove all the old members of the Police Board, he fired a considerable portion of the police force staff for political disloyalty as well. Throughout the war the police would limp along at two-thirds its antebellum strength because of this loyalty purge.[17]

From the perspective of the Provost Marshal, however, the purging of the St. Louis police was really a matter of putting first things first. Good public order could never be achieved as long as the root of the entire rebellion, southern sympathizers, continued to hold so much formal power in the city. The Provost Marshal had no choice but to first secure the control of the police and the military arms in the city. Beyond that, the Provost Marshal had to be concerned about the sites of cultural influence, like the press, the schools, and the pulpit. In the first few weeks of martial law, the Provost Marshal would also order the commissioner of the public schools to purge the schools of southern sympathizing teachers, as he had the police force. He would keep a careful watch over the most outspoken of the southern sympathizing clergy in the city, eventually arresting and banishing some of them. He would ban the circulation in the city of southern sympathizing newspapers published elsewhere.[18]

While the purging of various key professions and the arrest and even imprisonment or banishment of leading southern sympathizers raised the hostility of some St. Louis citizens, especially her southern sympathizing citizens, at least the ground for the Provost Marshal's actions were clear. They were at war. These men were disloyal to the Union war effort. From this perspective, the disorderly behavior of the Union troops was more problematic for Union authorities. Who or what was the legitimate enemy in this case? There was no declared war on men who betrayed their home by violating their domestic commitments, as there was a declared war against men who divided the bigger house of the Union by their political disloyalties. While it was clearly the responsibility of the Union military to expect orderly behavior out of their men while in active service, how far should or could military force extend over how enlisted men spent their pay while on leave or convalescing in the city's hospitals? While many local citizens may have been outraged at the behavior of the army captain with his "wife," the notorious Jennie Atwood, was it really the purview of the military to intercede in such matters?[19]

On August 26, some two weeks into martial law, McKinistry decided that some further action to control disorderly behavior was required. Noting a "disturbance of the public peace" that could be traced to the "unauthorized and improper sale of liquor to soldiers by irresponsible and ill disposed persons," he ordered "all saloons and barrooms and other places kept for the retailing of spirituous and intoxicating liquors in the city, except saloons connected with the principal hotels be closed." Perhaps this order on the part of the Provost Marshal simply indicated the somewhat tardy dedication of the Provost Marshal to maintaining reasonable order on the part of Union troops in St. Louis. He may have come to recognize that his initial regulation of Sunday and late hour business by saloons was insufficient to the task of maintaining minimally good order. The order came not a minute too soon, according to one St. Louis citizen, "Amongst the hail storm of proclamations now let loose, this is one that should have been out long ago, you see so many of these drunken defenders of our liberties that it is time to put a stop to them."[20]

It was, however, also widely rumored at the time that what really prompted the closure of the saloons was the fact that General Lyon's funeral cortege was on its way from the southwest corner of the state and would arrive in St. Louis at any moment. General Lyon, the driving force behind the successful invasion of the state by Union forces, was mortally wounded while leading a charge at the Battle of Wilson's Creek. As the slain hero of the Union military forces in the state, the movement of his casket with full military honors through the city raised the specter of yet another violent clash between soldiers and civilians. The free flow of liquor promised to increase the difficulty of an already difficult situation, amplifying the militancy of southern sympathizers on the one hand, while increasing the hostility and potential for wild behavior on the part of Union forces on the other. The movement of Lyon's body in state through the city warranted the closure of the saloons and other drinking places by the Provost Marshal then because it was an event that so clearly threatened to grease the wheels of southern sympathizing opposition on the one hand while escalating poor "Home Guard" behavior on the part of Union troops on the other.[21]

While the arrival of Lyon's body was an event that brought drink and its associated businesses to the attention of the Provost Marshal because it brought the excesses of low-life culture into direct and potentially damaging connection with the political war he was attempting to fight against southern sympathizing Home Traitors, his order to shut down the saloons in response was an attempt to bring his war against the political Home Traitors into line with his war against domestic disorder. The Provost Marshal never attempted to absolutely restrict drinking or saloons from soldiers, rather his policy was to render drink harmless to the pursuit of the Union war effort, whether the harm to the war effort came from the association of drink with political disloyalty on the one hand or domestic disloyalty on the other. In order to reopen for business, saloons had to agree to certain limits in serving liquor to soldiers. They were restricted from serving hard liquor to common soldiers altogether and could only serve malt liquor in moderation. Common soldiers were not to frequent "low" saloons under any circumstances. What defined a saloon as "low" was the presence of prostitutes plying their trade. By keeping the saloons strictly separate from the brothels, and limiting the extent of soldier drunkenness, the military hoped to be able to control the worst forms of social disorder that the troops generated. They hoped to shore up the line between the respectable and disrespectable households that the behavior of the disorderly Home Guard, like the army captain, threatened to undermine.[22]

Not only were saloons required to serve only beer to enlisted men and serve it in responsible quantities, they were also required to post signs indicating their political loyalty to the Union. One citizen, R. J. Howard, wrote in enthusiastic support of this new policy in October of 1861. "Nothing," he suggested, "during the present rebellion has, in my opinion, done more to squelsh treason in our city, than your order requiring the keepers of whiskey shops to attest their fidelity to the Government by placing the placard attesting that fidelity in a conspicuous place in their barrooms." While requiring public testimonials of Union loyalty may have contributed to reducing "Hurrahs for Jefferson Davis," that is overt acts of political disloyalty, the Provost Marshal's new regulations appeared to make only minimal inroads into the problems posed by disorderly behavior on the part of Union soldiers. One citizen described his experience of walking down to the levee with one departing regiment shortly after the crackdown on the saloons. "It was a shame," he wrote, "to see the men tumble about and fall down in their ranks, half the regiment must have been drunk, they actually fell while marching, and while they were halting on the Levee they broke ranks and rushed into the whiskey shops. The first and second regiment of the Home Guard left this afternoon and every one of the company wagons had some that was so drunk they were unable to walk."[23]

While saloonkeepers were willing to post "loyalty" signs if required to do so, they were considerably less inclined to comply with limits on their marketing practices. Politics was one thing, but business was business. The Provost Marshal encountered immediate and militant resistance to his stepped up regulations from outraged saloonkeepers. Shortly after his initial order to shut down all the city's saloons on August 26, he was informed by some of his men on guard that "certain parties, owners of liquor saloons," planned to remain open despite this order. Indeed, according to the Provost Guard report, the shopkeepers not only intended to remain open for business during the transit of General Lyon's funeral cortege through the city, but they were even prepared to defend that right, having "made arrangements of such a nature as will result in serious riot," if their business was blocked. McKinistry's response to this rumored resistance was to detail 100 men to the location of the known saloon resisters, and the next day to order the arrest of every saloonkeeper whose saloon was open without the proper permit.[24]

This initial crackdown was, then, only the opening salvo of a war, sometimes hidden, sometimes open, between the cultural lowlifes of St. Louis, the saloonkeepers, the gamblers, the prostitutes, and the Union authorities. The only way that the Provost Marshal was able to maintain some minimal compliance with his regulations was by constantly patrolling the low areas of the city and periodically arresting both soldiers and saloon-keepers who were caught in violation of the regulations. At the most extreme, the Provost Marshal was driven to shutting down saloons and arresting their owners, as with his initial encounter with the saloonkeepers and the Lyon funeral march. With promises of good behavior, saloonkeepers were generally released after a few days and allowed to reopen their businesses. In the worst of cases of repeat violators, or saloonkeepers who were guilty not only of serving liquor to soldiers, but also of providing a venue for prostitution, saloons and dancehalls were sometimes closed permanently. Of course, a saloon that was shutdown in one location under one name could always reopen elsewhere under another.[25]

Despite the Provost Marshal's power to order regular surveillance of low areas of the city and to arrest and even imprison offending soldiers and citizens, this was a war that he could never really win, and not just because of the militant resistance of saloonkeepers. The Provost Marshal could not win this war because of the active collusion on the part of some Union soldiers as well. Records of the rounds of the Provost Guard in the low areas of the city indicate that night after night, some men were willing to pay the price of arrest for the privilege of frequenting low saloons and drinking to excess. Perhaps they were willing to take the risk of arrest because despite the nightly arrests, the Provost Guard was actually not much of a match for the combined efforts of the saloonkeepers and soldiers. Together, saloonkeepers and enlisted men figured out ways around the Provost Marshal's regulations. One way of avoiding the discipline of the guard was to acquire a suit of civilian clothing and pass as an ordinary citizen. Quite a black market in such clothing appeared in St. Louis, and judging from the frequency of the Provost Marshal's orders attempting to quash it, was fairly successful. In 1863, the Provost Marshal went so far as to order all soldiers arrested in civilian clothes in saloons to be treated as deserters. After one particularly extreme case, the Provost Guard recommended that the post commander actually make a general search of the Benton Barracks and confiscate all the civilian clothing in possession of the troops. As the guard noted, "Soldiers are in the habit of buying citizens clothing in this city, for the purpose of wearing in town to evade the orders of the Post Commander, and also to enable them to desert. Near forty men have thus escaped from the 40 and 41st Mo within the past two weeks."[26]

Not only could soldiers elude the nightly rounds of the Provost Guard by donning civilian clothing, but they could also do so simply by donning a portion of an officers uniform, as officers were exempt from the Provost Marshal's regulations. The exemption of officers not only created another way for enlisted men to evade the regulations of the Provost Marshal, but it also provided a ready excuse for saloonkeepers who could claim that they actually thought that they were serving officers. It created confusion for the nightly Provost Guard as well, they, after all, were left to sort out on the spot, who could and who could not frequent which saloons. Sometimes sheer braggadocio won the day, as when entire cavalry units convinced the guard that they, like their officers, were exempt from the Provost Marshal's rulings. Certainly the fact that access to liquor was a privilege of rank, or just the conviction of entitlement on the part of men who did not have the rank but had the confidence to claim their right to the privilege anyway, could not have sent a message to enlisted men that reinforced the authority of the Provost Marshal's regulations concerning drink.[27]

While access to alcohol in moderation was difficult for the Provost Marshal to achieve, access to prostitutes was arguably even more difficult to control. On the face of it, the Provost Marshal's policy was one of no tolerance for any association between saloons, and in particular any association between the supply of alcohol, and prostitution. However, once again, officers were exempt from this rule and allowed the privilege of frequenting saloons and dancehalls where the women present were openly acknowledged by the guard to be prostitutes. As long as the guard determined, on its nightly rounds, that the officers and the prostitutes were conducting themselves in an orderly fashion, they passed them by. It required an extreme flaunting of good order, for instance, prostitutes on the dance floor with officers sporting portions of their uniforms, to bring down the wrath of the guard on the officers. While enlisted men were denied such open access to prostitutes, with the collusion of saloonkeepers they also once again found ways around the Provost Guard. One of the favorite ploys of saloonkeepers was to claim that the women working in their bars were not in fact prostitutes at all, but were instead "beer jerkers," that is legitimate employees of the saloon whose job it was to serve beer to the soldiers. In other cases, the women present in bars claimed to be entertainers, singers in fact at what were termed, "concert saloons."[28]

Throughout the war, the police commissioner repeatedly recommended that the City Council amend ordinances regulating the licensing of beer saloons where "young girls are employed to carry refreshments to visitors." In their 1862 report to the mayor, they described the practice as "an increasing evil" of "demoralizing tendency" for young girls, many of whom, "by their dress and conduct appear to be prostitutes or on the way to becoming such." While the police commissioner was willing to entertain the possibility that these young women really did begin in these jobs as "female waiters," as the saloonkeepers claimed, they suggested that they nonetheless fairly quickly fell into the trade of prostitution. In a way the very purported innocence of these young women made the occupation of beer jerking more reprehensible, and the saloons themselves more derelict, as locales for the recruitment of new prostitutes on the one hand and the corruption of enlisted men and civilians on the other.[29]

This phenomenon of the "low" saloon as a motor of domestic corruption, as a site to bring together unattached young military men and innocent women, both presumably of respectable households, and render them disrespectable in the worst possible fashion was exactly the phenomenon the Provost Marshal's regulations were designed to avoid. If growth in the occupation of beer jerker was any indication, and certainly the annual police reports indicated as much, the Provost Marshal's policies with regard to the growth of these saloons were no match for the draw of illicit sexual practices, any more than they were successful in restricting consumption of hard liquor or liquor to excess. Not only did the Provost Marshal appear to be losing ground on the issue of recruitment in saloons, but they also had difficulty with saloonkeepers who kept "boardinghouses" attached to their saloons, boardinghouses that were frequently more or less brothels. The Provost Marshal ruled that while soldiers on leave might board at these establishments, they could not cross over and also drink in the bars, following their general policy of attempting to render the saloon and soldiers drinking as respectable as possible by structurally separating it from prostitutes and certainly from brothels.[30]

This boardinghouse rule so disgusted three soldiers who arrived in St. Louis on furlough that they went personally to appeal to the Provost Marshal. As one of them commented, "soldiers in this town are nothing but dogs without collars." Another soldier, E. W. Prewitt, determined to argue the case in writing to the Provost Marshal. According to Prewitt, enlisted men taking their furlough in St. Louis had a right to enjoy it as they would. The fact that veterans who had served their country honorably in the field, came to St. Louis to spend their hard bought furlough and found themselves liable to arrest simply for frequenting a saloon attached to their boardinghouse struck him as an intolerable insult. "Many men among these veterans," he wrote, "feel that the honors given them on their return are but empty compliments, if they are to be refused the liberty of enjoying their short respite from the duties of the camp and the field." Veterans, he suggested, would have little disposition to encourage recruiting, or reenlist themselves, in the face of this kind of disrespectful treatment. "I have seen several men," he concluded, "who were on the point of volunteering who have retired from that purpose when they have found that Veterans who had been feted by the city were subject to these hardships."[31]

Not only did this soldier assert what he considered to be his right to spend his leisure time as he would, he came to the defense of those saloonkeepers who broke the Provost Marshal's regulations as well. He pointed to the case of one loyal Union saloonkeeper, Charles Abel, "a man who has recruited more than 400 men for the service and is daily bringing new recruits," whose saloon was closed simply for serving liquor to boarding soldiers. This loyal saloonkeeper had, at all times, followed the letter of the Provost Marshal's other rulings concerning alcohol, having "at all times refused to sell liquor to soldiers, but who has (as is the custom in the city) given a glass of beer (when sober and orderly) to them." Now his business was virtually ruined by the "over zeal" of the troops currently doing guard duty in the city. It struck the soldier as being particularly unfair that this saloonkeeper's business should be shut down over the issue of serving boarding soldiers when in "every saloon in the city" soldiers were sold proscribed alcohol. The Provost Marshal responded to this soldier's lengthy complain by ordering that the case be investigated and relief granted, but only in so far as it was possible to do so under the standing order. The basic principle, that of attempting to separate disorderly behavior, especially prostitution, from otherwise respectable drinking establishments, was to be maintained.[32]

The Provost Marshal certainly faced daunting challenges in his efforts to dissociate soldiers and the saloons they frequented from the low and disorderly of the city. Saloonkeepers and soldiers felt entitled to enjoy their leisure and run their businesses as they saw fit. The behavior of some officers only seemed to validate enlisted men's ideas of how fully empowered men were entitled to behave. The fathers of the city government were not much better as respectable role models, as they, year after year, refused to give the police the kind of ordinance against "female waiters," that they needed in order to really crack down on low saloons as generators of prostitutes and prostitution. Even the Provost Marshal's own guard was on occasion reported for being drunk while on rounds and for unnecessarily entering and dallying in proscribed dens that it was their duty to patrol, not frequent. At the same time, between the increased patronage offered by the troops, the profitability of the trade to saloonkeepers and property owners, ordinary residents in neighborhoods became only more hard pressed to defend the peace of their neighborhoods as they had previously known them.[33]

One poor beleaguered citizen wrote repeatedly to the Provost Marshal about the conditions of his neighborhood around 4th and Vine, an area of growing saloons and prostitution. In writing to the Provost Marshal, he first made it clear that he had already appealed to the civilian authorities without success. He politely requested some assistance, not just about one saloon in particular, but about the sort of traffic it generated, drunken men on the streets and prostitutes arriving in carriages at all hours to organize their own business. He collected signatures from a dozen other respectable households in the neighborhood and found a night watchman who was willing to testify and back up the neighbor's complaints. He suggested that if the Provost Marshal did not take action, he would be forced to move his family elsewhere. Finally, in desperation this householder was moved to take up direct action when the carriages arriving and departing with prostitutes began parking in front of his own house. He went out and told them to leave, but as he explained to the Provost Marshal, he was then accosted by the saloonkeeper who reportedly said, "God damn you what right have you got to interfere with me. I pay my rent and license and them that like to drink here shall drink and I swear to god the first time you cross my path I'll kill you." The woman in the carriage chimed in with, "You suck my arse, you god damned son of a bitch."[34]

The desperate neighborhood resident made a point of reporting the word-for-word conversation so that the Provost Marshal would hopefully finally see just how militant and aggressive these lowlifes were. They were threatening, after all, to kill him. With this information, the Provost Marshal finally took action against the saloon, ordering that it might continue in

business, but only if all "fancy women and loose characters be kept away."
Here we see the Provost Marshal's policy of attempting to separate drinking within reasonable bounds from prostitution as it appeared to the
respectable citizen. While soldiers and saloonkeepers experienced this
policy as a violation of their rights as free men, for neighborhood residents, the policy of outlawing "low" saloons was a halfway measure as well.
The respectable citizen had to accept the fact that the offending saloon
was still open to sell liquor to rowdy drinkers, but at least the worst affront,
the open solicitation of men by prostitutes was eliminated. Indeed the
prostitute provided the basis for a compromise of sorts between the
warring parties—the saloonkeeper could keep his business, at least
the drinking portion of it—the male citizen could pursue his leisure, at
least his drinking, and the neighbors could have some expansion of
respectability in the neighborhood. All that was required was the removal
of the prostitute.[35]

The prostitute could even be blamed for other disorderly excesses of
the soldiers, as the complaint of an army captain, Amos Foster, to the
Provost Marshal in April of 1863 illustrates. Captain Foster was so unfor-
tunate as to have his office located behind the Monitor Saloon, a business
that he described as constituting "intolerable nuisance . . . like other
saloons of its character a general resort for drunken soldiers." What apparently drove him to finally file a formal complaint against the saloon was the
appearance on his doorstep of five soldiers, two officers and three enlisted
men, who came out the back of the saloon drunk and climbed the back
stairs to his office saying that they had been sent from the saloon to, "look
after some women who they were told live up here." The officer went on in
his complaint to the Provost Marshal to note that "concert saloons," like
the Monitor, were "mere traps for unsophisticated soldiers." He, himself,
had been forced to order one of his clerks back to his regiment in the field
after he was "fleeced" out of six dollars at a drunken spree at another similar saloon. "These places," he concluded, "always have a crowd of whores,
thieves and gamblers in attendance. So if one method will not secure their
end, another will."[36]

Here the soldier is portrayed not as the manly veteran intent upon
spending his leisure as he will, but rather as the innocent victim, plied with
liquor, tempted by loose women, and in the end, leaving with his pockets
empty. Another officer, in proposing a policy for the "numerous low bawdy
houses" in the city, even went so far as to suggest that the abuse of liquor
by the soldiers was really the responsibility of the whores, not the soldiers.
"It is a notorious fact that the majority of the liquor obtained by soldiers is
procured through the vile agency of these public prostitutes. Who pur-
chase liquor and give it to soldiers at their rooms thus enticing them into
miserable dens where numerous cases of stealing are perpetuated and
seducing the soldier from his good conduct by the vile allurements they so
well know how to practice." While this officer blamed prostitutes for soldier's abuse of liquor, he was quick to note that a good soldier, particularly

one who had spent his enlistment in the field, would "naturally enough feel inclined" to visit such women. His intention was not to actually shut down brothels, then, but rather to "contract it to some extent." "I do this well knowing," he wrote, "that I cannot entirely prevent it."[37]

What he proposed was a policy that would once again hold the prostitute, and not the soldier responsible. He proposed sending military authorities to inform madams that if they were to admit soldiers, all the occupants of their houses would be arrested and turned over to the city workhouse. For the troops, he proposed a "stern lecture." Of course this holding the prostitute responsible, while the offending male customer went free, was the typical antebellum approach to the prostitute. It reflected the larger cultural assumptions that surrounded "fallen women," as sinks of hopeless corruption, and of brothels as houses of "ill fame," granted only a tenuous and conditional right to existence. It also reflected the antebellum right of men to exercise their "liberties" as they would as long as they did not cut too deeply into the stability of their legitimate households. From the outset in St. Louis, the policy of martial law followed along these basic precepts. So while initially the Provost Marshal tried to create good domestic order simply by limiting hours of the saloons and other establishments of popular culture, and failing that, by shutting down "low saloons," he finally, on September 26, one month into martial law, went further, going to the corrupt root of disorderly behavior, the houses of ill fame, and banished the most notorious brothel keepers from the city.[38]

Even brothels had their defenders, however. So while Jennie Atwood disappeared from the city after the Provost Marshal's initial order to banish the brothel keepers, not all the crew were so easily removed from the social body. There was, for example, Kate Graham. Although she was banished in September of 1861 alongside Jennie Atwood, a petition from her neighbors a year later asking the Provost Marshal to relieve them of "one of the greatest nuisances possible," would indicate that the order was never carried out. Kate Graham apparently continued to operate a disorderly house with impunity, "a rendezvous," according to her outraged neighbor's petition, "for all the worst characters in the city . . . a crib of the lowest sort . . . the resort of thieves, shoulder letters, prostitutes, pimps, gamblers and low priced hack drivers." In response to this protest from her neighbors, the Provost Marshal once again went after her business, shutting it down in the fall of 1862. Even this second action did not mark the end of Kate Graham and her disorderly house. In October of 1862, her landlord, Madison Miller, appealed to the Provost Marshal to allow her to reopen her business. "A tenant of mine," he wrote, "Mrs. Graham has had her House shut up as I think without cause. If you can I wish you would allow her to open by so doing you will oblige Madison Miller." Whoever Madison Miller was, he knew his rights as a property owner and a businessman. As with the persistence of "low" saloonkeepers, even brothel keepers could lay claim to a place in the economic life of the city and it was their status as proprietors, or their profitability to proprietors, like Madison Miller, that afforded some protection in the face of the petitions of respectable householders.[39]

And then there was John Gallagher, the only man banished with the female brothel keepers. A saloonkeeper, Gallagher's crime was like that of Charles Abel, the loyal saloonkeeper, that of keeping a "boardinghouse" attached to his saloon, in this case a boardinghouse so obviously the resort of prostitutes as to render Gallagher a brothel keeper worthy of being banished alongside the most notorious madams in the city. Gallagher, however, was spared banishment because his neighbors submitted a petition to the Provost Marshal on his behalf. In his case, his neighbors claimed that some horrible mistake had been committed. The neighbor, the saloonkeeper Gallagher had always, "borne good character" and had never been arrested in the past. Perhaps more importantly, the saloonkeeper was a "married man, having a wife and several children depending upon him for support." His banishment would therefore work a "great hardship," not just upon himself, but upon his family as well. Even low saloonkeepers like Gallagher could be rendered respectable by laying claim to his position as a loyal father and husband. Only the prostitute stood outside the circle of domestic redemption. The charges of domestic traitorship of the Home Guard could be mitigated and responsibility could be moved off Union soldiers and even off loyal saloonkeepers by this focus on the prostitute and her house. Even respectable women, the most offended of St. Louis citizens who lined the street the day that Jennie Atwood strolled by with her army captain, and certainly the women who mobbed Mrs. Knox's brothel when the husband spent the family's last dime, even these women and perhaps particularly these women, were willing to see the whore as the party most responsible for the disloyal behavior of the their men.[40]

The prostitute emerged as a critical figure, then, in the Provost Marshal's war against domestic disloyalty, and while this was a real war, that is a conflict that entailed real arrests and the actual banishment of some prostitutes along with the arrest of saloonkeepers and disorderly soldiers, it was never a war that actually had any hope or even actually intended to abolish prostitution. Indeed, prostitution actually grew during the war, taking up whole new blocks of the city. Union authorities openly admitted that their policy with regard to brothels was never about ending the trade, but rather about "contracting it somewhat." The war of the Union authorities was rather about maintaining the line between respectable and disorderly households, a line that was seriously stressed by the presence of the tens of thousands of unattached young men that moved through the city in the course of the war.

What the Provost Marshal encountered in this war for respectability was an ever-moving line, a line that the Union authorities attempted to shore up at the points of greatest stress and potential or actual damage to the Union cause. They responded as best they were able to the complaints of outraged citizens who found their neighborhoods overrun by drunken soldiers and lowlife, without cutting too deeply into the well-being of legitimate and even illegitimate proprietors. What the Provost Marshal did then about prostitutes and low saloons, he did to defend the Union war interests. If he could promote the war effort by shutting down a brothel, he did. If he could promote the war effort by reopening a "low" saloon, he did. While seriously undercut by the behavior of some Union troops and the force of profit and economic self-interest on the part of some saloon-keepers and some city fathers, the Provost Marshal found a critical ally in the fact that gender mattered to the citizens of St. Louis in their assessment of responsibility for sexual traitorship. The more the number of troops grew, the more the wounded poured through the city's hospitals, the more the Union policy failed to staunch the growth of low saloons and brothels, the larger the figure of the prostitute and the madam loomed as the purported root cause of domestic disorder and disloyalty. At least some boys would be boys. And some girls would be beer jerkers, concert singers, prostitutes, keepers of houses of ill fame, arrested and banished.

CHAPTER 5

"STAND BY YOUR MAN": THE LADIES MEMORIAL ASSOCIATION AND THE RECONSTRUCTION OF SOUTHERN WHITE MANHOOD

Two days after Robert E. Lee signed the armistice with Ulysses S. Grant at Appomattox, signifying the end of the long and bitter Civil War, the *Augusta Chronicle*, a major southern newspaper, published an editorial entitled "Female Influence and Energy." The author argued that women were much better suited to withstand life's failures and defeats than men: "Those disasters which break down the spirit of man and prostrate him in the dust seem to call forth all the energies of the softer sex." While single men who encountered defeat in life were apt to descend into "waste and self neglect," the spirits of married men were sustained by the influence of this positive "female energy." "Relieved by domestic endearments and self respect," defeated men could be "kept alive by finding that, though abroad may be all darkness and humiliation, yet there is still a little world at home of which he is monarch."[1]

Historians of southern women have taken widely differing positions on the impact that the defeat of the Confederacy and the accompanying emancipation of the slaves had on white women and white gender roles. Over 20 years ago, in her pathbreaking work, *The Southern Lady*, Anne Firor Scott argued that the war "opened every door for women." She attributed this outcome to the combined effect of white women's independent activities during the war and the blow that emancipation and defeat presented to patriarchal power. More recently, historians have been less sanguine about the emancipatory possibilities that the postwar social order offered to southern white women. The gains that women made during the war in forming autonomous public organizations, entering wage labor, and directing their own households are viewed as temporary expedients that evaporated at war's end, as rapidly as the cause that generated them in the first place.[2]

Regardless of which position historians espouse, they share the underlying assumption that improvement in women's status was based on their ability to become more independent. The war created this opportunity for women, if only because it required a massive departure of men to the front. As a consequence, Confederate women were forced to become autonomous, as heads of households or wage earners, for instance, if only to guarantee their own and their children's survival. It is this aspect of the war, the way it structurally drew women out of their dependent status into the independent place previously occupied by their men, that has absorbed much of the attention of historians. From this perspective, the end of the war and the return of the men home would naturally lead to a decline, if not an outright reversal, in women's independence.

It is not surprising, then, that historians have given little consideration to the role that "female influence," as depicted by the Augusta editorial, might have played in the postwar empowerment of southern white women.[3] Yet it is precisely in the arena of postwar gender relations that the possibility for a new form of postwar empowerment among southern white women existed. Indeed, the editor concludes his analysis of the war's impact on postwar gender relations with a classic antebellum gender analogy. Before the war, southern white men were like the "towering oak," while southern white women were the "clinging vine." In these "happier days" the vine "twined its graceful foliage about the oak and has been lifted by him into the sunshine." The Civil War passed over this southern landscape like a violent storm, however, and the oak was "riven by a thunderbolt," its spine cracked. The once clinging ivy now had the possibility of a new role to play. It could hold the splintered oak erect, if it would only "cling around with its caressing tendrils and bind up its shattered brow."[4]

White southern men had indeed suffered multiple defeats with the fall of the Confederacy, in relation to northern men as well as in relation to the southern slave population. Even those white southerners who had never supported the war effort were left to confront the economic devastation and dislocation that the Confederate defeat brought to all white men, regardless of political affiliation. Confronted with a myriad of military, political, and economic defeats, their women certainly found themselves in a critical position. Would they continue to pursue the apparently independent roles the war had opened to them? Or, would they "stand by their men," and in that way play a critical role in the reconstruction, rather than the further deconstruction, of southern white manhood?

The Ladies Memorial Associations that were formed in the South in the war's immediate aftermath were clearly dedicated to the reconstruction of southern white men. These associations took as their first charge the care of the most defeated of Confederate men—those who actually fell in the conflict, the Confederate dead. They saw to it that these men received a decent burial, that the sacrifice of their lives was honored at least once a year on Confederate Memorial Day, and that their story was emblazoned on monuments to the Confederate soldier that are to be found to this day in every southern town of any size.[5]

This organization has been almost universally overlooked by historians to this day; perhaps no better testimony exists as to its success in subordinating its own identity to the salvation of southern white manhood. And this despite the fact that besides women's church auxiliaries, the Ladies

Memorial Associations had by far the largest membership of any women's organizations in the South, certainly through the 1870s and perhaps into the 1880s. Its influence outside its immediate membership was also substantial. The Augusta, Georgia, association, for example, regularly organized hundreds of schoolchildren to decorate the graves of the Confederate dead on Memorial Day. The ceremony to lay the cornerstone of the town's Confederate Monument drew a huge crowd, the largest in the town's history, and the actual unveiling of the monument in 1878 was even larger, estimated by the local press to exceed twenty thousand.[6]

What explains historians' neglect of this organization? Perhaps it is because the subject is gender as a *relationship*, that is to say the proposition that men are *made* in relation to women, and women are *made* in relation to men, a deeply contested proposition. For historians of women, who view the establishment of women's voluntary organizations in the nineteenth century as the beginning of the women's rights struggle as a mass movement, organizations like the Ladies Memorial Associations, which were overtly dedicated to the rehabilitation of their men, are something of an embarrassment. For historians of the Confederate memorial tradition and veterans' organizations, the recognition that the apparently manly pursuit of telling old war stories, of being "real" men, was initially constructed by the postwar activities of their mothers and wives is also perhaps best overlooked.[7]

Perhaps the hesitancy of historians to explore this form of "female energy" goes even deeper to the blind, unreasoning love that binds us one to the other. Historians are perhaps more comfortable discussing less subjective forces that bind men and women together, such as the excesses of patriarchal authority, the benefits of paternalistic benevolence, or the pressure of economic necessity. The Ladies Memorial Association, however, had no such hesitation. Out of the raw, abraded ends of their attachment to their fallen husbands, fathers, and sons, out of the massive carnage that the Civil War represented for them, they committed themselves to perpetuate what they, at least, still had the power to perpetuate, the binding tie of "mother love." Frequently, the pattern of officeholding in the organization was explained by the extent of maternal loss these women experienced as a result of the war. Presidents, for instance, would have lost the most sons, vice presidents would just have one unclaimed on some unknown battlefield.[8]

Whereas historians of women have been inclined to view women's voluntary associations as a basis for women's struggle for independence, they can just as easily be viewed as an extension of women's "dependent" domestic role as mothers of men. Indeed, "mother love" was with Confederate men at the war's outset, for while the soldiers' aid societies sprang up across the South in the first months of the war to meet the basic structural need for women's labor in order to properly outfit the soldiers, it was frequently the very depth of their domestic attachment to their husbands and sons that inspired this labor. As one soldiers' aid society explained in its initial call for volunteers, "We will in this small offering of service secure to ourselves the heartfelt satisfaction that patriotism always inspires, and this will serve as solace to each of us for the absence of those whose lives are so dear to us."[9] As the soldiers began returning from the front, wounded and diseased, these women transformed their labor to match the soldiers' new needs. They set up hospitals and Wayside Homes to hopefully nurse these men back to health. Here, perhaps even more forcefully than in the initial construction of uniforms, Confederate women's labor was infused with their own desire to preserve their own particular domestic ties. As they labored over men otherwise unknown to them, they prayed fervently that their own sons and husbands might be spared a similar fate, or that if they should be wounded they might receive the same loving care at the hands of some other woman.

It was in this context of wartime hospital and nursing work that Confederate women first took up the task of caring for the Confederate dead. When men died under their care, the women were the ones who laid them out, saw to it that they received a fitting burial, and took care of their graves. After the war, it was these soldiers' aid societies that transformed themselves into the Ladies Memorial Associations. As they had clothed, fed, nursed, and buried soldiers in the war, so now would they care for their graves and for their memory.[10]

As in the case of the wartime aid societies, part of the reason for the continued existence of Ladies Memorial Associations was purely practical. The immediate physical problems of the Confederate dead went far beyond simply tending the graves of those men who had died unknown or unclaimed by their kindred during the war. The poor condition of war cemeteries everywhere begged for attention. Burial sites were frequently in a deplorable state, and poorly marked graves threatened to lose their identity altogether. Even more daunting was the problem of the battle-fields themselves, where soldiers had been buried in mass graves or simply covered over in shallow trenches where they fell. The work of bringing home the Confederate dead, establishing special sections in graveyards for their remains, and raising the funds for standardized grave markers frequently took these organizations years of work.[11]

A proper burial, however, was not the end of these women's postwar activity but the beginning. For as much as the plight of the Confederate dead continued to call forth the labor of southern white women, even more did it call forth the underlying attachment between mothers and sons, husbands and wives, brothers and sisters that had inspired that labor from the war's outset. Here is where the defeat of the Confederacy and its soldiers came to play a critical role, for if the Confederacy had been successful, women undoubtedly would have cared for the graves of their own men, but the responsibility for some how "memorializing" or honoring and recognizing the Confederate cause would not have fallen upon this normally private and individualized act of mourning. The victorious soldier is honored by his nation. Even a defeated nation can still honor its dead, but in the case of the Confederacy there was no nation, so the domestic tie between these women and their lost men bore the weight of that political burden.[12]

This politicization of domestic relations is perhaps most visible in the establishment of that central Confederate memorial tradition, Confederate Memorial Day, by the Ladies Memorial Associations in the year following the war. In March 1866, the Columbus Ladies Memorial Association issued a call published widely in the southern press for women throughout the South to "aid us in the effort to set apart a certain day to be observed, from the Potomac to the Rio Grande, and to be handed down through time as a religious custom of the South, to wreathe the graves of our martyred dead with flowers." In its initial call, the association went on to elaborate the day's larger meaning, a meaning that would become a standard explanation not only for Confederate Memorial Day, but also for the Confederate memorial tradition and ultimately for the war itself: because they "all did their duty. . . . They died for their country." The association argued that the larger issues of right and wrong, of victory or defeat, were irrelevant in the face of the basic sacrifice these men had made. For these women as women, the larger issues of why the South fought were irrelevant. They loved these men regardless of the war's rationale and outcome.[13]

From the perspective of the Columbus Ladies Memorial Association, it was more than simply convenient that Confederate defeat had occurred in the spring, when flowers were readily available for grave decoration. As they noted in their history of the origins of Confederate Memorial Day some 30 years later, in settling on April 26 they had hoped to encourage the citizenry to draw the connection between their own Confederate dead and the resurrection and ascension of Christ. "Like the hope that spread over the earth on the morning of the Resurrection," they recorded, "so the soft light of this sentiment shone over Dixie, and when April came, love wreathed her roses where the soldiers sleep." Wrapping themselves in this domesticized Christian rhetoric, these women went on to assert the primacy of their own role in this resurrection of the war dead. "Whose task," they queried, "had this been even in Biblical times?" "When the smoke cleared away, where do we find the devoted women? Where were Mary Magdalene and the other Mary after the crucifixion?"[14] According to the Columbus Ladies Memorial Association, it was "mother love" that would raise the Confederate dead, if only on monuments of stone.

Their own relationship to these men provided the ideological as well as material basis for the memorialization. The Confederate dead deserved to be honored, not for the cause they had lost—not for political power or racial hegemony—but simply because they had done their "duty" and "sacrificed" their lives for the defense of southern women and children. "For what did the South fight?" the Ladies Memorial Associations queried. "Not," they answered, "for the institution of slavery." "That," they asserted, "was a mere incident in the great drama. Let the true answer ring from the lips of every Memorial orator for generations to come." The "true answer" was that Confederate men fought not to preserve slavery, but to preserve their *own* "liberties" as free men, liberties that were embodied in their position as heads of their own households that allowed them to "protect" their dependents in the antebellum South and during the war itself.[15]

Of course, this perspective overlooked the fact that it was precisely the position of African Americans as slaves in white households that supported these men's "liberties" before the war. In the face of the emancipation of the slaves, white southern men were rendered more dependent on those household dependents that remained to them. They turned to their women and their children to validate them, to create out of their own continued subordination the basis for their reconstruction as honorable men, even in the face of their defeat in relation to northern men and the southern freedpeople. For their part, the Ladies Memorial Associations rose to the occasion by moving white women to the very center of the war's causality. "No one," they asserted, "could refuse us the simple privilege of paying honor to those who died defending the life, honor and happiness of southern women."[16]

The expanded public role that the Ladies Memorial Associations assumed for the purpose of valorizing their men put them potentially at cross-purposes in this effort to "stand by their men." The problem was how to provide a means for the reconstruction of their men's self-image without reconstructing themselves in the process—or at least without appearing to do so. As a result, the Ladies Memorial Associations worked to maintain the conventional forms of public gender subordination even as they eroded its underlying substance. They gave over conventionally "male" aspects of public organizational activities—public speech making, managing the construction finances for monuments, reordering graveyards, and negotiating with building contractors—to prominent men. They asserted their commitment to male representation forthrightly and perhaps somewhat defensively in the local press. "Southern women," one association wrote, "frankly acknowledge their dependence on southern men and waiving women's rights and parliamentary usages, they claim the privilege of having their public announcements made by gentlemen." They claimed that this behavior was only to be expected, because "Southern ladies naturally shrink from contact with the outside world."[17]

This association explained the meaning of its memorial activities in the most gender-conservative frame possible. Theirs was a defensive movement, a response to the incursions that the war had made into the domestic arena. The war had essentially turned domestic life inside out. The Ladies Memorial Associations continued to be active in a public world, now rendered structurally domestic as a result. This constituted no assertion of women's individual rights, autonomy, or equality with men. Quite the contrary, this constituted a continued attachment to domesticity—albeit a domesticity that, because of unforeseen circumstances, had been compelled to assume a public and even a political face. As the Augusta Ladies

Memorial Association expressed it, rather than being committed to "women's rights," its organization was based on domestic loss, a loss that with the Confederate dead, but radiated out to include a militarily, economically, and politically defeated white southern manhood in general.[18]

What did it mean for the larger southern social order that, despite the defeat of southern white men and the enlarged public role that their women continued to occupy as a result, these women continued to eschew direct responsibility for their actions and instead turned their postwar public empowerment toward undergirding a social construction of white manhood that had otherwise lost its material moorings with the emancipation of the slaves and the economic devastation of the war? An argument can be made that this strategy of "standing by your man" served to ease the transition to a society in which white women would increasingly be called upon to stand by themselves or stand with the aid of other women. This is perhaps most clearly evident in the establishment of homes for Confederate widows and orphans in the war's aftermath.

As the Ladies Memorial Associations took up "protecting" the Confederate dead, so too did they assume the responsibility for "protecting" their widows and orphans by establishing public homes for the most destitute. In Charleston, the Home for Mothers, Widows and Daughters of Confederate Soldiers was established through the efforts of Mrs. Mary Amarintha Snowden, who was also one of the founding members of the Charleston Ladies Memorial Association and its president during her lifetime. Within six months of its establishment, the home had 70 inmates, 50 of whom attended the home's school. In educating the younger generation to become "self helping and self respecting working women," such homes assisted in moving some of the younger generation of white women into a more autonomous position.[19]

Neither the establishment of these public homes nor the increased employment of white women that they facilitated was understood to be a response to the systemic decline of white men's ability to "protect" their women and children that the war had set in motion; instead, these women were able to wrap their activity in the reassuring mantle of the Confederate dead, insisting that the last wish of the dying soldier was that his family be provided for, even if it fell to women to do so. Far from undermining the position of postwar white manhood, these women presented themselves as actually contributing to it through the medium of the Confederate dead and their continuing needs. This connection between elite women's increased voluntary activity and the needs of the Confederate widows and orphans became a standard line of argument for such women in the years following the war.[20]

Nonetheless, a case can be made for the roots of white women's progressive reform activity in the postwar South in the establishment of these homes for needy Confederate widows and their children. Some of the women who began their public organizational work in these Confederate widows' homes of the 1860s and 1870s went on to form the King's

Daughters, the Women's Exchanges, and the Woman's Christian Temperance Unions (WCTU) of the 1880s.[21] Unfortunately, no such positive construction can be placed on the racial politics created by the continued subordination of white women to the task of the reconstruction of white manhood. Perhaps the clearest illustration of this is the Ku Klux Klan.

The Klan was formed ostensibly as a social club on December 24, 1866 by six young Confederate veterans in Pulaski, Tennessee, who dressed up in sheets and rode through the streets. According to one early Klan history African Americans "thought they had seen ghosts from the nearby battlefields, and had with haste gone back to their former masters, only too willing to work."[22] From this day forward, Klansmen appeared in their ghostly attire, demanding buckets of water, as men on battlefields were known to be in great thirst. Whether the freedpeople or their white supporters believed this ruse or not, the larger point is that the Klan carried their attachment to the Confederate dead one step further than the Ladies Memorial Associations. They made the dead ride again.[23] Who better to maintain the old social and racial order than the Confederate dead themselves? Who better to make war on black reconstruction than those men who had given their lives to the preservation of the antebellum southern social order and white men's position in it?

In 1867, the Klan held a convention in Nashville, Tennessee, to form a united organization. Before this convention, some Klan representatives asked Robert E. Lee to lead this newly unified regional order. Here the parallel to the Confederacy is clear, for as the Klan represented the Confederate soldier reborn, who better to lead them than their old commander in chief? Lee, in declining this honor, was reputed to have advised the Klan to "keep it as you have it, a protective organization." The statement of organizational purpose adopted at the Nashville convention in 1867 reflected this advice, with its commitment to "protect the weak, the innocent, the defenseless from indignities, wrongs and outrages of the lawless, the violent and the brutal; to relieve the injured and oppressed, succor the suffering, especially the widows and orphans of the Confederate soldiers."[24]

The Klan's mission of protecting the "weak" and the "innocent," especially the widows and orphans of the Confederate dead, closely parallels the Ladies Memorial Associations' vision of what the war was all about. The preservation of the institution of slavery became a mere "incident" in the war, an adjunct of the "real" reason Confederate men went to war—to protect their homes, especially their women. Similarly, the racial terrorism of the Klan was viewed not from the position of its African American victims, over whom southern whites had lost control with the demise of slavery, but rather from the position of those whose allegiance they continued to hold, the loyal white women of the South.

The first histories of the Klan were generally written by the participants themselves or their descendants. These works perpetuated this vision of the Klan as an organization primarily committed to the protection of the white population.[25] Several of these histories were written by women who were the daughters of original Klansmen. In 1924, for instance, Susan Lawrence Davis published *The Authentic History of the KKK, 1865–1877*. Her father was one of the founding members of the Alabama Klan, and she claimed to have known much of the KKK leadership personally. She dedicated her work, however, to "her mother, Sarah Ann (McClelland) Davis and the other southern women who designed and manufactured with their Own fingers the Regalia of the Ku Klux Klansmen and the trappings for their horses." Another Klan history coauthored by a woman, Mrs. W. B. Romine, placed a similar emphasis on the critical role women played in providing uniforms for the Klan. The Romines claimed that ex-Confederate women designed and made more than four hundred thousand Klan robes for both rider and horse and that "not a word was said by these women to anyone about them and not one single secret concerning them was ever revealed."[26]

Why is so much significance attributed in these histories to Klan robes? The parallel to the Civil War is apparent. As southern white women "stood by their men" by forming soldiers' aid societies to make their uniforms, so southern white women "stood by their men" in this reincarnation of the Confederate dead. The differences in the uniforms are instructive, however, because they point to a substantive reconstruction of white male identity. Although initially Klan uniforms varied widely, a standard uniform eventually emerged. The white sheet with the red cross on the upper right shoulder undoubtedly symbolized many things to the wearers—it was clearly "ghostly," it represented "white supremacy," but in the Romines' and Davis's explanation, it was white primarily to symbolize the central aim of the Klan, the "purity and preservation of the home." Indeed, Davis went so far as to portray the Klan as being a woman's organization, arguing that while "southern men and women supported the Civil War, southern women and men supported the Klan." Here the order is significant; while white men lost the Civil War, Davis argued that white women, acting indirectly through the Klan, finally won the war for "home rule," redeeming the South from Radical Reconstruction.[27]

While white southern men may have been redeemed by 1877 from Radical Reconstruction, that is, from a racial or regional reconstruction, the basis for that redemption was a gendered one. Consider, for instance, Davis's description of the Klan's Grand Wizard, General Nathan Bedford Forrest. During the war, Davis tells us, Forrest never drank, he always held religious services in his tent on Sundays, and he prayed before battle. He also had a "profound respect" for womanhood and was a "devoted husband." Indeed, his wife, Mary Montgomery Forrest, was his "inspiration." Whether Forrest actually exhibited these qualities, Davis holds him up as the exemplar of the characteristics that postwar white men should embody. Like the "White Life for Two" advocated by the WCTU, Davis was proposing the "white sheet for two."[28]

This vision of the Klan as an organization of "self sacrificing" men simply doing their duty to protect their women and children from an African

American population rendered threatening by the influence of rapacious northern white carpetbaggers was not seriously revised by historians until the 1960s. At that point, the original Klan histories written from the gendered perspective of the early participants were dismissed out of hand. As William Randall argued in his work, *The KKK: A Century of Infamy*, the 1867 Nashville statement of principle was "high sounding and innocuous," a mere rationale for the racial terrorism that was the Klan's real purpose.[29]

In 1898, Charlotte Perkins Gilman wrote what was arguably the nineteenth century's most devastating indictment of indirect female influence. In *Women and Economics*, Gilman argued that the ills of the capitalist social order—poverty, class exploitation, and violence—could be attributed directly to the subordinate status of women and the domestic realm as a whole. Because women in their roles as mothers and wives were essentially the servants of men, they raised sons and affirmed husbands in the belief that men's needs were the only valid ones. Through their loving service, they taught their men to be greedy and self-centered in relation to the larger world. Because these self-centered men needed to "support" such women, they took this greedy and self-centered construction of themselves out into the larger social order, doing whatever was necessary—robbing, oppressing, and exploiting others—to meet their women's domestic needs. Gilman argued, therefore, that the truly radical solution to problems of poverty, conflict, and oppression in industrial capitalist society is the destruction of women's indirect influence. When women were directly integrated into public life, motherhood would be freed from its need to serve; the result would be a more humane manhood.[30]

Gilman would have done well to turn her attention to the situation of the postwar South. Like so many northerners of New England extraction, she apparently assumed that there were no lessons for her there. If, however, she had considered the social trajectory of this region in the late nineteenth century, she would have found a striking affirmation of her argument for the connection between the continued subordination of women, particularly elite white women, and the violence and exploitation of the working classes by the KKK. However, she also would have confronted a devastating refutation of her proposed solution to this problem: the integration of women's previously privatized domestic labor into public life. In the postwar South this step toward the integration of white women and white domestic relations into the public arena not only failed to undercut white male domination, it in fact served to reinforce it.

CHAPTER 6

"You Can't Change History By Moving a Rock": Gender, Race, and the Cultural Politics of Confederate Memorialization

On August 16, 1974, in the depths of the Missouri summer heat, and when most university students were far from campus, the city of Columbia quietly removed a five-and-a-half-ton Confederate Memorial from the center of the University of Missouri campus. Placing the pink granite boulder on a flat bed truck trailer, workers transported it to an outlying weed-infested field in a city park. There it stood, its original 1935 bronze plaque of dedication to the "valor and patriotism of Confederate Soldiers of Boone County," virtually obscured by the spray paint and graffiti of a younger generation of students.[1] This ignominious end was hardly the future that the local chapter of the United Daughters of the Confederacy envisioned for the Rock when they first unveiled it with great pomp and ceremony some 40 years earlier. With their eyes trained firmly on the past, as their motto, "lest we forget," would indicate, the women of the UDC hoped that the Rock would continue to serve to bind the generations that followed them to a memory of what was for them still, even in the early twentieth century, a lived experience of the Civil War and Civil War loss.[2]

What they could not imagine in 1935 was that the real threat to their memories would arise from the members of a younger generation of university students. Not only would some white students forget the sacrifices of their forbearers who fought and died for the Confederacy, but also others would not be their descendants at all. By the late 1960s, African American students had arrived on the University of Missouri campus in sufficient numbers to present an alternative relationship to the "valor and patriotism" of the Confederacy that the Rock was intended to perpetuate. The struggle that emerged concerning the proper location of the Confederate Rock was therefore in many ways part of a larger cultural struggle over how and in what ways the campus in particular, and the surrounding community more generally, would be racially integrated. Could or would the legacy of the white South continue to be the largely unquestioned hegemonic culture at the university? Could or would the culture of the descendants of white slave holders simply coexist with the cultural legacy of the descendants of ex-slaves? And what role would white women play in this moment of potential cultural renegotiation? For when the United Daughters of the Confederacy placed the Rock at the center of the campus in 1935, they acted out of their position as cultural arbiters, as keepers of the public memory through their role as guardians of the white male Confederate past. Would the younger generation of white women choose to perpetuate their strategy of standing by their men, or would they use the new cultural configuration offered by the change in the racial order to establish a new and more autonomous race and gender politics for white women?[3]

The Columbia Chapter of the United Daughters of the Confederacy was formed in 1903. Of the 30 founding members, 23 were "real" daughters of the Confederacy, that is, their fathers, or some other male relation, actually fought for the Confederacy. The chapter was named after John S. Marmaduke, a distinguished Confederate general who hailed from the region, and whose niece was a member of the group. A poem written in 1925 by one charter member of the Columbia chapter about this namesake reveals the ways in which the naming of chapters was more than an effort to honor one man. The poem, "UDC Ideals," points out the noble and manly qualities of all the men from Missouri who served the Confederate cause.

> John S. Marmaduke, noble man
> Among Missouri's best he stood
> Brave and true, as all men are
> Who love their country and their God:
>
> Leader of men he was born to be
> With his heaven endowed capacity
> Of brain and blood, he dared to show
> What men were made of sixty years ago
>
> John S. Marmaduke, Oh how souls are thrilled
> Every UDC Heart is filled
> With renewed zeal the torch to wave
> Borne by hands of men so brave.

The last two stanzas made the Daughters' claim to their father's war, which became a central tenet of the organization.

> Drooped and flickered tho ne'er
> Trailed in the dust,
> Caught up by hands true to the trust
> Held aloft in the hearts and lives
> Of the Daughters in Nineteen twenty five

The Children too shall know the truth
and point to All, in North or South
The Path that noble manhood trod
And leave the victory with our God.[4]

The fathers, despite their courage and valor, may have nearly "trailed" the Confederate flag in the dust, but now their daughters would keep it aloft and even pass it on to their children. Here the UDC proposed to do on a cultural level what their fathers had failed to do, that is, win the war for the South. This white cultural war began formally as soon as the military war was lost, with the formation of such groups as Ladies Memorial Associations across the South. These associations were dedicated to the proper burial of their men, and with those burials, ceremonies rich in respectful symbolism.

The informal cultural war can be traced back even further, into the experiences of Confederate civilians on the home front, a "second front" upon which the war was also fought. The women who initially formed the Columbia UDC in 1903 had particularly strong reasons to feel that Missouri women had made significant wartime contributions to this second front. Columbia, located along the Missouri River in the heart of Boone County, was a major slaveholding area of the state, where a majority of the white men who fought in the Civil War, fought for the Confederacy. While their men were off in the battlefields, the "first front," women were left to deal with their own sort of war. Their town and their county were contested territory, with occupying Union troops and Confederate guerillas, or bushwhackers, pitted against one another.[5]

The story of Mary Tucker, a member of the Columbia UDC in the 1920s illustrates this two-front experience of war in Missouri. While her father was off fighting on the "first front" with the Missouri State Guard against the advancing Union forces in the state in the summer of 1861, Union troops were sacking her family home before the Battle of Carthage. She was forced to flee with her mother to St. Louis after their home was burnt to the ground and their stores destroyed. In the following summer, her father was killed at the Battle of Pea Ridge, the last serious effort of the Missouri Confederate forces to control the state. By the end of the war, Tucker had also lost her husband and her brother. Perhaps not surprisingly, Mary Tucker and her mother became militant members of the second-front war and were arrested, imprisoned, and eventually banished from the city of St. Louis for aiding Confederate spies.[6]

In the early twentieth century, the Missouri UDC took up the task of preserving home front stories of Confederate sympathizing Missouri women like Mary Tucker. Their more public efforts were devoted to memorializing their men's experiences on the first front. They worked hard to secure the reputation of their men based on stories of honorable behavior on the battlefield. In addition, UDC women stressed the valor of women on the second front, focusing on the ways in which women's commonplace daily activities were transformed into important political and public acts. They told the story, for instance, of a neglected grave on a farm some seven miles northwest of Columbia marked only with the single word, "Benedict." Benedict was the name of a commissioned officer of the Confederate Army who fell ill while on a recruiting mission in the Columbia area. He was hidden on the farm of Confederate sympathizers, where despite the diligent efforts of the women of the family to nurse him back to health, he died. According to the UDC's telling, the county was so "overrun" by "federals" it was impossible to give the man a decent public burial, and instead the immediate neighbors were forced to gather together secretly, during the dead of night, and to convey the body to its final resting place, marking it only with a stone engraved with the one word, "Benedict."[7]

Not only did the UDC lay claim to valor and courage for the activities of Confederate sympathizers on the second front, they also demanded recognition for the ultimate sacrifice, the loss of life that fighting on the second front cost its participants. While their men had sacrificed their lives on the battlefield, civilians on the home front also lost members of their families and their community to guerilla warfare. One chapter member, Ann Hickam, recounted the deaths of four of her close neighbors at the hands of Union troops in a paper she read before the Columbia UDC in the 1920s. The first, she claimed, was a "young man not yet out of his teens," who was "shot through his heart, and in the agonies of death was pierced through the throat by a bayonet and left dead and unburied." According to Hickam, friends of the family "risked their lives," to bring his body home to his sisters. "We were," as she put it, "almost afraid to bury our dead in those troubled times." The next victim was her nearest neighbor. Federal soldiers also met him on the road and even though he pleaded with them to spare his life, if only because of his wife and six children, they shot him dead. A few days later another man was killed, also the father of a large family and a few days later his wife died of a broken heart. Obviously these were the kind of immediate, devastating, personal experiences that people could not easily forget. The experiences were fused in a particularly intense way with women's traditional domestic activities. As Ann Hickam concluded in her account almost 60 years later, "all these sad and harrowing things happened in the small circle of our own neighborhood."[8]

After the war officially ended, ex-Confederate women across the South converted their wartime soldiers aid societies, which had fed, clothed, and nursed the soldiers during the war, into Ladies Memorial Associations that took up the task of memorializing the dead. In contrast, Missouri women found it difficult to form such organizations. This difficulty arose because the state had remained in the Union, and had been convulsed by guerilla warfare. Only in St. Louis, where large numbers of Confederate prisoners of war died in the local hospitals, and in Springfield, where the state's one major formal battle, the Battle of Wilson's Creek, created more than a thousand casualties, were women able to start public memorial organizations. As was the case elsewhere in the South, the Springfield Monument Association struggled to reinter the dead. In this case, the members sought to move bodies from a temporary location in the open field in front of the county courthouse, where they had been hastily buried in the August heat. The association raised the funds successfully for a Confederate Cemetery, and later acquired standard grave markers. In the rest of the state, commemoration of the war dead was necessarily observed as a private matter because guerilla fighting tended to leave the dead, frequently civilians, scattered across the landscape.[9]

It was not until the late nineteenth century that Missouri ex-Confederate women found the necessity and the opportunity to publicly organize, and memorialize, their wartime experience. In the 1890s, ex-Confederate Missouri women formed the first chapter of the Daughters of the Confederacy in order to secure the construction of a Confederate Soldiers' Home in the state. Perhaps in recognition of the extent of civilian involvement in actual warfare in the state, the Missouri Confederate Home would be the only soldiers' home in the country to admit women along with men. By the turn of the century, mounting problems associated with the proper memorialization of this Confederate generation spurred local chapters of the Daughters of the Confederacy in Missouri to consolidate their resources in the formation of the *United* Daughters of the Confederacy. In 1901, 40 years after the Battle of Wilson's Creek, the Missouri UDC erected the first public monument to the Confederate dead in the state.[10]

Confronted by the generational realities of aging and death, the UDC was acutely aware of the fact that they needed not only to care for the aging veterans but also to preserve the memory of the Confederate generation that was passing away before their very eyes. They needed lasting gravestones and monuments to stand as a testament to their vision of the past. Perhaps more importantly they needed to transmit their stories to the younger generation that was quickly losing any firsthand contact with the war. At the dedication of the Confederate Rock on June 3, of 1935, the local UDC chapter brought veterans, the youngest of whom was 87, from the Confederate Soldiers' Home some 40 miles away in Higginsville, in order to have living participants of the war present at the dedication. At this point even the "daughters" themselves were passing on. The officers of the organization who stood beside the aging denizens of the Confederate Home were the granddaughters of noted war heroes. The mayor of the city, R. Searcy Pollard, who pledged at the dedication that the city would always keep a light burning over the monument, was himself a grandson of J. J. Searcy who in the summer of 1861 led the Columbia Home Guard out of Columbia to defend the state against the invading Union armies at the Battle of Boonville.[11]

These grandsons and granddaughters hoped that the placement of the Confederate Rock on the University of Missouri campus would have the effect of perpetuating the memory of their families' wartime sacrifices long after the last actual participants in the war were gone. Indeed, the dedication of the memorial on campus in 1935 was the culmination of a generation of successful effort on the part of these women not only to care for, bury, and memorialize the passing of the Confederate generation, but also to leave an active mark on their descendants. There was for example, the local elementary school, Robert E. Lee Elementary, home of the "Patriots," which they decorated with pictures of Lee and Jefferson Davis and provided with histories of the Civil War that met their approval. At the University of Missouri, the UDC formed a close relationship with the Kappa Alpha fraternity, meeting with them at the fraternity's Chapter House to celebrate Lee's birthday and other significant dates on the Confederate calendar. At one such event, Mr. Crowe, a grandson of a Confederate soldier, extended a particularly warm welcome to the UDC and formally extended to them the use of the Kappa Alpha's Chapter House any time. As the UDC noted in the minutes of their next meeting, "the cordial welcome and evident care in decorating for our coming gives the Kappa Alpha Boys a warm place in the hearts of the Daughters." The UDC expressed the warmth of their affection for the Kappa Alpha Boys by passing a motion to have a Confederate Flag made for them and for the Confederate Soldiers' Home in Higgensville.[12]

Admittedly, not all the UDC's efforts of cultural preservation succeeded. They petitioned the state legislature to designate a Gray and a Blue wing at the university's main library. It remained unnamed, but the Missouri Historical Society, housed in what they intended to be the "Gray" wing of the library labored tirelessly throughout the 1930s to collect over 1,500 records of Confederate soldiers who served from the state. Floyd Shoemaker, the secretary and librarian of the State Historical Society and editor of the *Missouri Historical Review*, was himself an avid supporter of Confederate memorialization, as was his wife, who was a member of the Columbia UDC Chapter. At a speech he gave in 1941 at the unveiling of a monument to three of Missouri's leading Confederates at the state capitol grounds, Shoemaker suggested that despite the monument they were gathered to dedicate on that day, the Confederate military experience remained largely unmarked in the state. It was rather the lived cultural tradition, "pride in southern tradition and southern ancestry," as he put it that, "binds to the present the spirit of the days of the Confederacy." Evidences of southern tradition could be found in "the love Missourians have for the strains of 'Dixie'," or in architecture, "the high columned porch so often associated with memories of old southern homes." It was then in the survival of these cultural forms, "the music, literature, legends, and architecture of the South, (that) we find the South of tradition living today." [13]

A generation later, in the early 1970s, students wondered how a memorial like the Confederate Rock, which they viewed as inappropriately political and arguably racist, could have been located on the campus in the first place. In 1935, however, women of the UDC thought that the world had finally righted itself. Through their public organizational work in honoring their men, they had honored themselves, their families and their southern culture more generally. They had finally won the battle of the second front. They had secured what they saw as an appropriate level of respect and recognition, of public space, for white southern descendants and their cultural forms in the state.

Then, in 1939, an African American named Lloyd Gaines won a suit against the university and gained admission to the school. In doing so, he became the first black student to be admitted to the university. This occurred only four short years after the UDC's crowning accomplishment in the Confederate Rock.

There was a place for African Americans in the world of the UDC, but it was not as students at the university. Indeed the local UDC Chapter even decorated the grave of one African American, "Uncle Jack Coates," along with the white Confederate soldiers buried in the city cemetery every year on Memorial Day. But "Uncle Jack" was honored as a loyal body servant to his master, not as a soldier in his own right. In a sense the "place" the UDC envisioned for African Americans was not dissimilar to the position women envisioned for themselves. That is to say, as loyal supporters of white men and as avid supporters of the second-front war. Of course the difference was that their men really were *their* men, while for their slaves their owners were in fact no "real" kin of theirs and this despite the "Uncle" in Jack Coates, or even the "Aunt" in Aunt Harris, "our black mammy," who was buried with her white owners in the same cemetery as Uncle Jack.[14]

While the UDC continued to celebrate those African Americans who appeared (at least to them) to be like members of their families, even advocating that a special pension be established for slaves who remained loyal to their owners during the Civil War, the black community in the state worked diligently to establish itself as a truly free people. While defeated white Confederates of the county and the state looked to their kin and community to perpetuate their culture, African Americans in mid-Missouri looked to their kin and community for the same purpose. While white women of the UDC asserted the honor and valor of their defeated men, and through that vehicle, the honor and worthiness of their white southern culture more generally, the black population of the state struggled to acquire an equal place for itself in the public cultural life of the state.[15]

This struggle on the part of the African Americans in the state sprang from the experience of Civil War, particularly guerilla war, and the same households that the UDC was so intent upon memorializing. The admission of Lloyd Gaines as a student to the university represented two trends. The first was simple: that a racially exclusionary society could no longer be maintained at public institutions such as the University of Missouri. Second, it represented something arguably of much wider cultural and social significance. For intimately intertwined with the recognition of a more racially egalitarian future in the state, was the emergence of a more racially egalitarian past, the public acknowledgement of which went right to the heart of the white, Confederate memory of themselves and their families in the region.

Just as the UDC was establishing a hegemonic place for the cultural politics of the second-front war, the admission of black students to the university represented the possibility that the black story would be presented in a form that white people in the state would hear. What that black story would reveal was that the war in mid-Missouri was actually a three-front war, fought not only on the first front of the formal military encounter and the second front of the white household, but also on the "third front" of the black household. Of course at the beginning of the war, black slaves were distributed throughout the white households of their owners, and it was precisely this dispersal throughout the white community that created the basis for the white women at the time, and the UDC ever afterward, to cling to their single-minded white vision of African Americans as servants in their households, and thus as loyal participants in their second-front war.[16]

In many ways, the experience of slaves in Boone County during the war was similar to that of their owners. The African American third-front war followed and emerged out of the fortunes of white civilians and their slaves on the second front. Until 1863, slaveholding households were largely stable in the area. This stability was secured in no small part by the Union troops that were stationed in the town of Columbia. However much white southern sympathizers may have resented the presence of these men and conspired against them, they had to recognize the usefulness of the Union military commitment to upholding the institution of slavery in the formally "loyal" border areas. Beginning in the fall of 1863, however, the Union military began a policy of active recruiting of slave men for the Union war effort. Slaves in the state were offered their freedom in exchange for their service as soldiers. Union officials sent out recruiting agents from St. Louis into the heart of the slaveholding regions like Boone County.[17]

This shift in Union policy marked the beginning of the end of slavery in the county and opened up the third front of the African American war. The county's white slaveholders resisted the change in Union policy. General Order #135 opened the door to black enlistment in Missouri in November of 1863, and opposition was strong. In Boone County, the Provost Marshal refused to accept any black enlistees and the recruiting agent returned to St. Louis in disgust. The local bushwhackers, some of whom were members of prominent local slaveowning families, threatened local black men with death if they enlisted. Nonetheless, more than 200 of the county's slaves ran away to the next county in the fall of 1863, where the Union accepted their enrollments. By May of 1864, 387 of the slave men of the county had enlisted. That number represented 69 percent of black males between 21 and 40 years of age in Boone County as of 1860. The overwhelming majority of these black enlistees would never return to their families, as the mortality rate of their regiment was above 75 percent.[18]

There were striking similarities between the white and black experiences of the war. Like their mistresses, slave women from the county suffered the loss of their men at the front. These black men, like their owners, had often been forced to run away in the dead of night in order to fight a war to uphold their beliefs. For the UDC, the story of Benedict was wrapped around the secrecy and danger that accompanied Confederate recruiting efforts in the county because of Union occupation. In the case of slave enlistments, it was the white slaveowners or white support for slavery in the county more generally, that made the enlistment for slaves into a similarly dangerous and difficult proposition. And just as white Confederate owners, who were serving at the battlefront, left behind women and children, so too, slave men left behind women and children to deal with a hostile occupying force. But while southern sympathizing women had to fear the random violence of the occupying Union forces against Confederate sympathizers, slave women faced a double-edged and potentially more serious threat. They faced possible violence from both their owners and bushwhackers.[19]

Two stories of slave women's activities illustrate the dangers they faced. As with the case of the southern sympathizing women of Boone County, who aided and assisted Confederate recruiters like Benedict, black slave women assisted the Union forces with critical information. The occupying Union military could only count on the loyalty of the black population because Confederate sympathy was so widespread in the slaveholding counties. Slaves carried out this assistance at great personal risk. One slave woman, Easter, came into the town of Columbia with her daughter to look for protection, after bushwhackers left a threatening note in the kitchen of her owner, a Mr. Samuel Davis, which read:

> From Camp Dixie, Boone County, Mo. Addressed to Samuel Davis' Black woman Easter. As you are known to be a notorious reporter, this is to inform you that if you are found in this county one-month after receiving this notice you will pull a rope. You must take all your brood with you and skedaddle like hell. We are determined to have no more of your damned reporting.[20]

Easter did indeed "skedaddle like hell" and was fortunate enough to reach the safety of the Union military outpost with her daughter and two other women. Another slave woman, identified in the military record only as "a negro woman slave of Edward Graves," was not so fortunate. She had taken advantage of the increasingly chaotic conditions of the county to run away to the town of Sturgeon. In the fall of 1864, she attempted to return to help some of the other slaves from her former household to escape as well. She started back to town with five other slaves from off the premises: a woman, a girl, a boy, and two small children. After proceeding several miles she was overtaken by three men disguised in Union uniforms. They took the slaves a distance into the woods and shot them all dead, hanging one woman before they shot her and returning the two small children to the white owner. The master was taken into custody by Union officials and charged with complicity in the killing.[21]

As these stories would indicate, the last year of the war saw a sharp increase in guerilla activity in the county aimed at the slave population, as not only the first front, but also the second front began to collapse. In the fall of 1863, when the new Union policy encouraged slave men to enlist in the Union army, local bushwhackers responded with the threat of death to any slaves they caught attempting to do so. By 1864, however, the institution of slavery was in such tatters in the state that the legislature voted in gradual emancipation, and by January of 1865, they acknowledged the death of the institution by voting in immediate abolition. In the county, the bushwhackers responded to the news of emancipation by posting notices that any blacks that sought paid work and any whites that hired them would be lynched. The guerillas gave the black population two weeks to leave the countryside, and pointedly insisted that all of the able bodied adult men who lived in the county must now enlist in the federal army. They apparently particularly feared the continued presence of any adult black men in the county now that they were free. They made good on their threats by lynching several freedmen who remained in the rural areas of the county. As one Union officer described the situation,

> I blush for my race when I discover the wicked barbarity of the late masters and mistresses of the recently freed persons of the counties heretofore named. I have no doubt but that the monster, Jim Jackson, is instigated by the late slaveholders to hang or shoot every negro he can find absent from the old plantations. Some few have driven their black people away from them with nothing to eat or scarcely to wear. So between Jackson and collaborators among the first families, the poor blacks are rapidly concentrating in the towns.[22]

Even with the close of the war in 1865, the freedpeople and the white southern sympathizers continued to share a conflicted, intertwined, and common history. They would both have the experience of having their stories of valor and sacrifice suppressed. In the war's immediate aftermath, the overwhelming majority of the white male citizens of the county were disenfranchised for their pro-Confederate stance during the war. They found themselves living in a county and a state firmly in the hands of their wartime enemies, the Radical Republicans. For the few black soldiers who survived the war to return to their families in the county, and for the much larger number of their wives, parents, and children who lived through the harrowing days of the home front during the Civil War in Boone County, the postwar era offered even less opportunity for the public celebration of their sacrifices to the triumphant Union war effort. The demands of fighting the war had destroyed the institution of slaveholding that had undergirded the white households of the county. But immediately afterward, the racial hierarchy was quickly reestablished through the system of de facto segregation.[23]

Union military victory was followed shortly by political domination of Missouri by the Republican Party. In a situation in which former Confederates had little power, they could at least attempt to retain control over the private relationship between themselves and their former slaves, albeit in a different form. They also sought to control the memory of the war. Many of the white citizens of Boone County claimed to respect and feel genuinely fond of their ex-slaves, often their domestic servants or farm laborers. Some whites in the county even assisted the newly freedpeople in their efforts to build their own separate communities, churches, and schools. Whites were at the same time militantly opposed to anything resembling racial equality. While they might be happy to celebrate the loyalty of the slavery generation as their faithful family retainers, a faithfulness that began in earnest with the test of the Civil War and persisted into emancipation, they clung to their vision of the freedpeople as an extension of their own experience of the war. There was nothing beyond the second front in their own vision. They created a narrative of the war that privileged whites' experience, even though blacks had demonstrated the same kind of wartime valor and sacrifice. Simply put, Boone County's ex-Confederate daughters claimed the power to commemorate the war on their own terms, as a story of white sacrifice and white valor alone.[24]

The death of the white Confederate generation fueled the rise of Confederate demoralization in Boone County. The death of the "old family retainers," the slavery generation, also fueled the rise of more militancy by a new generation of African Americans. Empowered by the struggles of the older generation to provide them with education and material opportunities they lacked, this younger generation formed the NAACP in the first decades of the twentieth century and began to press for greater social and economic opportunities for the African American population of the state. And by the time of the dedication of the Confederate Rock, or shortly thereafter, they finally found in the person of Lloyd Gaines the possibility of breaching the highest bastion of exclusionary public education, the University of Missouri.[25]

Shortly after winning his case and being formally admitted to the university, Lloyd Gaines disappeared while on a train coming to enroll at the school. His body was never found. The message was clear. Despite their legal breakthrough, blacks were not welcome as equals at the University of Missouri. African Americans did not even attempt to attend the university again until the 1950s, and even then, their numbers were small. Black enrollment swelled in the late 1960s, but on campus they found an entrenched white southern and Confederate culture. The Kappa Alphas still flew the Confederate Flag and read the Ordinances of Secession at "Old South Days" every year, the band played "Dixie" at Tiger football games, and women regularly posed on the Confederate Rock for pictures in the school annual.[26]

A particularly hostile encounter between black and white students centered on the Confederate flag and led to the formation of the first black student organization in the 1968–1969 school year. By that time, African American students numbered between three and four hundred on campus. At a Missouri football game, a few black students responded to the custom of waving Confederate flags by waving a black flag. The response to their gesture was a small riot. At some point in the brawl a university policeman drew a gun on one of the black flag wavers and said, "We don't do things like this here" (or according to another account, "You SOB, you drop that flag or I'll blow your brains out"). After the incident, African American students formed the Legion of Black Collegians. The following fall they established a publication, the *Black Out*. In their publication, black students explained why they thought it necessary to form a separate organization. As one article explained, black students were tired of being "constantly regarded as a silent minority . . . ignored by the main stream of campus life." Another offered a more militant explanation, describing the University of Missouri, "alias 'Little Dixie' " as a "society of Racism." According to this writer, "If George Wallace were to walk though the dorms of this University his heart would be overflowing with pride. The number of Confederate flags that would meet his eyes could make an old veteran bigot glad. . . . The monument rock dedicated to the Confederacy would fill his eyes with tears of happiness and make him want to embrace the white faculty and staff of this University, who are all his loyal comrades."[27]

This writer went on to describe the university as one large plantation. He described the central administration building as "The Big House," which "stands in all its old southern splendor and basks in its deep southern environment." The "overseers" of this plantation, he wrote, "otherwise known as the 'security police' still have their guns . . . They fit perfectly into the system and have no qualms about doing the jobs 'Big Massa' calls down for them. The security police don't know that this is 1969 and slavery ended one hundred and three years ago. . . ." Black students were, according to this writer, "125 miles from nowhere" and therefore in no position to fight the sort of "political revolution," that was going on in major urban areas.[28]

Here the *Black Out* editorial referred to the location of the University of Missouri in the middle of the state, and far from either Kansas City or St. Louis, major urban centers with large African American populations. Ironies abound here, since in the nineteenth century, the river counties in the center of the state had constituted the center of the black population. At the time of the Civil War, for instance, slaves constituted 25 percent of the population of Boone County. After the war, freedwomen and -men quickly left rural areas, and moved to local towns and eventually to big cities like St. Louis, Kansas City, or Chicago. Thus by the time African Americans were able to return to mid-Missouri as students at the university, they really did face the worst of both possible worlds, an area with a deep slaveholding tradition where many of the black population who had provided the initial basis for that culture had long since departed. Recognizing the impossibility of a direct "political revolution," the *Black Out* quite astutely proposed to foment a "revolution of cultural change," and proceeded to take aim at the very aspects of southern culture that the UDC had labored so diligently to promote.[29]

Black students expected to find no "reinforcements" among the white students, but reinforcements, were, in fact, forthcoming and from an unlikely place—from white women. Some white women of the younger generation abandoned, at least for the moment, the older generation's role as keeper of men's reputation for honor and valor in the war. Instead, the younger group took up the challenge of establishing a place for women on campus in their own right. The demands of African American and white women students converged in the early 1970s, as both groups demanded more women and black faculty as well as course work that focused on the historical and contemporary contributions of women and minorities to the culture at large. The fall of 1971 marked a banner year for both groups, as the Black Studies minor was established on campus along with the first course offering that focused entirely on women. In connection with this nascent women's studies program, the Association of Women Students brought in a series of speakers. The first speakers of the series were actually two women, Gloria Steinem, by this time a well-known spokesperson for the Women's Liberation Movement, and Dorothy Pitman, a pioneer in establishing New York City's child day care program. Steinem did not disappoint her audience, as she proceeded to "tear down every myth held sacred by oppressors of women." She expressed amazement that "a school of close to 20,000 students still has only one black faculty member and a handful of female professors." She called for a coalition of blacks and white women on campus, because, as she put it, "together you can work some changes, but if you don't get together the establishment will try to run you against each other."[30]

As Steinem argued, "It is up to us to make the white male more aware of the intrinsic value of the individual . . . Only then will the human race stop dividing itself because of outward differences." She assumed white men were responsible for racism because they refused to recognize the "individuality" of both white women and blacks. The politics of a number of white women students appeared to be oppositional to the goals of the UDC through their support of feminists such as Steinem and the Women's Studies program. Rather than viewing male honor as something to be cherished, many of the younger generation of white women regarded it as highly suspect. Rather than "standing by their men," this younger generation attempted to ally itself with blacks and other social groups subordinated to white male dominance. As Steinem claimed, "(white) women have more empathy with blacks because both have been victims of the white man's discrimination." Steinem did acknowledge that the parallel between African Americans and white women was not complete, since "women may have lost their identities, but blacks are losing their lives."[31]

In her speech, Steinem singled out the Confederate Rock and the rebel flag waving over the Kappa Alpha fraternity house as two symbolic manifestations of the extent of racial exclusion blacks faced on the campus. She followed the lead of the black students on campus, which had just the previous year published a full-page picture of the Confederate Rock in their publication with the caption "Is Racism Fostered Here?" This query apparently received little attention from the overwhelmingly white student body. However, on October 6, less than a week after Gloria Steinem castigated the Rock, the UM-C student senate passed a resolution calling it "offensive and insulting to blacks and to all who sincerely desire an end to black oppression." They asked the City of Columbia to remove the offending boulder as soon as possible. According to coverage in the town newspaper, this resolution on the part of the students constituted a "belated controversy" surrounding a "long ignored red granite boulder" that had taken Columbia residents "by surprise." Of course, the citizens referred to were not the 10 percent of the population who were black and certainly not the readers of the local student black press. Importantly, it was white women who raised the issue of racism symbolized by the Rock.[32]

News stories covering the MSA motion stirred an immediate controversy among the townspeople. "Party Line," an audience participation program on one of the local radio station, was flooded with calls about the Confederate Rock. The president of the MSA claimed to have received "menacing and obscene phone calls" in response to the students' request. Citizens wrote numerous letters to the editor, a whole range of reasons were given for why the Rock should remain on campus. Townspeople believed that the Rock stood for public recognition of their heritage. All others were outsiders, in their view. Gloria Steinem came in for criticism on this score. As one writer asserted, "Here's an astounding example of a New York City resident, an acknowledged traveling rabble rouser, coming into Columbia, being paid by the student government association to sound off, who then tells people in the Central Missouri city how they should handle their historical monuments." Even the students were viewed as "transients" by some townspeople. As one letter concluded, "How ridiculous can one get? If the Student Senate has nothing better to do than try to stir up ill feeling between the races—they should go home."[33]

What the younger generation of white women students began, black women completed. In 1971, the Rock remained in place, despite the first formal request to remove it. In 1974, however, Angela Davis came to speak on campus. After her speech, the Legion of Black Collegians sent a list of demands to the university's administrators including asking that the Confederate Rock be removed from campus and that it be warehoused somewhere outside of public view. That summer the Rock was frequently defaced, and some local townspeople formed a patrol to guard it at night. Authorities became concerned that serious conflict between students and townspeople seemed likely to break out. Late in the summer of 1974, before the students returned, the city sent in a truck and workers to remove the Rock to a remote field in an outlying city park.[34]

This move was not, of course, exactly what the black students had demanded. The Rock was still in the public domain, however far off the beaten track. It was also not acceptable to at least some of the townspeople, especially the members of the United Daughters of the Confederacy and the county's Historical Society. These groups hired a lawyer and joined forces with the townspeople most concerned with preserving the (white, southern) history of the town. They first arranged to have the Rock moved to the grounds of the Historical Society, and finally, after a formal hearing before the county judge, to have the Rock, at public expense, permanently relocated in front of the county courthouse. No students appeared at the hearing to contest the placement of the Rock in front of the courthouse and it rests there to this day. It appeared to have been enough of an accomplishment to remove what to many had become a marker of a certain kind of race and gender politics from university grounds. In doing so they asserted the existence of a different kind of university "family," a "family" where African Americans were students and faculty rather than slaves and servants and where white women were present in their own right rather than as their father's daughters or their husband's wives.[35]

This new and in many ways fraught alliance between white women and black people would bring substantial changes to the university in the years to come—enhancing Black and Women's Studies programs, increasing the numbers of black and women faculty, staff, and students. The Rock, for the moment, appeared not to be an issue. Its previous location on campus was converted into an open speakers circle where all were free to speak.

But in the 1980s, there was a revival of the memorialization of the Civil War in Missouri and across the country more generally. The Sons of Confederate Veterans was re-formed in the state and began to spearhead memorial activities like the reenactment of Civil War battles, the placement of new markers on Confederate graves, and the annual celebration of Decoration Day. In Columbia, the SCV arranged to have a concrete walkway built up to the Confederate Rock to make it more accessible to the public and began to use it as the location of their annual gathering to memorialize the county's Confederate dead. In 1988, the United Confederate Veterans in Columbia paid to have a ramp built to the Rock to allow better public access to it at its courthouse location. And in the early 1990s, some townspeople once again began to celebrate Memorial Day at the Rock, not unlike that first day on June 3, 1935.[36]

By the early 1990s, however, the resurgence of Confederate commemorative activities met with organized resistance from the African American population of Missouri just as it had a generation earlier when the Rock was rolled off campus and down to the courthouse. The state NAACP actively opposed this return to a celebration of Confederate heritage, pointing out that what represented valor and courage of the common soldier to the SCV and other heritage groups in the state, represented a history of slavery and oppression to the state's African Americans. By 1994, pressure from the NAACP and other groups and individuals who viewed the Confederate memorialization as inherently racist, caused William Jewell College to refuse to allow the ceremony honoring the reburial of Jesse James to be conducted on their campus in Liberty, Missouri. The issue was not so much the reburial of a notorious Civil War guerilla and postwar outlaw, as it was the use of the Missouri Confederate flag, with which the organizers proposed to drape the casket. According to campus officials, the dark blue Missouri Confederate battle flag, while "not resembling the more familiar and controversial 'stars and bars'," was "still judged by school officials to be a 'racially' inflammatory symbol." School policy, according to one official, "equated Confederate flags with Nazi uniforms and Ku Klux Klan attire".[37]

The question of Confederate memorialization returned to the University of Missouri campus in the fall of 2001 when two students decided to hang a 3 by 4 foot Confederate flag in their dorm window. Other students on their floor protested and a petition was circulated and signed. Passersby frequently responded to the flag with calls of "racist." Nonetheless the two undergraduates persisted, arguing along with the larger Confederate memorial movement in the state, that the flag represented "southern pride and rebellion," not, as their neighbor on their floor suggested, "oppression and prejudice." Officials at the University of Missouri hesitated to take action against the flag because they feared a "tough legal battle," if they tried to force the students to remove it. More to the point, one administrator noted, the problem was one of "differing cultural views trying to live peacefully together."[38]

And so we might ask, what has changed? Can you change history by moving a rock? This question was taken up by the school's town newspaper when the students first proposed the idea in 1971. As they put it, "A rock is a rock. It just sits there minding its own business . . . Probably not even aware that it is racist. How much can you expect of a rock? The rock can symbolize racism, or anything else a passerby wants it to. . . . You can't change history by moving a rock." In so far as the Rock was a reflection of larger social changes in the racial and gender climate of the University of Missouri, it certainly did at least *reflect* difference. Across the state in the 1990s, the rise of Confederate memorialization met stiff resistance and frequent failures, indicating that the public culture had indeed learned a different, blacker, telling of the past. In this new racial climate, we might expect that the Rock would have received the same negative response as the flag hung in the Gillette Hall window. We might expect a return to the kind of pitched battle that created the need to move the Rock in the 1970s. Instead, we find little renewed protest against the Rock and its rememorialization, and even the addition of a new Civil War monument alongside the Confederate Rock.[39]

In October of 2001, while students were breaking into the dorm room in Gillette Hall and throwing a broken television through the window where the Confederate flag was hung, Civil War reenactors lined up, with Confederate as well as the Union flags waving to dedicate the new Civil War monument. Photo coverage of the event shows a young black girl laying a wreath from all the black school children in the county at the base of the monument and black members of the town's citizenry sitting in the front row of the audience. What this reveals is not simply a blackening of the memorializing event itself, but the history that undergirds it. The Confederate Rock was dedicated solely to the white dead of the county, but the new monument now includes the names of 26 black soldiers who gave their lives in the Union war effort, a number that surpasses the 24 white Union dead from the county. The recognition and inclusion of the third front has transformed the meaning of memorial events like the dedication of Columbia's new Civil War monument.[40]

This is not to say that all is race happiness in central Missouri. Even the new monument, while including black Union dead, critically undercounts the participation of African Americans in the war. There were, for instance, a number of slaves who ran away to enlist in the nearby county because Boone County was too conservative to have its own military recruiter. It seems likely that if their names are added to the monument, the county's black Union dead will not just outnumber the white Union dead, but will outnumber the total white, both Union and Confederate. When bounded by the experience of the UDC's white women and the standpoint of the second front, what appeared to be a white southern story in 1935 turns out, with the collapse of the tight weld between the first and second front and the politics of standing by your man, to have been a black story all along. Who knows what the Civil War and its memorialization will become in Columbia and the former slaveholding states more generally as we move ever further away from the patriarchal slaveholding households and the race and gender politics of those households that generated secession and war.[41]

PART 2

GENDER, RACE, AND CLASS IN THE MAKING OF THE NEW SOUTH

CHAPTER 7

PATERNALISM AND PROTEST IN AUGUSTA'S COTTON MILLS: WHAT'S GENDER GOT TO DO WITH IT?

With the publication in 1921 of this classic work *The Rise of the Cotton Mills*, the historian Broadus Mitchell set the framework for discussions of the nature of the mill workforce and the mill owner in the southern textile industry. According to Mitchell, the development of that industry in the late nineteenth century was benign and benevolent. The white southerners who established mills wanted to promote the betterment of their communities and ameliorate the condition of the growing ranks of the rural and urban poor created by the economic decline of southern agriculture. In establishing textile mills, local capitalists were empowered to offer these less fortunate white members of the community remunerative employment when their farms failed. They often supplied improved housing, started schools for children, and helped to finance mill churches. Altogether, Mitchell concluded, mill owners behaved more like fathers than like employers to "their" mill people, and the workers responded with gratitude and intense loyalty to the men who had created a better way of life for them. It was unfortunately true that these mill owners paid workers miserable wages and worked them long hours, while making handsome profits from their employees' labor. However, since the profit motive was basically secondary to the mill owners' desire to promote class relations that would mirror those found in a happy family Mitchell expressed his hope that this one blight on the industry would soon be eliminated.[1]

Of course, this "one blight" on the industry, the exploitative nature of labor–capitalist relations, was not eliminated. Revisionist historians have taken Mitchell to task for his failure to recognize the centrality of the profit motive among mill owners and have criticized him for his assumption that millworkers were active and happy participants in the myth of paternalism.[2] Perhaps the most telling evidence for the revisionist critique is the bitter and protracted series of strikes that racked the late-nineteenth-century southern textile industry, first in 1886 and again in 1898. Centered in Augusta, where the largest concentration of southern millworkers was employed during much of the period, the strikes demonstrated the divergent interests of capital and labor.[3] Standing united as a group in the 1886 strike, 3,000 workers in the Augusta cotton mills joined the Union en masse in resistance to wage cuts and long hours. They persisted in their protest against deteriorating labor conditions despite months of lockouts, threatened and actual eviction from their homes, life in tents in the dead of winter, the threat of their replacement by black labor, and the failure of national Union support. In their determination to secure a just wage and decent working conditions, these workers demonstrated a solidarity and a level of resistance to the overwhelming power of the employing class arrayed against them that seems diametrically opposed to Mitchell's picture of the dependent and grateful worker. In their stiff-necked determination to strike for their rights, these workers appear instead to exemplify what historians understand to be the legacy of their rural, yeoman heritage, much as their fathers had as common soldiers in the long and bloody Civil War a generation earlier.[4]

But can these strikes really be taken as evidence of a separate, class-based culture among millworkers? Unlike their counterparts in northern industry, southern textile workers never succeeded in organizing permanent Union structures in the nineteenth century. Even in Augusta, the center of class conflict and Union organization in the southern textile industry, one could argue that two strikes, however bitter, over a 60-year period did not necessarily undermine the mill owners' basic position as benevolent paternalists in the workplace. In a more recent history of southern textile workers, appropriately entitled *Like a Family*, Jacquelyn Hall and her coauthors have refocused the question of class politics away from workplace organization and returned to the centrality of the family as the critical basis for worker autonomy and cultural integrity. They argue that although workers were largely unable to alter their position in the cotton mills through labor organization during the nineteenth century, they were able to turn to their families for self-expression and survival. While the mill owners may have viewed their workers as docile and dependent members of one big mill family, that is, *their* mill family, workers themselves maintained their autonomy as a group through their experience of family as discrete and separate from that of the mill owner. Thus, Hall and her coauthors believe the workers' families created not the basis for labor's acquiescence, as Mitchell thought, but the bedrock of labor's separate interests as a class.[5]

The arguments of Hall and her coauthors concerning the cultural significance of the family bear a striking resemblance to those advanced by historians of slavery. Historians point out that although the slaveowner may have envisioned the slave plantation as his or her "family, black and white," slaves in actuality took refuge in their own kin structures and used them to create the basis for a culture independent of planter domination. Historians of slave culture have demonstrated that despite the power of the owner, slave men acted as fathers to their families — they undertook to provide for and protect their wives, children, and larger kin networks.[6]

Similarly, revisionist historians of millworkers, who have taken issue with the mill owners' claims to paternalism, have been intent upon proving that millworking men undertook to protect and provide for their own. These historians cite the independent labor organization of the millworkers, and their militant action in strikes, as evidence for their position. Melton McLaurin entitled his book on the textile industry *Paternalism and Protest* because his discussion of labor relations centered on this issue. He described the factory-owner as the purported "paternalist" and the factory worker as the "protestor" of the hegemony of the mill owner.[7]

In McLaurin's account, both the paternalists and the protestors are assumed to be men. However, if one examines the phenomenon of mill paternalism more closely, one discovers that not all its adherents in fact were men. The "benevolent" activities generally attributed to mill paternalists, such as the establishment of mission churches, schools for mill children, lay care, and hospitals, were actually much more likely to be the work of their wives, daughters, or the women of their class. While mill-owning men may have financed the initial costs of church or school structures, it was frequently their women who engaged in the daily work of "maternalism." Similarly, an analysis of the "typical" millworker and striker reveals that they were usually women or children. Not only was the workforce composed largely of women and children, but a sizeable percentage of mill households were headed by women as well. In Augusta, before 1880, statistics indicate that more than 40 percent of all mill households were headed by women. Even this number underestimates the extent to which mill households were headed by women, because female-headed families, being generally less well off than male-headed families, were much more likely to board in a larger household than to live by themselves.[8]

So if women in Augusta played critical roles, both as "paternalists" and as "protestors," then why has this question of middle-class benevolence and working-class militancy been framed by so many historians of the textile industry in such male terms? Perhaps millworkers have been routinely presented by historians as though they were all men because acknowledging the role of women would serve to dilute the case for the "manhood" of millworking men. Again, the history of antebellum slave studies is instructive. In much the same fashion, some historians of slavery have focused their energies on rehabilitating the "fatherhood" of the male slave, a fatherhood that takes as its paradigmatic model the gender roles of the slaveholding planter class. It is this underlying commitment to the elite white model of both fatherhood and motherhood that leads historians to turn a blind eye to the range of contributions that slave women made to their households. Similarly, the role of women both in the textile workforce and as heads of their own households is ignored because it is counterproductive to historians' efforts to make a case for the manhood of millworking men patterned after the gender roles of mill-owning men.[9]

Thus for all the focus on paternalism—who has it, who doesn't—there is still no real history of manhood as a historical category of analysis capable of changing its form and meaning with the changing race and class order that the development of the urban industrial world of the textile mills created. When Broadus Mitchell argues that the mill owners were like paternalistic slaveholders, and when Melton McLaurin counters with the millworking men "resisting" as protestors, or even when Hall paints a comforting picture of the mill family united like the fingers on a hand, none of them directly confronts the question if mill-owning men took up the "paternalistic" legacy of slaveholders in their role as mill employers, what or where did that leave millworking men? Indeed, historians seem to assume that despite the widening class divisions of industrial society, where millworking men now had nothing but their labor to sell and mill-owning and -managing men were left as the sole "heads" of the business, millworking men could still somehow occupy the "paternal" role, as defined by a single standard set by the experience of elite white property-holding men.

Although historians of southern textiles have focused on the concept of "father," manhood is not a fixed entity that they can somehow prove belonged to all men irrespective of their class or race location in the social order. Manhood, like womanhood, was constructed out of particular historical contexts. The move toward an urban, industrial society that the textile industry spearheaded in the South and in Augusta in particular, can therefore be understood as creating a state of flux and uncertainty in pre-existing definitions of manhood. It is instructive to examine whether mill-working men continued to view themselves as men in the preindustrial sense of the term after becoming "hands" in another man's operation. In the context of the antebellum South, this would have placed them in a permanently dependent position like that of women and slaves. From this perspective, the outbreak of militant labor organizing and strikes in Augusta in the 1880s and 1890s can be understood as part of a larger process of renegotiation of what it meant to be a free white man in late-nineteenth-century Georgia.[10]

Millworkers in the Old South

The discussion of this process starts with the origins of the mills in Augusta and the question, What does gender have to do with it? If being a mill "hand" was so antithetical to what southern white men understood to be their proper place as "heads" of their own economically independent households, how did the mills get started in antebellum Augusta in the first place? The construction of the mills occurred because they reinforced the larger patriarchal social order. Mill owners provided employment to women and children, especially rural widows and their children, who had no adult male heads of household to work the family farm. These women came to Augusta in the hope of finding labor for themselves or their children, or public support from the benevolent resources of the city's churches and government. What they found in antebellum Augusta, especially before the construction of the first textile mill in 1847, was not very encouraging. The main form of employment for women throughout the nineteenth century was domestic labor. In the South, white women found this avenue of employment generally closed to them, because it was regarded as the province of black women, either slave or free. Without education or capital, white southern women found that they could not take up schoolteaching, enter into a small business like a grocery, or keep a boardinghouse, the other main forms of employment for white women in the town. That left the possibility of sewing for a living, which, given the limited alternatives for remunerative employment for women of this class and station, created a surplus of needlewomen and low wages.[11]

Catherine Rowland, the wife of a prominent Augusta cotton factor, described the plight of one widowed woman and her daughter who were reduced to the support that sewing could provide. "I went this afternoon to see Harriet Tyndall, poor girl. . . . What a sad life is hers having to support herself and her mother by her needle and her mother in a perfectly helpless condition being both blind and palsied."[12] No amount of "plying her needle" could compensate for the structural position in which women like the Tyndalls found themselves in the rural, patriarchal, slave-based economy of antebellum Georgia. Nevertheless, the migration of women and children to the city did open the way for the eventual amelioration of their condition through the establishment, in 1847, of Augusta's first cotton mill. As the price of cotton declined in the 1840s, it shook loose the most economically marginal of rural families from their land. They moved to town, which undercut the economic health of the town in general, as profits from cotton factoring fell off and rural demand for the town's goods declined. This economic slump was further compounded by the extension of the railroad to factoring towns farther west, particularly to Macon, which also reduced Augusta's rural trade.[13]

The destitution in the ranks of the poor, especially women and children, combined with sluggish rural demand and low prices for cotton, motivated several prominent men to consider establishing a textile factory. By making cotton profitable even in unprofitable times, a mill would bolster the sagging urban economy, employ the destitute, and make a profit for the investors. Although Augusta was located on the Savannah River, the establishment of such a mill required the construction of a canal to improve waterpower. The actual construction of the Augusta Factory in 1847 represented a new opportunity for destitute women and children, a more profitable investment outlet for the town's merchants and businessmen, and an incentive toward a wholesale program of urban improvement.

This convergence of charitable benevolence, public improvement, and private profit is a marvelous example of the configuration of forces that Broadus Mitchell's analysis would lead one to expect. That is, it created the structural space for the position of the paternalistic mill owner, "father" to his dependent millworkers on the one hand, powerful male profit maker on the other. It was, however, precisely the logic of antebellum, white, rural gender relations embedded in a slave-based, cotton producing economy that enabled patriarchal benevolence and capitalist industrial development to go hand in hand. It might seem that the establishment of such a mill would violate the commitment of slaveholders and yeoman farmers alike to an autonomous existence grounded in their status as independent producers. But it was precisely the underside of this male autonomy and independence, the dependent position of women and children within these male-headed households that formed the structural basis for the paternalistic nature of labor relations within the mills. As long as the industry remained marginal, as it did in the antebellum period, as long as the work experience of women and children remained subordinate and marginal to the work experience of most white men, then the mills, rather than violating the antebellum understanding of what it meant to be a free man, actually served to reinforce it.

What happened to the harmonious and apparently benevolent nature of labor relations when the textile industry, rather than representing a marginal spin-off of the predominantly rural, patriarchal family structure of the antebellum economy, moved to the center of the economic life of the town? During the Civil War, when this first began to happen, events served to intensify the convergence of profitability, benevolence, and community promotion. The larger economic and social forces that had created the space for the mill owner as a paternalistic figure—and that had fostered the construction of the Augusta Factory—intensified. Wartime conditions increased the demand for textile goods dramatically, improved the profitability of the industry, and enlarged the supply of women and children in the town looking for some kind of work to replace the labor of their fathers and husbands who were at the front. As a result, the Augusta Factory became, according to its postbellum president, John Phinizy, a virtual "gold mine." At the same time it enhanced its benevolent reputation by offering employment to household members of men who were at the front.[14] The initial period of antebellum mill construction was one of "father lack." The war, a period of massive expansion of textile production intimately connected to "hyper-father lack," increased the numbers of women and children pouring into Augusta, especially in the last two years of the war, as they searched for some form of employment or charity to compensate for their absent brothers, husbands, and sons.

After the war, high prices for textiles and the persistence of a surplus of eager hands allowed the mill to pay dividends beginning with a high of 20 percent per annum in 1865. It paid this rate until 1873, when it lowered its dividends to 12 percent, which it paid throughout the remainder of the decade.[15] At the same time the persistence, in fact the slight increase, of widowed women and their children in the workforce and the community allowed mill owners and managers to boast of their good working conditions and harmonious labor relations. As one Augusta capitalist described the situation of female textile workers to the Senate Investigatory Committee on Relations between Labor and Capital in 1883, "You take a girl and put her into a sewing house here and she has got to work very hard to make 50 cents a day, and many of them cannot do that. . . . A woman can make $1.00 to $1.25 a day and you cannot put an ordinary woman at any work outside a factory at which she can make that much."[16]

What constituted good wages for a woman constituted poor wages for a man. In the logic of a patriarchal social order, this was reasonable. Men's wages were pegged to the cost of supporting a household, at least in theory, while women's wages were considered to be additional supplements to that of the male head of household. The smooth functioning of the mills was, in this logic, intimately connected with the replication in the factory of the larger social order of gendered dominance and subordination, wherein the men held the skilled and supervisory roles and only the women and the children actually functioned as "hands" under someone else's direction. As one Augusta capitalist explained to the Senate committee, "The worst thing in a factory is a sixteen year old boy; he will give more trouble than anybody else. . . . I make it a rule to put a woman to every loom where I can, but I am obliged to have men to fix the looms and put in the beams and various other things. However, if I could, I would not have a man in the weaving room except those that do the heavy labor. . . . the women do a great deal better."[17] As the president of the Augusta Factory concluded, "The men really do very little work except to watch the others and take care of the labor of the machinery. The actual operatives are nearly all female."[18]

Even as these mill men spoke, however, forces were at work that would lead to the rapid conversion of white men into mill operatives. Declining prices for cotton combined with the high profits of the Augusta Factory provided the incentive for yet another major expansion of the textile industry in Augusta in the late 1870s. The resultant expansion of the Augusta Factory and the construction of six new mills increased the total mill workforce dramatically, from some 700 employed in the mid-1870s to close to 3,000 by the mid-1880s. The construction of these mills was made possible by the enterprise of local townsmen in the face of declining cotton prices and by the simultaneous development of a largely new form of surplus labor created by the increased incidence of economic failure among hinterland yeoman farmers. As a result, migrants to the city included an ever-increasing proportion of male-headed households. The gender composition of the mill workforce and of the typical mill family began to shift dramatically. The total employment of men in the town's mills increased from 23 percent in 1880 to 39 percent in 1890, while the percentage of women declined from 52 to 43 and the percentage of children employed also declined from 25 to 18.[19] This gender shift was also apparent in the larger mill community as the percentage of mill households headed by women began to decline, from 43 in 1880 to 27 in 1900.[20]

Although the Augusta Factory persisted in its policy of hiring only white women and children as operatives, the newer mills had to accept more men. The president of one of these newly established mills, William Sibley, was inclined to put a good face on the increased employment of adult white men in his mill. In his testimony before the Senate committee, he asserted that the increased employment of entire families, that is, male-headed households, actually contributed to the "reliability" of his labor force.[21] This increased reliability resulted from the greater stability of these men who, according to Sibley, were more likely to persist in the mill workforce than those who were single. The familial position of men, as heads of households, rather than as footloose 16-year-old boys, made their increased participation in the mill workforce desirable.

The Knights of Labor

It was this familial status of the new male operatives, however, that contributed to the formation of the town's first textile Union, Knights of Labor Local 5030, in 1884 and to the outbreak of labor militancy in the strike of 1886. Although historians have considered the role of several factors in this emergence of autonomous organization among Augusta's workers, including the mills' concentrated urban location and the depressed economic conditions that then prevailed, no one has considered the contribution that the increased participation of men in the mill workforce or in the mill family might have made to labor organization and labor militancy.[22] Even a brief consideration of the politics of the Knights local and the course of the 1886 strike it mounted makes the role that larger gender structures played in the conflict apparent.

First, the name of the organization, the *Knights* of Labors makes one think of *men* as the honorable defenders of labor. They were prepared to do battle. Of course, the Knights were originally named not by southern textile workers but by northern workers. But for southern white men the image of the chivalrous knight protecting his own was probably even more powerful than it was in the North. These laboring men called themselves knights at the same time the rural world of horse-riding men passed away. Indeed, the organization itself has been understood by labor historians as a last-gasp effort on the part of the skilled worker and the small farmer to hang on to their preindustrial position in the face of the spread of urban industrial capitalism in the late nineteenth century.[23]

Not every adult white man was destined to be economically independent, as was largely the case in preindustrial, rural Georgia, but the advent of large-scale industrial production did not necessarily signal the end of this old form of manly independence. According to the Knights, by joining together the workers could hope to combine their own capital, form cooperatives, and continue to own the means of production, albeit collectively. In the Knights' vision the textile workers in Augusta would have to pool their resources together to eventually own and run one of the town's textile mills.

Much has been made of the unrealistic nature of this vision and its connection to the decline of the Knights of Labor. In particular, historians have pointed to the way the national organizations' commitment to the cooperative vision ran into conflict with the rank and file's desire to eat. The Knights aimed at a general reform of industrial capitalism that would reestablish them as relatively economically independent, but the immediate pressures to provide sufficient wages to support their households demanded their attention. The Knights of Labor faced a dilemma. On the one hand, they hoped to retain or reestablish their old position of authority as men who ran their own business and households. On the other hand, they needed to make a living through the new economic forms that were emerging, if only to support those households.

In the particular context of the textile industry, the Knights also had to make common cause with the rank and file of the textile workforce, the unskilled women and child laborers. This proved problematic. In Augusta, an attempt to form Local 5080 in 1884 was defeated. In 1886, membership increased for a time because of a walkout by the entire mill workforce of 3000. The organized skilled workmen of the mill community found themselves confronted with the challenge of protecting their own positions in the workplace and their own dependent family members while simultaneously shouldering responsibility for the needs of the entire mill community. They did, indeed, find themselves like knights on the battlefield arrayed against the men of the mill-owning class. The question was, who could play the "manly" role? Who could really protect and provide?

The demand for Union recognition precipitated the strike. The mill owners were determined to reject this demand because it affronted their property rights as capitalists, and it cut to the very heart of the traditional structure of labor relations grounded in the dependent familial status to which female and child employees were subject. Knights Local 5030 had the temerity to suggest that the Union, not the mill owner, represented the larger interests of millworking women and children—that the Union, not the mill owner would stand as the father figure of millworking families. Implicitly repudiating the paternalistic and benevolent claims of the mill owners, these adult male trade Unionists issued demands that would explicitly enhance their own familial roles. They called for a wage increase and for concessions that specifically recognized their independence and autonomy, such as the abolition of the pass system that, according to the Union, "lower[ed] the dignity of manhood." By promoting their own individual autonomy, millworkers hoped to improve the position of mill-working women and children and advance the interests of their entire class.[24]

When the Union was initially formed, Augusta's capitalists tried simply to ignore it. The issuance of the Union demands in January 1886 and the walkout of the most skilled male operatives in July of that year, which halted production, forced mill owners to act. They formed their own organization, the Southern Manufacturers' Association, and responded to the militancy of the workers by locking out the entire mill workforce in early August. From the capitalists' perspective, this action was intended to force workers to recognize their dependent relationship to the mills, and by extension to their "paternalistic" employers, and to see the foolhardiness of seeking class autonomy through the Union. As one prominent textile capitalist advised Augusta mill owners: "Crush the Knights beyond resurrection, they present a greater threat to the mills than the depression of the last two or three years, or any threat in the last twenty years. . . . Stamp out the Knights then and now, and make it amongst the operatives discreditable for one to admit that they even belonged to the organization. When they get good and starved and utterly ruined, they will turn upon and murder [J. S.] Meynardie and the other leaders of the organization."[25]

Women, especially widows and their children, were expected to be the Union's weakest link. Shortly after the general lockout, the local paper sent a reporter down to the mill neighborhood to inquire into the attitudes of the women in the community. "Will the women support the strike?" the reporter asked one male worker. "Yes, they will be the last to give in," he replied.[26] The Union's ability to support its members, however, was becoming increasingly precarious. The strikers, especially widows and their children, were dependent upon the support of the national organization to put bread on their tables. When the national organization decided to cut off this support at the end of August, the Augusta local sent one last desperate plea to the organization: "Do for God's sake render us such assistance as will hush the bitter wails of hungry children and poor, ill-treated widows and thin little orphan children—General Master Workman, you may think this an overdrawn picture, but God knows 'the half is not told.' "[27]

A stalemate ensued. Despite the increasing misery in their ranks, the workers would not capitulate, and the capitalists would not acknowledge their right to organize. At this point local Union forces were in shambles, deserted by the national organization, and suffering ever more intensely with the deepening winter chill. Finally, in early November, the capitalists agreed to negotiate. The workers failed to win any of their demands, and the Union collapsed shortly thereafter. The capitalists had addressed their biggest grievance, and at least tacitly acknowledged their autonomy, when they recognized the Union's right to exist. The local paper advised the workers to "go back to work and accept the settlement. There is honor in defeat, remember those who are dependent upon you!"[28]

Male operatives learned they had entered into a new kind of the dependent status as hands in someone else's workplace. Their very resistance, unionizing, and striking constituted a vehicle for the internalization of this knowledge. This lesson in "feminization," which women learned in childhood, many of these men found bitterly galling. Their previous experience as yeomen farmers and independent household heads stood in sharp contrast to their new situation. At the same time, capitalists were forced to recognize that this influx of adult male operatives had altered their relationship to the mill community. Indeed, while the increased presence of adult male wage earners represented a degradation of their own individual relationship to production, it simultaneously enhanced the prospects for independence and autonomy for the working-class community as a whole. For millworking women and children were now increasingly empowered by their very dependence upon the men of their own families, a dependence that finally allowed them at least a modicum of liberation from the harsher and more exploitative life they could expect when they stood in direct relationship to mill employment and the mill owner alone.

CHAPTER 8

THE DE GRAFFENRIED CONTROVERSY: CLASS, RACE, AND GENDER IN THE NEW SOUTH

I n the winter of 1891, Clare de Graffenried, an investigator with the U.S. Bureau of Labor assigned to research the condition of wage-earning women and children, published an article in *Century Magazine* entitled "The Georgia Cracker in the Cotton Mills."[1] In it she discussed the condition of the state's textile millworkers on the basis of hundreds of interviews that she had conducted among millworkers throughout the state, analyzed the factors she thought were responsible for labor conditions in the industry, and suggested how they might be ameliorated. The article met with approbation in the northern press and was widely cited as an authoritative statement of the condition of southern textile workers. In the South, however, it engendered widespread hostility and rejection. Journals as varied in political allegiance as the *Manufacturers' Record*, an organ of southern business, and the *Wool Hat*, a Georgia Populist weekly, disputed the accuracy of the article and thereby created what came to be termed in the local press "The De Graffenried Controversy."[2]

This controversy bears close examination because in it are refracted relations of class, race, and gender that developed in the late-nineteenth-century South. In one sense, the hostile response that De Graffenried's critique elicited from all sectors of southern white society simply reflected the ways in which the regional context of economic subordination and racial hierarchy set limits upon the sort of progressive reform of industrial capitalism that was then spreading rapidly in the North. At the same time, however, these very regional characteristics gave rise to a unique type of gender politics in which new and more intensified forms of white female domesticity could be offered as substitutes for confronting the apparently intractable relations of race and class. In particular the response of Rebecca Felton, a prominent Georgia social reformer and political activist who produced the most sustained rebuttal to De Graffenried's critique, reveals the way in which the development of gender politics was shaped by the distinctive relationship between home and workplace that characterized the economic and racial structure of the South in the decades after the Civil War.

De Graffenried's 1891 article opened with a description of the depressed living conditions of the state's millworkers. Housing was "barrack-like" with no yards, porches, or even doorsteps. Many houses lacked even "a stove in the last stages of rust and decrepitude," and women still labored over a "sooty fireplace . . . decked with an old-time crane and pots . . . ." Bare floors were "begrimed with the tread of animals"; there was no running water or "outhouse, in the whole community."[3] Houses were cold, drafty, and frequently overcrowded. Poor drainage led to frequent outbreaks of malaria that reached epidemic proportions.

Perhaps the best that could be said for the textile operatives' housing was that the occupants were rarely there. De Graffenried found children as young as five or six, and women approaching their sixties, all working in the mills. Young infants, brought to the mills by their working mothers, were "reared amid machinery, their cradle often a box of bobbins, their coverlet the hanks of yarn." It was not unusual to find three generations of women working side by side, from sunrise to sunset, some eleven and a half hours a day, five and a half days a week. Unfortunately for the health of these women and their children, however, the mill environment represented no improvement over their homes. The hot "steaming atmosphere" necessary for the production of textiles turned "ordinary unsodden human flesh . . . limp and helpless." Standing long hours, bent in unnatural ways over machinery, took its own toll, especially on the children.

> Unmarried women of thirty are wrinkled, bent, and haggard. . . . Sickly faces, stooping shoulders, shriveled flesh, suggest that normal girlhood never existed. . . . A slouching gait; a drooping chest, . . . a dull, heavy eye; yellow, blotched complexion; dead-looking hair; stained lips, destitute of color and revealing broken teeth—these are the dower of girlhood in the mills.[4]

De Graffenried was particularly concerned with what she perceived to be the pernicious consequences of the widespread employment of young children and their mothers. Because economic necessity forced married women to work for wages, they had little time or energy left to run efficient households. The poverty of their living conditions was exacerbated by their absence from home. "The mothers being immured in the factories, family life is a travesty. . . . The bareness of their unlovely abodes is more abject than the direst poverty can excuse." The legacy of child and adolescent labor was adult women without the skills to make the most efficient use of what domestic resources they had. Housing was sparsely furnished in part because the "faculty for adornment, for beautifying their belongings, is a missing sense." "Sickly faces" reflected not only a lifetime of hard labor in the mills, but also an "unhealthy and inefficient" domestic life. "Everywhere they use snuff and tobacco, and subsist on scanty, innutritious diet. . . . the butt of ridicule, shiftless and inconsequent, always poor though always working."[5]

The destructive relationship between family life and the workplace had set in motion a self-perpetuating, downward cycle. Women spent their lives in the mill and not at home feeding and training their children. Because the children were forced into the mills, at least in part as a result of domestic inefficiency, they grew up without acquiring the skills necessary to establish a different kind of family themselves, thus perpetuating the cycle into the next generation. De Graffenried gives the example of the experience of one child, Mary Belle Surrelle Jones, "a wizened midget of eight," whose father was dead and who had begun to work in the factory at the age of five.

> I wur eight yur ole come er Chewsdy when maw drawed my fus pay. Don' have money much offen; maw she gimme er quarter laist buthday. Maw's hur in er mill, en paw's hur, en Sailly she he'ps maw spool' ca'se she hain't big 'nough ter piece ainds. Sailly she's six, en maw hain't got nary one ter leave her wid, so she bring her ter mill. No'm I hain't got no book-learnin'. Yais, 'm, I dips. Overseert' other mill, he says, "Calline, dip snuff," says he; "cas'se, ef yer don't, blue dye'll pizen yer."[6]

Such children, integrated too soon into the adult life of the factory, were "early taught the alphabet of sin." Rarely able to attend school, they lived in total ignorance of life outside the mills. At night they returned home to overcrowded living conditions where "whole families huddle together irrespective of sex or relationship," and "moral distinctions are unknown. . . ." Not surprisingly, women married early and took the marital relation lightly. "The instability of the conjugal bond and the indifference with which marriage is often regarded are evidenced by the boasting of many matrons as to the ease with which they have rid themselves of objectionable partners. . . . Ultimately, then, the family as a social unit dissolved under the pressures of poor living and working conditions, and in turn the family's disintegration destroyed the hope for a more enlightened younger generation."[7]

What caused the distortion of these women's and children's lives? De Graffenried rejected the possibility that they were inherently debased and therefore personally responsible for their plight. "The normal Georgia cracker under all her nicotine stains overflows in simplicity and unperverted goodness." "Dissoluteness of life and speech are rather an excrescence than a vital disease." Instead, she looked to the set of social relations that created the structure of their lives, in particular their relations with men. "A most potent factor in this abuse is that the fathers will not work and the little ones must." Although virtually the entire community of women and children were to be found in the mills, the adult men could usually be located "about the single store of the village, lounging, whittling sticks, and sunning their big, lazy frames. . . ." The working of a small plot of land and an occasional hunting trip for food were their excuses for avoiding mill labor. Not only did the men refuse to enter the mills, but they also refused to do the heavier work around the house, leaving it to their already overworked women to haul the water and chop the wood. "His lordship descends to no duties so menial."[8]

Wage-earning women and children were thus asked to bear more than their share of life's burdens. They could not be expected to work long hours in the mill and at the same time maintain a healthful household, or, in the children's case, to acquire the skills that they would need in adult life. De Graffenried found the propensity of "meek wives or fond daughters" to excuse this behavior on the part of their men "pathetic and exasperating." She gave the example of one young woman who "claims that her stalwart husband has 'been er-cuttin' wood'; yet when closely questioned she is obliged to admit his worthlessness: 'fur mos' two years now he hain't er-binner.' "[9] As long as men were neglectful of their familial responsibilities and the women and children accepted and even rationalized their behavior, women and children would continue to be called upon to try to make both ends meet and most likely would fall short in the attempt.

But women's dismal domestic relations with their men were, according to De Graffenried, only half the problem. The other half of the equation was their relationship with their employers, the mill owners. These men contributed to the depressed condition of their employees through their willingness to employ young children and to work them and their mothers' long hours under poor conditions. "Year after year bills to prevent the employment of children under ten and twelve are defeated in the legislature, less from objection to the measure than from criminal indifference and because a time clause has been added reducing the hours of labor; and this curtailment, the manufacturers feel, would be disasterous [*sic*] to their interests."[10]

Some manufacturers did try to reform their workers' living conditions. De Graffenried gave the example of one mill owner who tried to institute a series of reforms. Improved housing was built, gardens were started, and schools were opened. The new houses "fell to pieces through neglect, or were burned up in drunken orgies." Operatives used the garden fences for fire wood and turned their hogs into the gardens, saying "Bacon's better'n garden sass any day." The school stood empty for lack of attendance. The mill owner finally gave up: "Though he speaks of them with mist in his eyes, [he] 'lets the poor devils alone.' " Other manufacturers tried to curtail the employment of children in the mills with equally limited success. "Often a wholesale dismissal takes place, quickened by protests of labor Unions; but under various pretexts the gnomelike toilers creep back, especially into the country and suburban mills because of the scarcity of hands."[11]

What was really called for, according to De Graffenried, was state intervention that would regulate working conditions while simultaneously improving domestic life. Only in this way could the destructive relationship between work and home life be broken and a new pattern set. The reforms most needed were a legislative prohibition on child labor together with a compulsory education law. Such reforms would remove children from the destructive environment of the factory and place them in the constructive environment of the schoolroom, where they could acquire the necessary skills and domestic habits to break out of the cycle of poverty.[12]

Once children, especially girls, were educated in the ways of a healthy domestic life, it would become possible to reform the diet and living conditions of the workers. Social pressure could be applied to the men so that not working would be perceived as shameful. "Scourge the idle men until, in Georgia, as in Maryland and parts of Maine, self-confessed failure and disgrace are implied when husbands put wives into the mill."[13] This pressure when successful would reduce the need for married women to labor in the mills and would give them more time for their homes and their children. Education in subjects like "scientific temperance" would help eradicate the use of alcohol and snuff. The money saved could again be applied to the reduction of married women's labor and the improvement of domestic living conditions. Instead of undermining domestic life, the worker's relationship to production could begin to support it and vice versa. The downward cycle could be reversed as a more productive domestic life would create a more skilled and diligent worker, and a more skilled worker could support a more productive home life. Referring to the results of protective legislation already in existence in Great Britain, De Graffenried asserted that "as a result of the educational requirements of the short time clause for all earners and the prohibition of night and over time work for women, the increased social welfare of the masses [is] apparent in the rise of wages, greater production of wealth per capita of population, fall in prices, and dimunition [*sic*] of pauperism and crime."[14]

The evidence and analysis contained in "The Georgia Cracker in the Cotton Mills" established De Graffenried as a pioneer in the field of progressive labor legislation. Her painstaking collection of data on the living and working conditions of Georgia's millworkers was enlisted to bolster her basic position that the public employment of women and children at the expense of their domestic lives was responsible for the depressed condition of the population as a whole. She advocated that a new alliance be formed between the state and the interests of the domestic arena in opposition to the excessive incursions of productive life. State intervention was necessary because wage-earning women and children lacked the social power to defend themselves against the encroachments of capitalism. Since women's labor spanned both the domestic and the productive spheres, more limited approaches to the problem—such as the organization of trade Unions or the attempt on the part of benevolent mill owners to reform domestic conditions—were doomed to failure because they did not address the determining conjuncture of women workers' lives, the relationship *between* the productive and the domestic spheres.[15]

Although De Graffenried's article was widely praised in the North and was even given the first prize for the best essay on wage-earning women by the American Economic Association, in the South it met with widespread hostility and rejection. The *Manufacturers' Record*, a journal representing southern business interests, began the so-called De Graffenried Controversy with an article in February 1891. It charged that rather than being an accurate statement of the condition of southern millworkers put forward by a sincere advocate of the interests of southern women, the study was actually part of a larger plot on the part of the "South-hating" *Century Magazine* to misrepresent "everything southern." "For years the South in one phase or another has been to Century contributors the butt for ridicule and misrepresentation."[16]

According to the *Manufacturers' Record*, the North had particular reason to malign the southern textile industry. For over a decade southern textile boosters had been pointing to the advantages the South held for the industry: the proximity to the staple, the inexpensive waterpower, the milder and more humid climate, and the lower cost of labor. Given these obvious advantages and the threat they posed to northern industry, the northern press had decided, according to the *Manufacturers' Record*, that it was necessary to undercut the nascent southern textile industry by impugning the reliability of the southern textile workforce.[17]

Southern mill owners looked about for someone to defend the industry and the Georgia Cracker against this "South-hating" attack. They found her in Rebecca Latimer Felton, one of the most politically powerful women in the state. Having begun her political career in the 1870s as her husband's (William H. Felton) campaign manager in his successful bid for the U.S. Senate, she had gone on in the 1880s to develop her own autonomous politics as a prominent member of the Georgia Woman's Christian Temperance Union and as the foremost promoter of convict lease reform in the state. By 1891, Felton was widely recognized within Democratic political circles both for her political acumen and for her prodigious talents as an editorialist.[18]

The actual request to Rebecca Felton for a rebuttal came in March 1891 from J. F. Hanson, one of the founders of and acting agent for the Bibb Manufacturing Company. Hanson was so incensed with De Graffenried's article "because of its injustice alike to cotton mill owners and operatives" that he initially considered writing the rebuttal himself.[19] He recognized, however, that it was preferable to have some "outside interest" take up the defense, even declining to present Felton's reply to *Century Magazine* for publication, stating "if it provokes controversy, the fact will not be overlooked that it was presented for publication by one identified with the interest Miss De Graffenried assailed."[20] Hanson wanted to avoid the issue of class interests and class divisions altogether and thought the focus should be on the common interests of mill owners and their operatives. "You will be amply able to do this," he wrote to Felton, "so far as Georgia is concerned. I regret that such is not the case in some of the Southern States where long hours, poor pay, and 'pluck me' stores enforces [*sic*] a system of abject slavery upon the poor mill operatives."[21]

In the case of the Georgia mills, Hanson wanted Felton to focus her entire attention upon the domestic conditions of the operatives.

Obviously southern mill owners were "not responsible" for what operatives did outside the mill; but the critique was such an insult to the "moral conditions prevailing among the operatives, most of whom are virtuous, and a large percentage intelligent," that Hanson was moved to come to their defense.[22] What began as an attempt to defend the industry against criticism was thus transformed into an act of paternalistic noblesse oblige. The potential for criticism of the industry was to be deflected onto domestic and gender issues. As a consequence, Hanson found Felton to be preferable to himself as a respondent, for she was on the right side of the gender divide. Being, as she described herself, "a woman's woman— I believe in my sex," Felton presumably understood women's domestic trials and responsibilities firsthand.[23] As Hanson concluded, "It seems appropriate that this work of a woman should be undone by one of her own sex, not to say state."[24]

Rebecca Felton was always prepared for a good scrap, and this time was no exception. As she told an audience of millworkers, "I was willing and ready before I was requested to reply to these unjust—untrue—and ungenerous statements—which I tried to do faithfully."[25] Originally Felton sent her rebuttal to *Century Magazine*. They, however, declined to publish it, stating, "You are sincerely impressed with the idea that she [De Graffenried] has not told the truth, and you seem to look upon her work as an attack upon the South. . . . but with entire respect for your opinion, and belief in your sincerity and good faith, we cannot accept this statement of the motives and action of Miss De Graffenried."[26] Consequently the article was published instead in the *Augusta Chronicle* (Georgia), in a city where over half the state's millworkers were employed.

In her article Rebecca Felton set out to defend the "honor of the state, of the cotton mill owners and the sex . . ." against "this thistle down of hate . . . scattered far and wide without protest over the whole Union . . ."[27] She argued that any intelligent, unbiased reader should have recognized the implausibility of De Graffenried's description of the condition of the southern white textile worker, for her evidence contradicted itself at every turn.[28] Moreover, the millworking population was composed of individuals, and their personal situations were not reducible to a type. De Graffenried's article was a poor attempt to convince the reading public that the "occasional black sheep" the "unregenerate exceptions" were the norm among millworkers.[29]

Although J. F. Hanson and other mill-owning interests in the state may have viewed Felton's defense as a way to deflect criticism away from the problems of capitalist industry, she perceived the problem primarily as one of gender and race rather than one of industry and class. She was particularly incensed with De Graffenried's description of the immorality of millworking women, what Felton described as "the sorest spot of all—the outrage upon womanly virtue and modesty." Through her description of the supposed degradation of white millworking women, De Graffenried created the basis, according to Felton, not only for undermining the further development of the southern textile industry, but she also simultaneously laid the ground for a northern attack on the legitimacy of white supremacy in the southern social order as a whole. While mill presidents and stockholders were in a position to defend themselves against spurious attacks against their industry, these hardworking poor white women who provided the raw material for De Graffenried's attack were not. They were innocent victims, pawns to larger sectional antagonisms.

Felton took it upon herself, then, to defend these "industrious, honest, virtuous, well behaved, law-abiding and God-fearing . . . women" against the charges of being "too indolent to dress modestly and too indifferent to the moral law to seek a divorce before exchanging husbands." For many of these poor, long-suffering women their self-respect was all they had in this world, and now De Graffenried threatened to rob them of even that small consolation in life.[30]

Felton's article was corroborated by the newspaper itself, which printed the text of interviews with local mill superintendents, schoolteachers, and ministers. According to the *Augusta Chronicle*, "what Mrs. Felton has essayed to show by argument," the *Chronicle* has "proven by actual facts . . ." in its interviews with these local experts. De Graffenried had erred in using "fantastic instances for types." The local mill population was described as being basically "industrious, thrifty, moral and progressive," and the move to the mills from the countryside was viewed as improving the general condition of the population rather than leading to its general deterioration, as De Graffenried claimed. As regarded the sexual mores of millworking women, the interviews were uniform in their support of Felton's claims. H. L. Witham, a superintendent of the Dartmouth Mills, pointed out that the morality of mill women was no different from that of "the same number of people of any other vocation in the same walk of life." He asserted that "cases of depravity" were unusual and that those that occurred "were due to the fact that a large portion of the operatives were country girls, who left their parents on the farm and come to work at the mills where, deprived of the guardianship of father and mother, a few occasionally go astray." Some of the interviewers were willing to grant that the "laxity of morals" De Graffenried described might exist in isolated rural mills. Professor F. M. Osborn, "principal of the Fifth Ward Grammar school," noted that "there are remote localities in the country, removed from the influence of city, churches and schools. . . . where Miss De Graffenried has found, perhaps, types of mill operative[s] which she has pictured, but it is manifestly improper to present these isolated examples as the factory operatives of Georgia."[31]

Obviously, any firsthand account is subject to bias, and certainly, testimony from individuals whose livelihoods were directly dependent upon the mills must be viewed with some skepticism. But the observations of contemporaries on the condition of the millworkers can be confirmed by the manuscript census returns. The relevant 1890 manuscript census is not extant, but the 1880 census gives striking support to the contentions of

Felton and the local experts. On the question of the sexual morality of millworking women, an analysis of all households in Augusta that contained at least one millworker, 364 households in all, revealed only three women who were listed as single with a child or children. Two of these women seemed to fit the pattern described by the interviewers, that is, young (17 in one case and 19 in another), without family, and boarding in households that contained none of their kin.[32]

Rather than evincing the dissolution of the family structure, as De Graffenried contended, the census data indicates the remarkable extent to which the family persisted as the basis of social organization in the community. Of the 364 millworking households, only two were entirely composed of non-kin members.[33] Unlike mill towns such as Lowell, Massachusetts, the large number of apparently unrelated young women attracted to millwork in Augusta were not lodged together in boarding-houses. Rather, they were absorbed into existing millworking families. Virtually every household in the study contained at least one boarder, usually a single woman or perhaps a widowed woman with young children. Frequently these female boarders were the same age as daughters of the family who also worked in the mills. This persistence of the family structure despite the differential attraction of young women to the community may help to explain the low incidence of illegitimate births.

On the whole, adult men in the community appeared to have been hard-working. Only one household confirmed the picture that De Graffenried drew of the male population as a whole, the lazy, no account father lying about while his wife worked in the mill to support him and their three-year-old child.[34] De Graffenried may have interviewed women who boasted of "the ease with which they have rid themselves of objectionable partners"; however, the census revealed only six women listed as married but living without husbands. There were 16 divorced women in the community, the majority of them living with their families of origin. To assume that these statistics reflected households where "moral distinctions are unknown" and where "whole families huddle together irrespective of sex or relationship"; as De Graffenried described them, does seem to be, as Felton contended, "unjust—untrue—and ungenerous."[35]

The critical difference between Felton's and De Graffenried's analyses lies in their respective understanding of the nature and structure of the typical mill family and therefore their understanding of the nature of the relationship between women's waged labor in the mills and the state of their domestic lives. De Graffenried assumed that the typical mill family was a two-parent household. Felton, in her defense of the mills, presented the typical mill family as composed of white widowed women and their children. The mills offered these women their only opportunity to obtain a living.[36] The mills offered a substitute shelter, a home to these women and their children. The mill owners were, in this sense, substituting for a lost father or husband. Rather than seeing the mill owner and the working conditions he created as complicitous in the moral degeneration of their workers, Felton viewed them as benefactors of working women. Felton recounted the testimony of one Confederate widow and her daughters who worked in an Atlanta mill.

> I lost my husband in the War. We lived on a rented farm. I tried to work the farm with three small children. I couldn't make bread, and pay the rent. I came here eight years ago. My son works in the city, at the carpenters trade. gets three dollars a day. My two daughters earn eighty and ninety cents each at the loom. I keep house and milk the cow. . . . We bless God every day for this shelter-good food and good clothes.[37]

The 1880 census data reveal a large percentage of women in this situation, at least among the Augusta mill population. Some 45 percent of all mill households were headed by women. Virtually all these women were older widows, generally aged 40 or over, of an appropriate age to have been widowed by the war. The majority did not work in the mills themselves but were dependent upon the support of their adolescent children, mostly daughters, who did. Actually, the percentage of female-headed families was higher than the number of female household heads would indicate because of the predominance of women as boarders, so that 70 percent of boarding families was also composed of widows and their children. Of course, millwork had always attracted this population, but war deaths served to increase their number by increasing the number of disrupted rural families.[38]

Although De Graffenried, herself a Georgian, had left the state during the economically depressed postwar period in order to find a better living in the nation's capital, how quickly, charged Felton, had she forgotten the dire condition of the struggling women of Georgia that she left behind.[39] No one could understand or properly evaluate the effect of the cotton mills upon the condition of the "Georgia Cracker" who failed to comprehend the larger context of regional conditions, an approach that was obviously missing from De Graffenried's analysis of the situation.

In an effort to redress the balance and to supply the regional context, Felton wrote an essay of her own entitled "Cotton Mill Labor in Georgia." In it, she explained the critical role the Civil War played in the development of the textile mills. The war left the state in "blackness and waste— ashes and desolation." The worst of the destruction fell upon poor rural white women, especially those who were widowed and left with children to support in a devastated economy. These women had no alternative but to try to make a living as their families always had, through agricultural labor—a type of labor that was, however, "unsuitable to the sex." Times were so hard in the postwar South that not even the minimal conditions necessary to the reproduction of life could be maintained. Fortunately, however, for the state and for the region as a whole, "patriotic Georgians" came to the aid of these women and children, constructing cotton mills and thereby offering them the possibility of a decent living.[40]

Rather than contributing to the decline of domestic life and to the degeneration of the race, as De Graffenried had argued, the mills were actually essential to the maintenance of any semblance of a respectable domestic life among poor white women; it removed them from the necessity of field labor, a labor that however "unsuited to the sex" was carried out by many black women. As arduous as working conditions in the mills were, they were less strenuous than farm labor, and, as a consequence, the mills made a critical contribution to the domestic integrity of poor white households. Of equal significance was the contribution that millwork made to upholding white supremacy by providing otherwise destitute white women with "feminine" employment opportunities that were denied to black women.[41]

A more sympathetic and prosouthern approach, according to Felton, would lead to the realization that the economic devastation and especially the loss of men in the war had created a situation within the region in which the interests of the mill owners and millworking women were the same. Felton understood their relationship as primarily domestic, in which distinctions of capital and labor played little part. She saw this domestic relationship in its racial and regional aspect—viewing the workers as white women seeking a substitute for their wrecked homes and the mill owners as "patriotic men" responding to the best interests of their race in offering these women "shelter" in the form of mill employment. Together these millworking women and mill-owning men were rescuing the South from its impoverished postwar condition.[42]

De Graffenried had found her own shelter in working for the government, and she had come to believe that it had a role to play in defending a basic level of shelter for all wage-earning women and children. By passing protective legislation the state could protect women against certain types of exploitation in the workplace and, through the passage of compulsory education laws, could promote women's role in the domestic arena. According to Felton, however, De Graffenried's application of this argument to the particular case of Georgia millworkers was fundamentally flawed by her failure to consider the peculiarities of the region. The most critical problem faced by southern white wage-earning women and children was not exploitation at the hands of capitalists but rather the danger that capitalists, faced with tough competition, might no longer be able to employ them at all. Southern wage-earning white women and children suffered not from the strength of southern capital but from its very weakness. De Graffenried was, therefore, mistaken in using the logic of class and gender to analyze the situation of southern women millworkers whose true predicament could be grasped only in regional and racial terms. Caught between the economic subordination of the region on the one hand and the commitment of white southerners to the perpetuation of racial hierarchy on the other, millworking women's best interests were served, according to Felton, by the shelter that was provided by capitalist mill owners who would be jeopardized by the misplaced compulsory protection that government regulation would create.

Because De Graffenried failed to recognize the economic constraints created by the subordinate position of the region as well as the social imperatives dictated by the regional commitment to white supremacy, Felton thought that she was unduly optimistic about the possibilities for reform. De Graffenried's model of reform came, in fact, from the British example, where she argued that the passage of factory regulation had resulted in a "rise of wages, greater production of wealth per capita of population, fall in prices and diminution of pauperism and crime."[43] De Graffenried believed that by breaking the downward cycle into poverty created by the detrimental relationship between home and workplace, protective legislation could redress the fundamental flaw in the system, thereby laying the foundations for a take-off into prosperity; an improved homelife would create a more hardworking and productive worker, and a more hardworking and productive worker would create the possibility for a more productive home life.

In publicizing the shocking living and working conditions of the millworkers, De Graffenried had intended not to insult them but rather to generate support for ameliorative reforms. In her view, "the duty of a patriotic Southerner was plain. Believing that right dealing would improve the poor whites, and thinking that examples from their low estate would teach more than many homilies, I wrote the Century paper . . . ."[44] Felton, who did not believe in the viability of such reform, saw the critique only as a heartless attack. With the possibility of any substantial labor reform out of the question, De Graffenried's criticism—in Felton's view—could only have the effect of demoralizing the state's workers, stripping them of their only real assets, their honor and their self-respect.[45]

Bitter exchanges between De Graffenried and Felton continued in the southern press for some time. Each woman questioned the legitimacy of the other as a true representative of the best interests of their sex. Each accused the other of having other first loyalties—loyalties of region or of class—that impinged upon their gender politics. De Graffenried responded initially to deny Felton's charge of her South-hating bias: "Mrs. Felton charges me with 'revengefulness,' with 'scattering the thistle-down of hate,' with 'unprovoked antagonism' to my own people, with 'sensationalism and incidental newsgathering' . . . with 'befouling the good name of my section because of bitter memories' and with a cruel heart. At these accusations I can afford to laugh."[46] De Graffenried then counter-charged that rather than being primarily concerned with the well-being of the white wage-earning woman, as she claimed, Felton was actually primarily interested in maintaining her powerful economic connections in the state in order to promote her own individual political gain as well as that of her politician husband.[47]

In the course of the controversy, De Graffenried presented herself as the objective social scientist and neutral civil servant above class or regional interests and Felton as the vote-mongering politician. Felton responded by arguing that although De Graffenried "tells your readers that

'I am a politician, or I'm nothing at all,' " Felton herself was the real free agent in the controversy. After all, De Graffenried had to be concerned about remaining in the good graces of the federal government, associated in Felton's mind with northern interests.[48]

For herself, Felton denied that she had any material interest in the southern textile industry. "I own not a dollar in factory stock, have not been paid a dollar by factory people to defend them . . . ." She assured her audience that if she had had De Graffenried's privileges, "her opportunities of European travel, as well as a general itinerary covering a period of years in the United States" she was sure she would "have been able to do justice to a poor but honorable class of white women. . . ." Felton called upon the state of Georgia or the U.S. government to give her the same opportunities to present her case to the public. "Pay me a handsome salary, as well as traveling expenses—I think I could find a better place to call attention to Georgia's degraded white population than The Century and other journals of that ilk."[49]

Of course, as a hardworking southern wife, Felton lacked De Graffenried's polish, undoubtedly the reason her "fair critic" thought she was "unable to write a review." If, however, Felton had any reason to regret her actions in the press, it was not, in her own mind, from the inadequacy of her scholarly gifts or her propensity to truckle to vested interests, as De Graffenried charged, but rather from her tendency to say exactly what she thought, regardless of the consequences. "I am not generally credited with 'supressing facts,' to please any party, faction or section. . . . I can only say, that when my heart and mind are overcharged with indignation and disgust, my impulsive words flow like white metal from the furnace door. It is my style, and like my nose, it is my own."[50]

Well aware of Felton's acid tongue and admiring her reputation as a social reformer as well, De Graffenried had attempted, before the controversy emerged in the press, to write privately to her. "When I heard that you would reply to my Century article, I was about to write to you that I would answer—though silence had been my previous course—and to express the wish that discussion, if discussion it might be called, should be conducted without bitterness. My intention was frustrated by hearing a few hours later that you had replied. . . ." De Graffenried went on in the letter to appeal to their common southern heritage, past acquaintance, and common interest in gender reform, and expressed her hope that she would be able to continue to regard Felton as "an ally in reforms."[51] De Graffenried closed her letter with a note concerning some pamphlets she enclosed from a working-girls' paper, *Far and Near.* "I trust you will have the inclination and find the time to read the pamphlets sent herewith. *Far and Near* is the working-girls' paper, which those of us who are interested in clubs for working girls have agreed to write for."[52] De Graffenried hoped that Felton would consider the newspapers further evidence of her commitment to the best interests of wage-earning women. De Graffenried clearly looked up to Felton, who was some 10 years her senior, and cared about the latter's good opinion. In light of the angry denunciations that were to follow in the public press, the conciliatory tone of De Graffenried's private letter is ironic and somewhat sad.[53]

In point of fact, De Graffenried's letter gave a more accurate picture of the two women and their relationship than did the accusations that they hurled at each other in the press. Despite their charges to the contrary, their class and regional backgrounds were strikingly similar. Both women were born into the elite of Georgia society during the heyday of the antebellum plantation economy. Rebecca Felton's father, Charles Latimer, and her husband, William H. Felton, were planters and slaveholders. Clare de Graffenried's father, William Kirkland de Graffenried, was a well-established lawyer in Macon. Both women received the best education available for women within the state at the time, and they were both talented students. Initially their families resisted secession, but eventually they came to accept and support the Confederacy, Clare de Graffenried's father as a member of Joseph E. Brown's cabinet and Rebecca Felton's husband as a volunteer surgeon for the military. Both families suffered serious personal and financial losses as a result of the war. Rebecca Felton lost her two children, referring to herself afterward as a "childless mother." Clare de Graffenried, who was an adolescent during the conflict, never married, perhaps because of the loss of so many young men during the war. Because of the financial reverses of their families, both women took up wage labor as schoolteachers after the war. After a few years, Rebecca Felton returned to domestic life before becoming her husband's campaign manager in his successful fight for the U.S. Senate. Clare de Graffenried moved to Washington, D.C., in the mid-1870s, where she continued to teach southern girls. In the mid-1880s she acquired her post with the U.S. Labor Bureau.[54]

The gender politics of both women were formed in the context of the experience of their region. With the coming of the war and the financial reverses of their families, they, like so many other women of the southern elite, found themselves forced to earn their own living for the first time. This combination of early class and racial privilege, followed by a rapid shift in elite gender roles, served to politicize both Felton and De Graffenried. Whereas prior to the war their vision would have been turned inward, toward the concerns of their particular families, the impact of their southern postwar experiences was to tear them out of their private domestic role and throw them into the world of wage-earning women. They both came away from this work identifying and sympathizing with the plight of white working-class women.

De Graffenried and Felton identified with white women as a social group intensely, and their sense of gender identity was compounded by a sense of debt. Both recognized that they owed to their less fortunate white wage-earning sisters much of their own personal opportunities to improve their lot in life. De Graffenried expressed her gratitude in an article entitled "The 'New Woman' and Her Debts" in which she described how the labor of women in the early textile mills of Great Britain and New England broke down the barriers against women's wage work in general and made possible the entrance of women like herself into the professions.

> I would like to speak now of the new woman's debt to the real working woman; to her who first leaped over the home threshold and broke the fetters of tradition that confined the gentler sex within the domestic sphere . . . by toiling 16 and 18 hours out of the 24, by living in stables, by being beaten and starved under employers drunk with avarice and power, these early mill hands—grandmothers, mothers, maidens, and tiny children—bought with blood and tears the right for women to compete industrially with men.[55]

Despite some improvements, women and young children in the United States still worked unconscionably long hours. In the British case, the Factory Act reforms had been secured by men of "rank, wealth and public spirit," and De Graffenried was "sorry to count no feminine helper among the reformers." In the United States, only the workers themselves appeared to be concerned to promote such labor reform. It was, therefore, most appropriately the responsibility of elite professional women like herself, who, "by virtue of ampler leisure, superior education, and social importance," have the position and influence to be a voice for reform in this country.[56] And how much more so in the southern case, where prejudice against women in the professions was more extreme and where few occupations were open to women of any class, although economic necessity forced them to compete with one another for whatever was available. This, according to De Graffenried, was the motivation behind her decision to write "The Georgia Cracker in the Cotton Mills."[57]

It was not simply the New Woman's debt, or in this case the New South Woman's debt, to her humbler wage-earning sister that should cause her to promote the interests of her gender in protective legislation, De Graffenried explained. The expansion of the state's commitment to the interests of women and, in particular, the expansion of the role of the schoolroom in the passage of child labor and compulsory education laws, would at the same time expand the significance and legitimacy of professional women's work as well. After all, the critical factor in creating proper domestic "standards," in De Graffenried's analysis, was the moralizing force of the classroom—that is, the role of the substitute mother in the new public domestic space, the professional role of New Women like herself. The sacrifices of wage-earning women, especially millworking women, had broken down prejudices against women's work in general and allowed for the development of the New Woman. The New Woman was, as a result, in a position to help promote the interests of less skilled women workers, and this advocacy would also serve to further her own interests by expanding the role and significance of women's domestic professions, particularly the role of schoolteachers.

In De Graffenried's analysis, class distinctions among women facilitated the development of gender solidarities. The relationship between elite and working-class women would lay the foundations for a shared gender politics that would be materially beneficial to both. As with her position on labor reform, De Graffenried's vision of gender politics was positive and optimistic. Although wage-earning women were exploited in the workplace and professional women were discriminated against because of their sex, the solution to the problems of both lay in their cross-class alliance, the fruits of which were already obvious in the emergence of the "New Woman" and in the possibility, therefore, for the reform of the conditions of wage-earning women.

Felton also viewed elite women as indebted to poor white women and saw elite women's politicization as critical to the development of social reforms. Unlike De Graffenried, however, Felton argued that the basis for that indebtedness was their common loss as white southerners rather than their common gain as productive citizens. Felton presented her regionalized form of gender analysis to the United Daughters of the Confederacy (UDC) at their national convention in 1893 in an appeal for better education and industrial training for poor white women: "The question today centers about the duty of white men and women to the helpless poor of their own race and color who went down in the unequal struggle of the sixties, and whose decendents [sic] are now helpless, in poverty and apathetic ignorance."[58]

Felton argued that the basis for elite women's bond with poor women lay not in the promotion of their mutual interests in the workplace but in their common domestic losses. Even in 1893, almost 30 years after the close of the Civil War, the wounds of widowhood and orphanage still bled in the South and threatened, without the concerted efforts of more privileged women, to bleed for yet another generation.[59]

Elite women were indebted to their poorer sisters not because of the economic opportunities these poor women's labors had created for them but rather because the poor whites' losses in their common war were deeper and more lasting than the planters' own. As a result, the poor white woman was in no position to carve out a new place for all women in the world of wage labor. Indeed, she was unable to find a viable place even for herself in the crippled postwar economy and languished, "helpless, in poverty and apathetic ignorance," in the decaying countryside. Felton told her audience the story of one such woman whom she had met while stumping the agricultural regions in support of the establishment of a state industrial and normal school for girls.

I made my appeal and was leaving the speaking stand in the grove, when a woman of about twenty-five years, met me, with tears streaming from her eyes. Said she, "This is the first word that has come to my ears since my soldier father was brought home and buried in yonder field, to show that anybody knew that poor white girls were entitled to an education like their brothers. It is too late to do me any good, I have had to work in the cornfield to keep bread in the mouths of the children since father died, but it will keep other girls, who are younger, but bless your heart, Mrs. Felton for thinking

of us! If you never get it, we know you have done all you could to help us."
The tearful face of that poor young woman is ever in my mind, in thinking
of this subject.[60]

According to Felton, conditions of life were so depressed among poor
rural white women that "statistics go to show that seventy-five percent of
all the insane women in asylums (came) from such poor neglected country
places." The worst problem these women faced was that the hardship and
monotony of their lives would lead to complete breakdown. "Their hopeless indifference to the condition of affairs that surround their homes and
their progeny, is perhaps the most aggravating of all problems in the mind
of the philanthropist and patriot."[61] These women needed to maintain
their pride and self-respect in the face of the daily trials that poverty
imposed upon them. They desperately needed to believe that life held
some opportunity, if not for themselves, then for their children. Felton
concluded her speech to the UDC with reference to the role played by the
De Graffenried article in the condition of these women.

> Some years ago, the Georgia Cracker in the cotton mills was held up to rude
> criticism in a Northern periodical, with illustrations of their dress, homes
> and ignorant surroundings, and when I recollected through what depths
> these women had traveled to reach even the wages of cotton mill existence,
> my feeling of sympathy was raised to the glowing heat of indignation and
> righteous wrath, against their enemies, that their low estate should be thus
> caricatured for a "heartless holiday," when poor widows and orphans were
> struggling to keep bread in the mouths of the dependent children.[62]

Felton so feared the demoralizing possibilities of De Graffenried's article
on the state's millworkers that she took it upon herself to tour the state
giving speeches concerning it to millworking women. At the Roswell Mills,
located outside Atlanta, she opened her speech by stressing the common
regional bond she felt with her audience.

> I have lived in the country nearly all my life. I am a Georgia Cracker. Whatever
> is of interest to you is of interest to me. Whatever of prosperity comes to
> you—rejoices me—for your sake and my own. Whatever of adversity has
> fallen to your share, consequent upon the Civil War has been shared by me.
> Your people are my people—your God is my God. Where you die—there!
> expect to die.[63]

Whatever existed in the way of class divisions between Felton and her
white millworking audience were nothing in the face of the difficulties
they had been through together as residents of the same region. Rather
than being bound together by their common experience as women in
relation to the productive arena, they were united through those cata-
clysms that had catapulted them into the work force in the first place,
through their common experience as white women of the war-torn South.

Their regional experience may have disrupted their domestic lives and brought them irreparable personal and economic loss, but it could also serve as a powerful force for social cohesion, a cohesion necessary to counterbalance the socially debilitating impact of poverty. Recognizing this, Felton urged her millworking audience to take pride in their regional identification and in the contribution that they were making to the economic recovery of the state.[64]

Felton claimed that some good could come out of the De Graffenried Controversy if it caused millworkers to recognize how much other southerners appreciated their contribution to the region, "how near they are to the great public heart." The inevitable economic hardships that fell to poor white southern women could be endured and possibly even minimized, as long as these women could maintain their self-respect and, perhaps even more important, the respect of southern society at large.[65] By leading respectable and frugal lives, millworking women could hope to preserve their good names and their families' domestic well-being. It was not, Felton insisted, lack of "education and money" that made people "vicious, low bred or beneath attention"; no matter what critics like De Graffenried implied. It was lack of pride in one's self and in one's region; and in the South, according to Felton, the second was tantamount to the first.

> No man or woman is to be looked down upon because they earn honest money and make a living. Sensible people never do look down upon honest poverty and who should care for the opinion of silly dudes and shallowpared critics? Don't allow any such silly notion to plague you my friends—or rob you of a moment's rest. Do your part well—there all honor lies![66]

Because Felton assumed that southern workingwomen could not hope for higher wages, shorter hours, or other improvements in their laboring lives, she was forced to rely upon a single-faceted approach to improving their condition, domestic reform. Only through the virtue and domestic expertise of the respectable poor could some minimal level of decency be maintained and some improvement be hoped for. While De Graffenried expected that her description of the degraded domestic life of Georgia Crackers would promote improvements in their working conditions, from Felton's perspective public charges of loose living would only worsen the sense of demoralization that had caused immorality among them in the first place. Because she believed that the condition of the millworkers rested on their own private initiative to a much greater degree than did De Graffenried, Felton was even more concerned than De Graffenried was about threats to the well-being of the millworking population that originated in the domestic arena. As she explained to her millworking audience:

> I see a demon, that will make a man beat his wife—aye, sometimes kill her— that will starve little children and oftentimes murder them outright—that

will rob little children and helpless women of their homes—that will deprive them of good clothes—that will forbid an education—that will take away all peace of mind. . . . I should be unworthy of the privilege that the almighty master has given me today—if I left this audience without entreating you to guard your homes your happiness—your prosperity—your offspring—your own life from the *Drink Demon*.[67]

Since drink turned men into beasts or at least robbed the family of its economic well-being, Felton concluded that it was nothing but a "public nuisance" and should be abolished. The only reason the trade continued was because powerful interests found it profitable. The solution, according to Felton, was for the state to intervene and prohibit the sale of liquor. For those who took the position that prohibition was a violation of personal liberty and an illegitimate intervention into private affairs on the part of the state, Felton argued that it depended largely on whose personal liberty was in question—the liberty of saloonkeepers and some deluded men or the masses of women and children who must suffer the consequences of men's drinking.[68]

The main opponent of the *"Drink Demon"* was the Woman's Christian Temperance Union, which Felton referred to as "Organized Mother Love." Here, according to Felton, who was one of the most prominent members of the WCTU in the state, was the appropriate arena for the development of southern gender politics. And just as she was more than willing to advocate state intervention when it concerned the domestic arena alone, she was militant in advocating the appropriateness of women's political activity in support of such domestic issues. As she explained to her millworking audience:

Ah! But some will say—you women might be quiet—you can't vote, you can't do anything! Exactly so—we have kept quiet for nearly a hundred years hoping to see relief come to the women of this country—and it hasn't come. How long must our children be slain? Friends—if a mad dog should come into my yard, and attempt to bite my child or myself—would you think me out of my place, if I killed him with a dull meat axe? If a snake was crawling over into the cradle, had its head drawn back for a stroke with its deadly fang—would you blame its mother to chop its head off with the kitchen knife? Ah! you would call that woman a brave woman . . . and yet are we to sit by while drink ruins our homes?[69]

So, while Felton saw the southern context as limiting the possibilities of reform within the workplace, the regional situation also enhanced the prospects for a politics of gender that would unite all white women in the demand for militant domestic reform. The very poverty of the economy, combined with the regional commitment to racial hierarchy, served to intensify the social significance of poor white women's domestic plight as the mothers of their race and made the political role of their advocates, elite women, critical to the perpetuation of the social order as a whole.[70]

It was elite white women's domestic virtue in promoting causes like public education and temperance reform, not state regulation of the factories, that had to compensate for the lack of economic opportunity in the South. What could not be earned through wages had to be obtained through better domestic order at home. Thus Felton had no objection to government involvement, and if the South could not afford to regulate the industry for fear of losing it, the state ought to intervene in the domestic arena to promote a more efficient domestic economy. In temperance speeches she gave throughout the state, Felton outlined the nature of the role that she envisioned southern white elite women playing in this process.

> Those of you that were spared—that survived—that escaped death on the battle field or slow wasting away in a hospital bunk. How can you forget what you owe to these dead soldiers? May God help you to see your duty! Friends—You owe these children an education. You owe them good laws, to live under—you owe them protection from dram shops—that consume their money and degrade their condition. It is a debt—and you are responsible for its payment.[71]

While De Graffenried envisioned a cross-class alliance among women that would enhance their gender role in the home by protecting their class interests in the workplace, Felton advocated an alliance based primarily on white women's common domestic position. The one public arena in which both Felton and De Graffenried accepted the need for state involvement was education. Felton's stress here on the need for better working-class schooling seems to bring her position very close to that of De Graffenried, but while both agreed that popular education was desirable, they envisioned it as serving very different ends.

For De Graffenried, education was part of a larger progressive program of state intervention that would extend the space for working-class domesticity by exempting children and, hopefully, mothers from the necessity of wage labor. For Felton, by contrast, the schoolroom was, in itself, an embodiment of the institutionalization and publicization of domesticity that the regional experience and particularly the commitment to white supremacy required. "Because these [poor white] girls are the coming mothers of the great majority of the Anglo-Saxon race in the South," she argued, and will "make or unmake the men of that era," it was in society's best interest that those who would rear the next generation be themselves placed under the tutelage of respectable elite women like Felton to fit them for their primary reproductive tasks.[72]

What Felton decisively rejected was De Graffenried's claim that state education had to be purchased at the expense of industrial capital through factory laws that "shall bar any child from eleven hours daily drudgery," as De Graffenried argued, or "shall call attention to the housing of operatives" and force mill owners to provide them with "better surroundings."[73]

For Felton, to "arouse our patriotic people to the necessity of educating our poor white girls" was desirable in itself, and if it succeeded "in building up and enlarging our various manufacturing industries, textile and mineral, by encouraging in the minds of our wage workers proper pride and emulation . . . then still further good was accomplished."[74]

Here is the critical point at which Felton's and De Graffenried's conceptions of social reform and gender politics unmistakably diverged. For De Graffenried, drawing on the precedents of northern society and Great Britain, elite and working-class women shared a common interest in progressive reforms that would regulate the conditions of factory labor and thereby redress the imbalance between domestic inadequacy and productive overwork. For Felton, however, this progressive solution was inappropriate to the peculiar conditions of the postwar South. She too wished to enhance the white working-class domestic economy but insisted that this had to be accomplished in a manner that was consistent with the continued expansion of industrial capitalism and the furtherance of white supremacy. Although the critical problem for progressive gender reform may have been to find the basis for a constructive relationship between women's domestic roles and their work roles, as De Graffenried argued, the material conditions of the South, as Felton described them, suggested that this ideal balance was not likely to be achieved.

In her essay on child labor, Clare de Graffenried took the position that with sufficient public exposure and political organization, any situation was reformable. "No evil is hopeless when its extent is known and its corrective is rigidly applied.[75] This was certainly her position in the so-called De Graffenried Controversy. As a consequence, Rebecca Felton was put in the uncomfortable position of being a self-proclaimed reformer who was forced to argue against the possibility of certain types of reform. This perhaps explains the vehemence of her response to De Graffenried and the manner in which she returned to the controversy in her speeches year after year. Although it may have been true that the competitive weakness of capitalism in the South necessitated the long hours of labor among millworking women and children, it was not a pleasant necessity to face, much less to feel grateful for. It was better on the whole to avoid the issue of child labor, which throughout the whole debate Felton conspicuously ignored. Focusing instead on the possibilities for the development of a distinctive southern white gender politics, she limited herself to the question of temperance and female education, around which an alliance between elite and poor white women might be immediately expected to form.

When De Graffenried wrote her article in 1891 she hoped that it would have the effect of stimulating the southern "leisure class" to promote the development of progressive reform. The response she received, particularly from Rebecca Felton, should perhaps have indicated to her the futility of the assumption that reform was possible in any situation so long as there was the requisite goodwill. In fact, no paternalistic landed class emerged in the South, as it did in Britain, to take up the interests of wage-earning women and children and to regulate industrial capitalists through the power of the state. On the contrary, the southern landed class continued to work to maintain an economic system and a set of political values that undercut the very possibility for the development of a modern industrial economy, much less an industrial economy in which the interests of capital would become increasingly dependent on the improvement in living standards and working conditions of the laboring class.[76]

Of course, De Graffenried was aware that in the United States a sense of noblesse oblige was sadly lacking among the elites, although given her own planter-class origins, she may have expected more from the southern planter class. Certainly in the North the achievement of protective legislation was not the result of elite paternalism but of pressure exerted by the workers themselves. In the South, however, labor had little success in organizing at all during this period.[77] Attempts were made to organize the textile industry by northern Unions, especially in response to the increased flight of northern capital and shops to the South in the late 1890s. However, the same argument was made against labor organization that was made against government legislation in Felton's critique. The "northern" Unions wanted to organize in the South in order to raise the cost of labor, wipe out the South's comparative advantage, and bring a halt to runaway shops and export of capital. Only a foolish worker would join a Union that would mean the elimination of his or her job.[78]

The difficulties of organizing textile Unions in the South were further exacerbated by the deplorable conditions among agricultural laborers, especially among black agricultural laborers. On those occasions when textile workers attempted to form Unions and went out on strike—for instance, in the Augusta textile strike of 1898—employers had no problem in replacing them with rural white laborers who were eager for the work.[79] And behind the growing tide of dispossessed rural white labor was a veritable sea of black agricultural labor, which employers threatened to draw upon if required. Working conditions in the mills may have been deplorable, as De Graffenried pointed out; but, as Felton argued, they were a privilege reserved for whites only and were considerably superior to the condition of day labor in the countryside. Thus both trade Unionists and progressive reformers in the southern textile industry found themselves hemmed in, threatened by the loss of jobs to northern industry on the one hand and by the availability of even "cheaper" southern rural labor on the other.[80]

The "progressive" solution in the South, as the Populists at times recognized, would have required that yeoman-class whites make common cause with black agricultural laborers to dismantle the plantation economy and thereby pave the way for economic modernization and growth. A new progressive agricultural elite, a more productive agriculture, and the end to the specter of black competition would have set the stage for the kind of economy and society that could have sustained the type of labor organization and governmental reform of capitalist enterprise that De Graffenried advocated—that is, an economy and society more like those of the North. The problem, then, for progressives such as De Graffenried was that in the southern context liberal reforms would have required a radical restructuring of the racial and economic order. As a self-proclaimed white supremacist, De Graffenried herself would have opposed such a radical change. In fact, her advocacy of protective legislation was partly motivated by her own desire to insure the "supremacy" of the white race. "This lethargy, this neglect [of poor whites], needs deep pondering, and I, to whom the supremacy of the white race is dear, believe that it should be widely proclaimed and quickly remedied."[81] Not only was De Graffenried committed to maintaining the racial status quo, so according to her interviews, were the millworkers themselves. She quoted a weaver in one Georgia mill:

> Fo' the war, honey, them 'ristocrats had all the plaintations, en houses, en fine doin's. Po' white folks was n't nowhar. We was glaid ter run er loom, en buy er pint uv 'lasses en live offen rich man's corn. Now, ev'ry cuss with er yaller steer is er-gittin rich. Even them niggers, bless yer soul, is er-buyin' uv er house. White folks cain't let them niggers be er lead mule. We's 'bleeged ter git up en git.[82]

Rebecca Felton recognized, as De Graffenried did not, that in the southern context the logic of a progressive solution to the problem of labor threatened the hierarchical divisions of race. In a choice between labor reform or maintenance of the racial status quo, Felton assumed that the millworkers would choose to maintain their superior position over the blacks. Similarly, she believed that if the choice was between their reputation for feminine virtue and the possibility of labor reform, millworkers would agree that the "sorest spot of all" was not poor working conditions but attacks such as those made by De Graffenried on their domestic self-respect. The state's millworkers who collected $60.00 to have a plaque placed on Rebecca Felton's grave in gratitude for her defense of their honor in the controversy certainly seem to have taken this position. Perhaps when they honored Felton with their hard-earned collection, they had the most realistic sense of where the possibility for the improvement of the lives of southern white wage-earning women and children resided. Given the existing racial and economic structure of the South, only the domestic arena remained.[83]

CHAPTER 9

REBECCA LATIMER FELTON AND THE PROBLEM OF PROTECTION IN THE NEW SOUTH

On November 21, 1922, women packed the galleries of the U.S. Senate. Delegations from every women's organization in Washington were present for the introduction of the first woman senator ever. Hale and hearty despite her 87 years, the new junior senator from Georgia rose to give her maiden speech. "The women of the country have reason to rejoice," she asserted. "This day a door has been opened to them that never was opened before."[1] Rebecca Latimer Felton had particular reason to rejoice, and to be proud, for not only was she the first woman to be so honored but, equally important to her, she was a woman of the South, of Georgia. As she later wrote, "It meant that a woman reared in the sheltered security of an antebellum plantation was to be the first of her sex to sit in the U.S. Senate. It was hard to realize. . . . Who in that day would have had the hardihood to predict that the time would come when Georgia women would hold public office?"[2]

Who would have had the hardihood to predict it even two years earlier, when the South, almost to a state, refused to ratify the Nineteenth Amendment? And who would have looked to the state of Georgia, whose legislators had rushed to be the first to go on record in opposition to the amendment?[3] Perhaps only Rebecca Felton herself, long a power in state Democratic circles, even without the vote, and savvy in the ways of southern politics and southern gender relations. Having grown up in the antebellum South, she understood the intensity of planter-class men's commitment to the protection and the subordination of their women. Having endured the hard years of Civil War and Reconstruction, she also understood the personal and economic necessities that had led to the new public roles that women took on during those years.[4] How to reconcile the old values of protection and seclusion with the new realities of independence and public status for women? This was critical problem of elite southern gender relations in the late-nineteenth-century South. It was in this context that Felton carved out a new role for herself. In negotiating these contradictory cross currents, she found a place for herself and for women of her class and race. She emerged as one of the preeminent new women of the New South.[5]

At first glance, Rebecca Latimer Felton's early life course gives little indication of her eventual emergence as a leading spokesperson for women's rights.[6] Born in 1835 on her family's plantation in DeKalb County, she grew up in a prosperous planter family. The oldest of the four Latimer children, she was particularly close to her father. Eventually, he sent her to live with kinfolk in the town of Madison so she could attend the Female College there and acquire the best higher education then available to women in the state. Upon graduating at age 17, Rebecca Latimer promptly married the graduation speaker, William Felton, a man of many talents: medical doctor, minister, planter, and politician.

For Rebecca Latimer Felton, the role of the plantation mistress, which she took up at 18, was one to which she had been reared. It was the life of her mother and her grandmother before her and the one she assumed her daughters would occupy after her. Even toward the end of her long life, in what had become a much different South, she continued to see the antebellum plantation mistress as a feminine ideal. "The mother of eleven children," she wrote of her grandmother, "her industry, her management and her executive ability in caring for and carrying out her household affairs are still wonderful memories." Such women presented, in Felton's estimation, *the* model for womanly endeavor and as such provided her with "examples in my own extended life."[7]

By the same token, Rebecca Latimer Felton's male ideal remained in many ways that of the antebellum planter class, men like her grandfather and father, whom she described as being as hardworking and as industrious as their wives. Her grandfather ran a grain mill and sawmill, along with his plantation, and her father combined plantation work with management of a tavern and local store. In Felton's recollection, these men cast a long shadow, a shadow that kept their women in the shade of the plantation, sheltered from the outside world. "The wife and mother," she wrote, "were like plants in the deep forest. Their softness and dependence were derived from the shade. A woman's home was the center as well as the circumference of her efforts for civilization or humanity."[8]

In her book *The Southern Lady*, Anne Scott has discussed the apparently contradictory role of the antebellum plantation mistress, caught between her authority and responsibility within the plantation and her subordination to the planter within both the household and the public arena.[9] Although some planter-class women expressed their discontent with this role through private outpourings in their diaries, Felton, at least in retrospect, understood that elite women's subordination was the price they paid for their class and race privileges. Few women anywhere, Felton argued, could lay claim to such a retinue of "servants," to such an extended domestic place. "No wonder," she concluded, "matrimony was the goal of the average woman's existence." The only acceptable alternative was that of the schoolmistress, and even she "usually married some man with slaves to wait on her." Better to be subordinate but wealthy, in Felton's view, than to be independent and poor.[10]

The planter's public power redounded to the private advantage of the lady. Her public subordination to him not only signified her recognition of his public position but also announced the extent of her own private domain. Through her exaggerated deference and public incapacity, the lady expressed the extent of her own domestic authority. To violate one's place in this world was to break an unspoken agreement, an implicit social balance of power. Only through a studied acceptance of one's place and a strict delineation of its limits could harmony reign. Precisely because elite women's class and racial authority was so substantial within the confines of the plantation, gendered proscriptions against activities outside of it were necessarily all the more intense. As George Fitzhugh so aptly put it in analyzing the nature of "women's rights" in the antebellum South, "In truth, woman, like children, has but one right, and that is the right to protection. The right to protection involves the obligation to obey. . . . If she be obedient, she is in little danger of maltreatment; if she stands upon her rights, is coarse and masculine, man loathes and despises her, and ends by abusing her."[11]

According to Rebecca Felton, women of the planter class rarely broke their end of this agreement. They "obeyed," that is, they minded their place. The rupturing of elite gender relations was the result of the hubris of planter-class men rather than the insubordination of planter-class women.[12] It was planter men who refused to compromise on the issue of slavery, who masterminded secession, and who thereby set in motion a series of events that would forever undermine their ability to offer "protection" to their dependents. It was the wholesale destruction wrought by the Civil War, especially the death and crippling of so many fighting men and the loss of their property in slaves, that eroded the privileged option of planter-class women, rendering them vulnerable to the forces that had long molded the lives of most southern women.

For women of the planter class, the decline of male protection and women's exposure to economic hardship was inextricably fused through the crucible of Civil War. Rebecca Felton repeatedly described the impact of the war in terms of her own unprotected "exposure" to the elemental forces of nature. "The War," she wrote, "broke on the South like a thunder clap from an almost clear sky" and brought with it a "four year hail storm."[13] The location of the Felton plantation, outside Cartersville in North Georgia and near a major railroad line, did indeed put them in the center of the storm. A main line of supply for the army of the West, the railroad brought the war to Cartersville early through an almost constant stream of soldiers and supplies and, increasingly, through the return of the wounded and dead. Felton suddenly found herself in the public arena, not as a result of any rejection of her domestic status but in an effort to protect it. There was now an entire army to care for, and women's place was where the hungry, ill clad, and wounded were. Felton helped organize the local Ladies Aid Society and became its first president. Members met the trains, provided food, and took in wounded soldiers who would not survive the rest of the trip. She cut up her dresses for uniforms and ended the war in homespun. Running out of coffee, sugar, and salt, she found substitutes.

Eventually, the strategic location of the Felton plantation made it necessary for Rebecca herself to find refuge. Her husband, who was then serving as a Confederate surgeon, was able to secure an old farm outside Macon. Here Rebecca, her two children, and what remained of their slaves lived out the last year of the war. What began with the loss of her private domestic status and the stripping of her household to support the war effort would finally end with the virtual destruction of life on the plantation, as she had known it. Invading troops razed the buildings, the slaves were emancipated, and her two surviving children died in the last year of the war from tainted water supplies and epidemic disease.[14]

To rehabilitate their plantation after the war, Rebecca and William Felton opened a school. Their neighbors were so impoverished that they frequently paid their children's tuition by working to rebuild the Felton's plantation. In the context of their common struggles, Rebecca Felton came to understand and in some sense to identify with the experience of her yeomen neighbors. She particularly identified with the plight of the women, perhaps widowed and most certainly rendered destitute by the war, who faced an even harder lot than she, "forced to work in the field," as she wrote, "or worse."[15]

The bonds forged with other Confederate women in the heat of battle were thus strengthened in the lingering misery of the postwar era; they would come to form the basis for Felton's political activities for the rest of her life. Left to their own devices, women like Rebecca Felton had become a "wonder to themselves."[16] Not only could they support themselves, but they could also aspire to making a vital contribution to the well-being of the less advantaged members of their own sex. As much as Felton came to value this new independence among women, however, she feared with a passion the economic necessity, the threat of "exposure" that drove it on. More than ever she valued her own domestic privilege, what was left of it.

Rebecca Latimer Felton was of two minds. Like other women throughout history, she agonized over the trade-offs between freedom and protection.[17] That which was "progressive" in her looked to the expansion of her own autonomy and that of other women as well. That which was fearful and threatened looked back longingly to the old days when protection and seclusion had been the experience of women of her race and class. She railed at those she held responsible for its decline. And *who* was responsible? Felton never answered this question in a consistent fashion, anymore than she ever made a clean break with the desirability of male "protection." As the years passed and elite women emerged more securely as public figures in their own right, Felton did begin to argue with mounting forcefulness that it was the men of her class who were responsible, because they were the ones who had allowed the profitability of slavery and the lure of the market to override their sense of responsibility to domestic dependents. The domestically responsible course, according to Felton, would have been to compromise with the North and agree to gradual and compensated emancipation. Instead, having grown "overblown" with their own self-importance, slaveowning men recklessly threw the entire plantation world into the crucible of war.[18]

At her most independent and outspoken, Felton was inclined to expound on the shortcomings of male dominance at great length. When confronted with the economic vulnerability that these shortcomings had created for women, however, she concluded that some male protection was preferable to none at all. To salvage what little remained of antebellum "protection," she was inclined to limit her criticism of patriarchal social relations, or at least to exempt those few individual men, like her father and husband, who initially opposed secession. In her dependent, vulnerable persona, she was inclined to criticize not patriarchy per se but those individual men whom she regarded as inadequate or downright dangerous. Gingerly criticizing hotheaded secessionists, she reserved her greatest ire for those two-faced scalawags who supported reconstruction governments and the empowerment of black freedmen. To Felton, the very existence of free blacks, not to mention their assumption of political authority, was a constant reminder of all the ways in which the planter patriarchy had failed.

Indeed, it was freedmen who engendered Felton's most intense feelings of animosity in the postwar context. Unable to confront fully the white man's failure to live up to his domestic responsibilities, she became preoccupied with the freedman's failure to live up to his. In her view, the decline of plantation life and the loss of the protected status it afforded plantation mistresses came to rest squarely on the shoulders of the ex-slaves, whose insubordination and refusal to work were safer targets for her frustrated outrage than were the men of her own class. Indeed, Felton's racial politics reflected her own experience of class power and gendered subordination. When the ownership of slaves had enabled the planter to shelter the women of his family on the plantation, Felton had perceived black slaves as diligent and loyal members of her world. In her reminiscences, the typical slave was the female domestic, who symbolized not only the planter's authority but the authority of the mistress as well. When the fall of slavery left her husband and others of his class economically and politically exposed, the prototypical black became the shiftless male laborer—a dangerous, threatening, foreboding figure, whom she envisioned as fundamentally out of his place in the postwar world, plundering her fields rather than laboring diligently in them.[19]

The collapse of the slave-based plantation economy created a virtually irreconcilable tension for Felton. Her desire for gender equity was countered by the devastating economic vulnerability she witnessed among the women around her, particularly among those who were without male "protection." It was this tension that drove her into the political arena. In the summer of 1874, William Felton entered the race for the U.S. Congress as an Independent, committed to representing the interests of the yeoman farmer in his upcountry county, Bartow. Rebecca Felton began her political career in support of her husband's candidacy, by acting as his campaign manager, scheduling his speaking engagements, arranging to have others speak for him, and writing numerous letters to the local press in response to attacks on his positions. For the Feltons, one legacy of the new womanly roles opened during the war was the possibility for a new kind of partnership in postwar politics. William Felton not only accommodated himself to his wife's new public activities but also actively facilitated her further political development. It was widely rumored, for instance, that Rebecca Felton not only wrote newspaper editorials in the doctor's defense, which she signed "Plowboy" or "Bartow," but wrote parts of his speeches as well.[20]

If this partnership reflected the possibilities created for more equitable relations between the sexes in the postwar South, the hostile public response reflected the larger social limitations imposed on couples that assumed such relative gender equality. Widespread derision of Rebecca Felton's participation in her husband's campaign reflected the fact that although new roles for women created the opportunity for more equitable gender relations, they were even more certain to create a gender backlash, particularly among economically and psychologically diminished men. Having been forced by the exigencies of the period to give up some aspects of their former dominance, many southern men clung with increased insistence to those forms that remained. The political sphere was the one arena to which women had virtually no entree in the 1870s and 1880s, and most southern white males, defeated and defensive, intended to maintain their sexual prerogatives there. As Rebecca Felton herself recalled, "I was called a 'petticoat reformer' and subject to plenty of ridicule, in public and in private."[21] Her husband was subject to ridicule as well. One local paper went so far as to entitle the announcement of William Felton's reelection to the U.S. Congress in 1878, "Mrs. Felton and Doctor Reelected."[22]

Beyond a certain point, the hostility Rebecca Felton's political assistance engendered became a liability to her husband and outweighed the benefits that her intelligence, argumentative skill, and political savvy brought. There were real limits to the degree to which William Felton's private acceptance and public support of her work could counteract the impact of a hostile public. Gender norms in the larger society thus set limits on the extent of equity between even the Feltons. Rebecca Felton could contribute her prodigious pen to her husband's speeches, but she had to mask her contributions and certainly could not speak for herself. She could write flaming editorials in defense of his campaign for the "plow boys" of Bartow County, but she could not sign those editorials in her own name. The Feltons' partnership was necessarily based on supporting the development of William Felton's career and the interests of William Felton's yeoman constituency. The emergence of Rebecca Felton's own political career awaited the development of a new political constituency in Georgia, a constituency that was shortly to take form throughout the New South.

It was the Woman's Christian Temperance Union (WCTU) that would provide Felton with an audience of her own for the first time. In 1881, Frances Willard, president of the WCTU, made her first southern organizing tour. Friends and supporters tried to dissuade her from making the trip in the first place. As one friend counseled, "It will be a most disastrous failure, for there are three great disadvantages under which you will labor—to go there as a woman, a Northern woman, and a Northern temperance woman."[23] Willard was therefore pleased at the warm reception her plea for home protection received from southern audiences. She was particularly heartened when Rebecca Latimer Felton joined the WCTU in 1886. Felton was a great asset to the fledgling organization, and the benefits were more than reciprocated. Regularly touring the state, she gave rousing speeches for the cause, holding forth against public ridicule and demonstrating that her powers as a speaker, if anything, exceeded her abilities in cold print. By the end of the decade, she had become one of the organization's most prominent orators.[24]

As important as the WCTU was for Felton's development as a public political figure, it was even more important for the way it allowed her to address the gender issue at the center of her concerns—the question of home protection. For Felton, the "drink demon" became a metaphor for the social consequences that the decline of the power of the individual planter and of agricultural life in general in the South had unleashed. In the burgeoning anonymity of the city and with the expansion of free labor, Felton found a threatening world, one full of the "glow of factory furnaces" and the "whirl of machinery." This was a world where a woman could not walk down a street in safety and where her children were particularly exposed and vulnerable. "Tonight," as she told one temperance audience, "there is not a city in Georgia where a decent woman's child can go, and be safe in its streets from the danger and temptation of liquor saloons."[25]

While the Civil War had dealt a crippling blow to the power of white southern men to protect their women, Felton now argued that the "drink demon" constituted an even more formidable threat. Drink promised to destroy what little protection remained to women and children by turning their fathers, husbands, and sons into useless drunkards. According to Felton, the temperance issue revealed the continuing, and in some ways increasingly critical, gap between the rightful place of domesticity in society and its subordinated second-class status in actuality. For a few "sin-cursed dollars, contended Felton, state legislators were even willing to bargain away the well-being of the entire younger generation." "I see them sell a license," she told her audience, "which says to the liquor dealer, you can for such a length of time destroy every man you can reach—not excepting my own son." "Friends, neighbors, citizens," queried Felton in one temperance speech, "what is this curse that walks in darkness and wastes at noonday? . . . Is it not the unholy gain that follows liquor selling—and the eternal loss that follows liquor drinking? . . . Oh Men of Georgia, when your hearts prompted you to legislate for hound dogs, and sand hill gophers—why haven't you protected your own offspring? It is this failure to protect that has raised the outcry of temperance women."[26]

As with the issue of slavery, the lure of profit continued to override and undercut men's allegiance to the domestic interests of their families and society as a whole. Now matters were far worse, though. At least under slavery, the subordination of elite women's domestic sphere had been in some measure balanced by the extraordinary profitability of the planter's economic system. Class privilege had served to soften the impact of domestic subordination. In the face of their declining economic position, Felton insisted that elite men now needed to legislate domestic "protection" through the agency of the state. No longer capable of simply controlling their own plantations as relatively self-contained social worlds, they were now called upon to actively represent the domestic interests of their women and children in the political arena. In her temperance speeches around the state, Felton encouraged men to cast their votes for properly "feminized" candidates: "Vote for true men—men who will do your will—men pledged to your protection. Oh Men of Georgia! Your votes will either make or unmake the boys of this generation. This is a crisis. Stand to your homes and vote for no man who will not pledge himself to save these boys."[27]

Insofar as men had failed to take up her challenge and represent women's domestic interests politically, they had, according to Felton, "impeached their own manhood." Women were left with no alternative but to enter the political arena themselves and lobby for a policy of prohibition in defense of their maternal roles. As in the case of women's wartime organization into Ladies Aid Societies, public organizational activity under such circumstances did not constitute a rejection of motherhood. Quite the contrary, according to Felton, it manifested the reemergence of a similar kind of militant commitment to domestic defense, an "organized mother love . . . ," "*Mother love* . . . stung to desperation . . . ," a "Mother love grown bold in its agony . . ."[28]

The WCTU's politics of empowering motherhood brought elite southern women like Rebecca Felton to the threshold of an exciting but paradoxical new world. Achieving a free and independent motherhood required a precarious balancing act for female politicians with gender as the key to their agenda. While history had taught elite women of Felton's generation that they had to be prepared to earn their own living, the meager prospects for real autonomy for women in the straitened postwar economy led them back to the desirability of access to male income. Felton therefore hesitated to advocate that young women set their sights on the acquisition of a career. She was more eager to see the basic structure of the family, especially the white farm family, reformed along more gender equitable lines.

In the 1890s, she took up speaking to rural audiences on the critical but undervalued role of women on the family farm. She urged farmers to recognize the contribution their wives made to farm operation. "In this day of scarce labor, I'd like to know what a farm in Georgia would amount to, as a home, unless there was a woman on it." Farmers, according to Felton, should discard the old adage "A dog, a woman and a walnut tree: The more you beat them the better they be" and replace it with greater respect and appreciation for wives and mothers. Rather than devote all his time and energy to his marketable crops, the farmer should realize that "the best crop a man ever raised in all his life was a crop of good obedient children."[29]

In 1891, Felton proposed a program to the state agricultural society that she called the "Wife's Farm." In recognition of the wife's contribution to the family farm, every farmer in the state should pledge himself to work a portion of his land as his "Wife's Farm." While the wife cooked the husband's breakfast, Felton suggested to her rural audiences, the husband should be out laboring in her fields. Felton assumed that the product of the "Wife's Farm" would be crops for home consumption rather than market production. In this way, the farmer could confront the "vexed question of commercial independence" while promoting the "contentment and happiness of the household."[30] A more balanced relationship between the interests of the family and the demands of the market would be the ultimate result of an agricultural system grounded in gender equity.

Felton claimed that the underlying message of domestic gender equity she offered her farmer audiences of the 1890s was similar to the advice she would have given the men of the antebellum planter class some 30 years earlier, had they asked. Confronted with the specter of a mounting agricultural depression, Felton herself saw the same dark vision: a vision in which southern agriculture and domesticity were undermined by white men's determination to pursue profit in the market at any human cost. Like the antebellum planter, the postwar farmer continued to orient himself toward a fickle market economy at the expense of the more solid and enduring interests of his family. Just as the planter's war had rendered him unable to protect his dependents, so the persistence of a market-oriented culture was once again threatening the very perpetuation of the farm family, leaving lower-class women and children unprotected and exposed.

In the aftermath of Civil War, when Felton herself felt overwhelmingly threatened, she focused her own fears onto the freedman. Unable to blame the husband who could no longer support her as he once had been able to do, she displaced her anger on the freedman who refused to return to his "place" in the postwar order of things. Once again, in the serious agricultural depression of the 1890s, her efforts to seek the roots of the problem in a diagnosis of gender imbalance and a program of domestic reform ended in race baiting. Felton was ultimately reduced to holding the black population, especially black men, responsible for the dire condition of white farm life. Since the most pressing need of the farm population was a "feeling of security in the homes we inhabit, where wives and daughters can be safely protected," it was all too easy to absolve the farmer for his failure to provide these and to visualize danger in terms of the threat of assault and rape on the part of black men. "I know of no evil, which more unsettles farm values and drives farmers to towns and other occupations than this lurking dread of outrage upon their helpless ones—in their homes and on the highways."[31]

Just how far out of balance Felton perceived southern gender relations to be in the 1890s can be seen in the lengths to which she took this argument. Poor white farm women in the 1890s were considerably more "vulnerable" and "exposed" than women of Felton's class had ever been, even in the darkest days of Reconstruction. During the 1890s, it seemed to Felton that poor white women were losing their economic security and that their very lives and physical safety were in jeopardy. In the image of the rape of a poor farm woman on an isolated and desolate country road or homestead, Felton found a graphically explicit and emotionally explosive symbol to express the intensity of her fears for the sanctity of motherhood and the necessity for domestic reform.

Despite her best efforts to promote the elevation of motherhood and the realm of reproduction within the farm family, the condition of farm women and children appeared only to deteriorate in the 1890s. If farm men would not or could not sustain their wives and children in a progressive fashion, who or what could? In fact, the failure of gender reform in the countryside caused Felton to appeal with ever more conviction and intensity to the membership of elite women's voluntary organizations. Both because of their dedication to empowering motherhood and because of their commitment to the supremacy of their race, elite white women should throw themselves into reform efforts to improve the lot of rural women and children. The best vehicle to achieve such reform, Felton argued in speech after speech, was to be found in the expansion of educational opportunities for poor youth, especially poor white girls. "Why do I particularly mention poor white girls?" she questioned an audience of the United Daughters of the Confederacy. "Because," she answered, "these girls are the coming mothers of the great majority of the Anglo-Saxon race in the South. The future of the race for the next fifty years is in their hands."[32]

By raising the specter of "race degeneration" in the impoverishment and powerlessness of white motherhood and by pointing to elite women as the only group likely to carry out the reforms necessary to improve the status of these women, Felton lent increased urgency and larger social significance to the organizational activities of elite white women. Should gender reform fail among the mass of the white population, the threat to the entire social structure was so critical that even the voluntary activities of elite women's organizations were not sufficient to the task at hand. Government intervention was required to place a floor below which white motherhood could not be allowed to sink. As much as elite women were the critical actors in voluntary familial reform activity, they were, like the WCTU before them, even more important as the key political pressure group that would move the government to regulate the family in the interests of an improved domestic life. In particular, women's organizations had to pressure the state government to pass compulsory education laws. It was not enough to improve the quality of rural schools. Children must be required to attend them. Furthermore, the ability of men and women to enter the familial relationship in the first place must be regulated by raising the age of consent and requiring marriage licenses and health certificates: "It will always be the intelligent home life of the nation which will hold our ship of state to its moorings as a republic and we can all appreciate the necessity of protecting home life and domestic interests. I believe as a method for the prevention of crime and for the protection of the helpless and innocent safeguards should be thrown around the issuance of marriage permits, known as marriage licenses. . . . A health certificate should have been required a hundred years ago-for the protection of the unborn."[33]

Ultimately, Felton was prepared to go so far as to demand sterilization for those women who were, in her opinion, incapable of maintaining a respectable family life. "Perhaps you may decide that my plan is too radical, but I do believe that a criminal woman should be made immune to childbearing as a punishment for crime," Felton asserted to her audience. Although she did not single out black women explicitly here, it would appear that Felton did have them particularly in mind when she proposed this scheme. Although she desired to "throw around another woman's daughter the safeguards which that less fortunate child needs" if the child was white, in the case of "erring" black women, she advocated compulsory curtailment of all reproductive capacity.[34] If the basis for racial superiority was grounded in an empowered white motherhood, as Rebecca Felton assumed, then the supposed racial inferiority of the black population must be reflected in a highly disorganized black motherhood and family. As she concluded in this speech,

> We have a problem to work out in this country—as to the best methods for the intelligent education of the colored race amongst us. That it is a serious problem no one will deny. Until we can find clean living, as a rule, and not simply as an exception in the colored homes of this country, we are simply walking over a hidden crater which may do as much general damage as Mt. Pelee did in the island of Martinique. The plan of prevention of crime, by making criminals immune to the propagation of their own species, would go very far towards shutting off influx of infanticides and brazen prostitution among the ignorant and shameless.[35]

Government intervention to protect white women and children and the actual elimination of some black women's ability to reproduce would, according to Felton, create the kind of motherhood that was critical to the larger economic, social, and political well-being of the South. It was precisely at this juncture of class, race, and gender relations in the late 1890s that Felton came to commit herself publicly to suffrage for white women.

Instead of supporting suffrage for women out of a recognition of the common interests of all women, regardless of race, or the desirability of autonomy for women for its own sake, Felton advocated the enfranchisement of white women precisely because she perceived them to be so vulnerable and threatened in a world where only they could be relied upon to protect their own domestic interests. She quickly became one of the most prominent spokespersons for the movement in the state. Like so many others in the North and South, her arguments in favor of the vote for women were not explicitly racist, but they were clearly exclusionary, couched in terms of empowering native-born white women to defend the greater interests of their motherhood.[36]

Indeed, Felton's commitment to white women's suffrage was a result of what she perceived to be a lifetime of failure on the part of white men to protect their wives and daughters and to give them sufficient space to discharge their maternal role. In Felton's view, when offered a choice between the interests of motherhood and the family or of profit and the market, most southern men had consistently chosen the latter, even when womanhood had been "exposed" as a result. The issue of woman suffrage offered southern men one last opportunity to redress the failure of their fathers and grandfathers by empowering their wives and daughters to represent directly the interests of domesticity. Although the "failure of statesmanship" that led to the Civil War was a result of white southern men's inability to recognize that "the time had come in the Providence of God to give every human life a chance for freedom," Felton hoped that the intervening generation of men had learned a lesson and would not engage in another "vain effort to hold . . . property rights," this time by continuing to control women rather than slaves.[37]

Fathers, according to Felton, should give their daughters the vote because they recognized the limits of their own ability to protect them and saw that they would be most effectively protected when empowered politically to protect themselves, especially against the power of an abusive mate.[38] Indeed, making women into citizens would create the basis for a more equitable and companionate relationship between husband and wife. Political gender equity would underwrite the construction of the family in its "best form," as a "school for tenderness—for sympathy—for self-sacrifice—for forgetfulness of self—and honest dealing as to privileges between husband and wife." The days of the "fox-hunting, hard drinking—high playing—reckless living country squire," who "played the tyrant in his home," were gone. They were as gone as the days of "our great-grand-mothers," who were "too busy with the spinning wheel and the loom to trouble their minds with elections and taxes."[39]

Rebecca Felton's hopes for a progressive politics of gender in the New South were to be disappointed when Georgia's legislators revealed themselves to be singularly recalcitrant. Even after the national Democratic party adopted woman suffrage as a part of its presidential platform in 1916, Georgia legislators continued to object almost to a man.

In Felton's mind, this behavior was reminiscent of that manifested by their fathers and grandfathers over 50 years before. By turning their backs on the national Democratic party, Georgia legislators had once again, Felton declared, "become a law unto yourself." History was apparently repeating itself. Prominent Georgia antisuffragist Mildred Rutherford testified before the legislature that a vote for the Nineteenth Amendment was tantamount to a vote for the Fifteenth, because granting the franchise to black women would serve to reopen the whole question of enfranchising black men. Nothing could be further from the truth, Felton countered before the state legislative committee. Instead of contributing to the decline of white supremacy by politically empowering the black population, the vote for women would make a critical contribution to it by empowering white motherhood.[40]

As elsewhere in the South, it was antisuffragists who first introduced racist arguments into the suffrage campaign, and, as elsewhere, Georgia's representatives supported the antisuffrage position by an overwhelming majority. According to Felton, this failure of state legislators to grant the vote to white women actually constituted a refusal to treat them as other than slaves. Although southern representatives tried to argue that they opposed the passage of the Nineteenth Amendment because of their "steadfast belief in states rights—their exalted and virginal devotion to the principle—handed down from father to son—ever since the Civil War," the real reason Georgia legislators refused to support suffrage for women, according to Felton, had nothing to do with defending states' rights or even white supremacy. The real reason was because these men were committed to their grandfathers' gender politics, which had now become hopelessly obsolete. "The truth of the whole business lies in their determination to hold the whip hand over the wives and mothers of the South!" They, however, would learn the same lesson that their grandfathers had before them: "I predict that woman suffrage will come to the South— despite the drastic and frantic opposition of nine-tenths of the Southern Democrats in Congress—at this time. They seem to be the lineal and legal heirs to all the *political debris of secession*. . . . They forget that the world is enfranchising its women as an act of right and justice . . . It is their ignorance of what the world is doing—that now obsesses them."[41]

Knowledge of what the world was doing was to come to the state legislators of Georgia sooner than perhaps even Rebecca Latimer Felton could have hoped. On August 26, 1920, the Nineteenth Amendment was finally ratified. That which Georgia state legislators had claimed to fear most, the forcible arrival of woman suffrage through a federal amendment, had come to pass. The response of the entrenched political powers was a curious one. The state that had rushed to go on record first in opposition to the passage of the Nineteenth Amendment made even better speed in moving to be the first state to place a woman in the U.S. Senate. When Tom Watson, a longtime political ally of the Feltons, died with his term in the U.S. Senate unfinished in 1922, it provided Governor Thomas Hardwick of Georgia with the requisite opportunity. He initially offered the appointment to Watson's wife, Georgia Durham Watson, but she declined the honor. He then offered the appointment to Rebecca Latimer Felton, who accepted.

Felton was immediately flooded with congratulatory mail, not only from the state of Georgia but from across the country as well. One correspondent wrote that the appointment had "taken New York by surprise and has electrified her. Men and women alike are thrilled and enthusiastic."[42] Not only was the appointment "well earned," concluded a second correspondent, but it also constituted an honor to all women. It was "one of the signs of the times; the hand-writing is on the wall. Women are rapidly coming into their own."[43] The newly formed National Woman's Party responded to the appointment by asking Rebecca Felton to join their list of "eminent women" and to accept the honorary chairmanship of their political council. As the vice president of the party, Alice Paul concluded, "Now that you are the first woman Senator your name has exceedingly great weight and we hope you will be willing to lend it to this campaign to secure a better lot for all women."[44]

For all her justified pride in the honor, Rebecca Latimer Felton must have been of two minds regarding the appointment. It reflected a due recognition of her political contributions to the state, and perhaps more important the changed status of women that had been effected as a result, but it was only a temporary, symbolic appointment, and her first Senate speech was also to be her last. As one correspondent pointed out, "Mr. Hardwick knows that Mrs. Felton has a following and Power in Georgia Superior to any Woman in the State, This Bunch of Flowers that He has tossed at your Feet does not cost Him anything yet, Since Women have been given the Franchise, his little Stunt is a Ballot winner. . . ."

"Now Mrs. Felton, Why not you run for the U.S. Senate?"[45] Why not, indeed? The appointment was in fact a half gesture of the sort that Felton had come to expect from the southern male establishment over a long and active political life. As such, it reflected the ambiguous state of southern gender relations, even after 60 years of crisis and change. The secluded status of elite white women had indeed ended, and nothing marked that fact more clearly than Rebecca Felton rising to give her acceptance speech on the floor of the U.S. Senate. Nevertheless, the purely symbolic nature of her appointment also reflected the reality that no clear-cut public position or power for women had yet emerged in the South.[46]

Just as the South was forever remaining old while becoming new, so, ever since the collapse of the traditional order during the Civil War and Reconstruction, had the new southern woman remained subordinate while becoming liberated. The ambivalent and contradictory story of Rebecca Latimer Felton should give us some idea of why this was the case. The life of this archetypal woman reformer reveals the dynamic of progressive self-assertion and reactionary resistance characteristic of the larger social order that she steadfastly sought to change. The very forces spurring the development of independence and autonomy among elite white women in the postwar South were at the same time frequently the bedrock of conservatism and reaction that impelled them backward to nostalgia for the hierarchies of patriarchy and race. The decline of the social and economic power of the planter class, which opened the door for the emergence of greater equity between the sexes, simultaneously reinforced the value of home "protection" and thus the ideal of gender dominance by men. White southerners' commitment to the "supremacy" of their race could be enlisted by gender reformers like Rebecca Felton to support the politics of empowering white motherhood. The larger consequence of the rigid racial hierarchy that emerged after the collapse of slavery was to deny the rights of black women as citizens and as mothers. Nevertheless, it was this denial that served to rationalize state legislators' opposition to granting the vote to white women as well. Ironic as it may appear in light of the Georgia legislature's refusal to ratify the Nineteenth Amendment less than three years earlier, the token appointment of Rebecca Felton as the first woman to sit in the U.S. Senate was perhaps the most fitting expression of the pattern of elite white gender relations that had developed in the postbellum South. As an honor graciously bestowed on her by her governor, not a right that Felton herself had earned, it marked the end, not the beginning, of a notable political career.

CHAPTER 10

REBECCA LATIMER FELTON AND THE WIFE'S FARM: THE CLASS AND RACIAL POLITICS OF GENDER REFORM

I t was the annual meeting of the Georgia Agricultural Society in the summer of 1897 on Tybee Island. The meeting hall was half-filled on that sultry August afternoon as Rebecca Latimer Felton took her place on the platform and commenced her speech, "Woman on the Farm." The news that Rebecca Felton was speaking spread quickly and the hall was soon filled to overflowing with members of the Society and interested guests from the nearby hotels. By this time, Felton had become a well-known lecturer and political figure in the state. Born into a planter-class family in Decatur, Georgia, in 1835, she married Dr. William Felton, a minister, doctor, and planter, at the age of 18 and became the mistress of a slave plantation outside Cartersville, Georgia. Dr. Felton was twice elected to the U.S. Congress in the 1870s and Rebecca gained her first political experience as his campaign manager. She acquired a reputation for being a tough and argumentative politician, largely as a result of her editorials in support of her husband's small farmer policies.[1]

By the time of her Tybee Island speech in 1897, Rebecca Latimer Felton had not only established herself as a force in farmer politics in the state; she had also, beginning in the 1880s, turned her considerable political energies toward the cause of improving the position of Georgia women as well. By the end of that decade, she was one of the leading figures in the Georgia Woman's Christian Temperance Union, speaking tirelessly across the state in support of this cause. In the late 1880s, Felton also campaigned in support of higher education for women, and with her support the Industrial and Normal School for women was established in Milledgeville. In 1891, she came to the public defense of Georgia's wage-earning women, in a debate published widely in the state press.[2]

Thus when Rebecca Latimer Felton rose to address the large crowd on that August day in 1897, she spoke with the force of more than 20 years' experience in farmer politics and more than a decade as a militant supporter of various gender reforms. Especially through her temperance work, she had acquired a reputation as a dynamic and contentious public speaker, and this undoubtedly contributed to the large crowd she drew

that day. Her audience was not to be disappointed, as Felton set out with
characteristic vigor to discuss her two deepest political commitments at
once: the position of women in southern society and the economic difficulties faced by the family farm. As the local press later commented, the
speech elicited "marked demonstrations of applause and frequent bursts
of laughter at her sharp sallies and frequent thrusts at the male portion of
the audience . . . [it] could not be termed otherwise than masterly."[3]

Indeed, Felton minced no words with the male portion of her white
farmer audience. She laid the ever declining state of southern agriculture
squarely on their doorstep: "You, gentlemen," she charged, "have tried
your prentice hand on this business for a century or over in Georgia, and
you succeed in special particulars, while you blunder always in essential
generalities." Southern farmers were always, according to Felton, "turning
the point of view toward the outside the world," when they should
consider, first and foremost, the inner life of the farm. Making reference to
her nearly 40 years of experience in agriculture, Felton noted: "it makes a
veteran like myself smile to hear you prate about foreign trade or the tariff,
silver and gold, metallic conferences and war with Spain as an excuse for
depression in business and low prices." Rather than focusing all their energies on these "special particulars," these concerns of the "outside world,"
Felton advised her audience to turn their energies toward the "inner life"
of the farm. The real problem of southern agriculture was the way in which
farmers were overly oriented toward market production, at the expense of
production of items that could be consumed directly by the farm family or
by local consumers. It was the continual glutting of the world market with
cotton, even in the face of the low prices it brought and the solid prices to
be had in domestic consumption items like bacon, lard, good butter, and
corn that bankrupted southern farms, forcing ever increasing numbers of
farm families to abandon the land and head for the cities.[4]

Indeed, in their lengthy discussions of world markets, tariff policies,
proper fertilizers, and agricultural techniques, farmers had missed a critical,
perhaps *the* critical factor, in the success of farming: the labor of women on
the family farm. Everyone seemed to have missed it, for while the U.S. census recorded the contributions of women to other areas of the economy,
"a sponge," Felton contended, "never more completely absorbed the water,
than did the men of this nation absorb and appropriate to themselves . . . farming and the general agriculture of the Union." This gendered
inequity was particularly striking in light of the seemingly endless contributions that women made to the farm economy. Rising well before dawn
and working past sunset, farm women frequently wore themselves down
to a "leather string" in the service of their families. Despite the heavy
demands of child rearing and household labor, they frequently sent what
little domestic help they could call their own, that of their young children,
out to the fields to help their husbands. They were even accustomed at the
end of a long day to taking the youngest baby out and working in the fields
themselves.[5]

In exchange for these tireless efforts, women received next to nothing. While farmers were free to fraternize in town on Saturday afternoons, their wives found themselves confined to the farm, without even the resources to attend a church service on Sunday. "How many women have you known," Felton queried her audience, "who didn't get a good pair of shoes and decent clothes at the end of the year—for twelve months of the hardest work—without a day's intermission from January to December?" Here Felton intentionally drew a parallel between the treatment of slave agricultural labor in the antebellum period and that of poor white farm women in the war's aftermath. Slaves, at least, had customarily received a new set of clothing once a year. Many farm women, according to Felton, could not even expect that. Indeed, she argued that such women found themselves in a state of "actual and peremptory bondage." Gender relations within the southern farm family offered up at least one case in which the old adage was realized, "The man and his wife are made one," and Felton concluded, "that one is the man."[6]

Men who went to town on Saturdays to hold forth about the state of "my crop," "my house," and "my farm," with their fellow farmers elicited Felton's particular wrath. With the emancipation of the slaves, only the subordination of their women remained to sustain their overly inflated sense of self. "If he did not have one slave," she charged, "he couldn't thus spread himself like a green bay tree, and bray like a son of thunder." Felton declared herself to be at a loss to know which feeling predominated when she considered this state of affairs, "disgust for the masculine tyrants" or "mortification at the slave-women who accept the yoke without a protest."[7]

While such farmers insisted upon treating their wives as mere extensions of themselves, or, at worst, as something akin to their farm animals, the antidote to such male hubris appeared to Felton to lie in the competing status of free labor. Where, she queried, would this puffed up farmer be on "his" farm if he had to *hire* the labor of a cook, a nurse, a washerwoman, and a seamstress to replace the contribution of his wife? "I wish I had the power," she asserted, "to put them over the cook stove and wash pot, until they would be willing to say 'our crop,' 'our farm,' and 'our' everything else." If Felton relied upon the analogy to slave labor relations as a touchstone to indicate the depths to which some farm men had fallen in their relations with farm women, she relied upon wage labor to deflate their exaggerated claims to sole credit for the farm by indicating the sort of conditions women might expect if they were treated as any other wage labor. She offered the example of a logging camp. If the cook was paid less than the cutters, there would surely be trouble. Yet women, Felton argued, "can cook and do all the domestic drudgery for half a century and nobody thinks she is entitled to spend a dollar to please herself."[8]

Despite the economic difficulties of the family farm, women, Felton informed her audience, never went on strike or demanded higher wages—or any wages for that matter. The more conditions deteriorated, the harder they worked. Clearly, this behavior bore a limited resemblance to that generated by exploitative labor relations, whether slave or free. Indeed, Felton's political strategy in her Tybee Island speech, despite her frequent allusions to the "actual and peremptoral bondage of farm women," was grounded in the assumption that gendered social relations were character- ized by a substantially different dynamic than either slave or free labor. After all, it was only because white farm women were *not* their husband's slaves that Felton could hope to shame men into a more equitable treat- ment by the comparison. Similarly, it was only because wage labor consti- tuted an increasingly prevalent *alternative* structure for the valuing of white farm women's otherwise unpaid domestic labor, that she could use it as a goad to drive southern farmers on toward a better treatment of women on the farm.[9]

Felton's use of these social analogies alternatively to shame and to goad the male members of her farmer audience reflected her underlying assumption that men could be expected to reform their own behavior in relation to women, at least if they were properly admonished or cajoled. Indeed, Felton assumed that, unlike the case of other forms of social dom- ination, there was no fundamental antagonism between the interests of the dominant and the nondominant in gender relations. What else was she doing at Tybee Island in appealing to farm men to reform their relations with their women? Gender equity could apparently be created simply by eliciting the good will of the male members of the audience alone. Farm men, Felton contended, should simply discard the old adage: "A dog, a woman and a walnut tree: the more you beat them the better they be," and replace it with a due recognition of the indispensible contribution that their wives made to the farm.[10]

Goodwill, however, was a slippery concept. It was, after all, not simply a question of becoming "better" or more virtuous men, an improved version of what they already were. Rather, Felton was appealing to them to become "different" men altogether. For how could they possibly come to really value their wives' dedication to the inner life of the farm as long as they themselves identified first with their market crops and their own public position? Only when farm men recognized domestic life as primary in the construction of their *own* sense of self-worth, in their *own* under- standing of what constituted the basis of their manhood, only then would they truly be able to value it in their wives. As Felton explained, what every farmer needed to realize in order to achieve an improved status for their wives was that the "best crop a *man* ever raised in all his life was a crop of good, obedient children."[11] Once he realized the limited significance of market crops and of the public arena in his own life, then he would have little trouble appreciating the value of his wife's contribution.

Not only was goodwill on the part of men a slippery concept in Felton's intellectual vocabulary, so was her understanding of female subordination. Indeed, in Felton's account, white farm women were as consumed by their attachment to *their* primary crop, children, as they were by the domination of men and by men's pursuit of the market. So when the farmer was in town, "braying like a son of thunder" about "his" crop and "his" farm, what, queried Felton, *actually* kept the wife at home? It was, she argued, as much a result of *her* attachment to the children and the household, as it was the consequence of her husband's domination of public space and the family purse strings. How else was one to understand the behavior of those women who responded only with a redoubled energy the more economically hard pressed the man became on "his" farm, the more totally absorbed he became by "his" troubled attachment to the market. What were those hardworking farm women doing reducing themselves to a "leather string," if not attempting to make up the gap between what their husbands had been able to wring from market agriculture and what they needed to keep the domestic establishment afloat? One welded, even "married," farm women to the other.

Felton actually had no desire to "liberate" women from marriage to the "inner life" of the family farm.[12] Instead, she saw this weld as providing the basis not only for the reform of gender relations, but also for the emancipation of the southern farmer and southern agriculture from what had become, in the postwar era, its thralldom to the market. Whatever independence was possible for both men and women appeared to Felton to lie in the promotion of a common recognition of their *mutual* subordination to the interests of the "inner life" of the farm. Six years earlier in 1891, Felton had proposed a program to the Georgia Agricultural Society that was calculated to do just that by turning farm production directly toward the interests of the family and away from the demands of the market. In a petition entitled "Southern Chivalry: The Wife's Farm—the Husband's Pledge!" Felton had appealed to what she described as the "crowning glory of the civilization of our Southland," the "chivalric" treatment of our "fair women."[13] Pointing to white southern men's long-standing claim to the shelter and protection of their women, she had argued that this "chivalric" tradition could then, in the context of the farm crisis, be most fittingly illustrated in the economic as well as the social sphere of life. The petition had asked that farmers set aside a portion of the farm as the "Wife's Farm." It would constitute, according to Felton, a concrete manifestation of the farmer's recognition of his wife's joint and equal contribution to the farm enterprise.

Having established this "Wife's Farm," the farmer should then join what Felton called the "Before Breakfast Club." While his wife was in the house cooking his breakfast, the farmer should, in a sort of direct labor exchange, be out working *her* fields. The crop produced on the "Wife's Farm" was to belong solely to the wife. And here Felton had assumed that the production of the farm would reflect the domestic attachment of the wife and the crops produced would be for home consumption rather than for market production. As a consequence, farmers would be empowered to confront the "vexed question of commercial independence," as they would finally find an alternative basis for production to replace their own endless and increasingly troubled pursuit of the market. At the same time, they would simultaneously promote the "contentment and happiness of the household," as a more balanced relationship between the interests of the family and the demands of the market would be the ultimate outcome of an agricultural system grounded in gender equity. Felton contended that progressive gender reform, the empowerment of the "female" or the "domestic" principle (and Felton assumed that they were one and the same) on the part of men would create the only sound basis for their emancipation from dependency on the market. Indeed, the emancipation of the farmer from his subordination to the market, in Felton's construction, was actually dependent on his own willingness to emancipate his wife. Not only should female gender roles provide the model for men, but men should also understand that gender relations were at the root of their class problems, that gender was in that sense a causal factor in economic development.

This program was unanimously adopted by the Georgia Agricultural Society in 1891 and Rebecca Latimer Felton was elected as president of the program. Local chapters were to be established in every county in the state. Rebecca Felton's assumption that men could be relied upon to reform their own behavior was apparently not without some foundation. Unfortunately, despite its auspicious beginning in 1891, the program proved to be short-lived. "Politics," Felton told her Tybee audience, were soon "consuming the nation and so the women's case went by default."[14] Here she made reference to the Populist movement that arose in the early 1890s. Relying upon men's traditional sources of public power, the Populists attempted to free the farmer from his burden of debt by using votes to create government supports for staple crop production. This effort failed, and in its demise Felton saw the further deterioration of the farmer's ability even to maintain, much less to promote, a more constructive relationship between the needs of his family and the demands of the market.[15]

The agricultural crisis of the 1890s was particularly devastating to Felton because it reminded her so forcefully of her own experience as a young mistress of a slave plantation in north Georgia, fully a generation earlier. At that time, white southern men made the fateful decision to secede from the Union in response to the mounting northern opposition to slavery. In doing so, they set in motion a series of events that exposed the "inner life" of the plantation mistress to an exploitative relationship with the market, in many cases for the first time. For Rebecca Felton this "exposure" began with the necessity of stripping her household in order to support the war effort, suffering through economic shortages, and ultimately leaving her home altogether as a refugee. By the war's end, she had lost both of her children to poor living conditions, her plantation was razed by passing troops, and her family's primary source of wealth, its slave property, was no more.

At least in retrospect, Felton thought that planter-class men should have compromised with the North and agreed to a gradual and *compensated* emancipation. She saw this as the domestically responsible course, for although it would have required a loss of the planters' exalted place in the world, it would have served to protect their families against domestic loss. Instead of taking this course, however, white southern men responded by becoming ever more militantly committed to what they viewed as their prerogatives as "free men." Indeed, according to Felton, the more the sectional crisis intensified, the more planter-class men, like southern farmers a generation later, puffed up about " 'my' crop, 'my' plantation, and 'my' slaves."[16]

And what of the plantation mistress herself? Although in the years after the war, Rebecca Latimer Felton became increasingly outspoken about the failure of "statesmanship" on the part of planters, at the time she had been notably silent. "I could not," she wrote in her recollections, "fight against my kindred in a struggle that meant life and death to them."[17] And beyond loyalty to her kin, there was the undeniable fact that as much as the single-minded pursuit of the market and slave ownership created the orientation of southern agriculture to production for the market, thereby empowering the "male" principle, the economic success it generated for those fortunate enough to own slave labor was in the economic interest of the *entire* planter class. Planter-class women benefited from the ownership of slave labor. The plantation mistresses' domestic domain was constructed, after all, from the labor of black "servants."[18]

Indeed, the brunt of the "masculinization" of southern slave economy was not borne by elite white women at all, but rather by slaves. For it was in the manner in which the planter class was empowered to own the reproductive capacity of their slaves that we find the real suppression of domestic life in the antebellum South. Plantation women experienced this domination of the domestic life of their slaves by the market interests of their class, only as a sort of echo effect. They resented the way that slavery within the plantation household empowered white men to engage in sexual relations with black women. Slave ownership enabled planter-class men to, as Felton put it, "defy the marriage law of the state" and keep "two households on the same plantation, one white and the other colored, and both women were afraid to make public outcry." Therein, concluded Felton, "lay the curse of slavery"—at least as far as the plantation mistress was concerned.[19]

Nonetheless, the success of the planters' market crops bought the acquiescence of the most powerful of southern women as surely as it bought the children of the least powerful. The very same planter who violated his marriage vows and kept "two households on the same plantation" was also, as another planter-class woman wrote, "the fountain from whom all blessings flow."[20] In the Civil War's aftermath, however, the benefits of white male domination within the planter class were thrown seriously out of balance through the death of the men, wartime destruction of the plantations, and the loss of wealth in slave ownership. And it was this decline in the personal and economic power of the planter-class male that launched Felton and other women into political careers as gender reformers in the postbellum period.[21]

Felton worked tirelessly for many causes, all aimed at constructing some new balance within white gender relations either by empowering white women to protect themselves in the marketplace, convincing white men to reform their behavior, or by using the power of the state to intercede on behalf of the white women and children. All her efforts, however, to create such substitutes for the lost patriarchal "protection" of the antebellum period proved in the face of the continued decline of southern agriculture in the postwar era to be only that—substitutes and poor ones at that. Although wage labor among white women increased, it was never sufficient to create a viable alternative to unpaid familial labor for farm women. And with the apparent failure of programs such as the "Wife's Farm" to create gender equity, the possibility for the creation of a "self-sufficient" white womanhood appeared ever more remote to Felton.[22]

In one final effort to promote gender equity in her Tybee Island speech, Felton turned her attention from the demise of the "Wife's Farm" to the possibility of at least saving the younger generation of white farm girls from the fate of their mothers. She encouraged her Tybee audience to work for improved educational opportunities for their daughters. Even here the possibility for improved conditions appeared doubtful to Felton. "Wake up, men of Georgia," she finally told her Tybee audience, "to the crisis now upon you!" She urged them to consider that their daughters would, after all, be the "coming mothers of the white race. . . . In the sight of heaven, I bring this note of warning and entreaty to you. What means all this lynching on our borders? You never heard of it in years past and gone. If you have one obligation in life before and beyond every other," she concluded, "it is your duty to motherhood."[23]

Here Felton made reference to three lynchings of black men that had occurred in the state a week prior to her speech, ostensibly for the rape of white women. And in so doing, she displaced the basis for the reform of white farm women's conditions from a struggle with their own men onto a conflict with anonymous black men. The basic problem of domestic life that she had hitherto analyzed in terms of the inequitable treatment of women was suddenly transformed into the threat of external racial violence. Even her analysis of the decline of southern agriculture suddenly veered away from her earlier focus on the peculiar regional weld of class and gender relations between the white farm family and the market, and reappeared in what she perceived as the menacing figure of the predatory black male. "I know of no evil," she asserted, "which more unsettles farm values and drives farmers to towns and other occupations than this lurking dread of outrage upon their helpless ones—in their homes and highways."[24]

This shift from progressive gender reform to reactionary race politics on Felton's part indicates that despite her lengthy criticism of farm men's treatment of women and her sincere efforts to "reconstruct" white manhood through reforms like the "Wife's Farm," she ultimately could not bring herself to break with the benefits of white male "protection" in 1897, any more than she could in 1861. From this perspective, the problem for white women was that rather than suffering from too much "manhood" in the southern social order, they were suffering from the fact that there was not enough to go around. "Not," as Felton put it, "manhood enough in the nation to put a sheltering arm about innocence and virtue." If white men could not reform their ideas of their proper place and establish a new, more equitable "manliness" in relation to their women, they could, perhaps, still establish it by asserting their supremacy over black men. In the case of the alleged rape of white women by black men, the failure of white manhood that could not be addressed through a more equitable treatment of white women could be assuaged, if only symbolically, through a suppression of black manhood. And so, Felton told her Tybee audience, "If it needs lynching to protect woman's dearest possession . . . I say 'lynch' a thousand times a week if necessary."[25]

This turn on Felton's part to a gender politics grounded in white supremacy indicated her own fears of the hopelessness for a gender politics grounded in economic, or class, equity with white men. Indeed Felton's political vision was ultimately grounded where most white women's labor was still located, on the family farm, subordinated, undervalued, and still dependent upon the good graces of white men. The closer white farm women came to being nothing but their husband's "slaves," the more Felton looked to the manner in which their common race privilege with their men could serve to protect them from such a fate. If the solution to the crisis of farm life could not lie in a change in white farm men's conception of the basis of their manhood or in their ability to improve the social and economic standing of their wives, then it would have to lie in their ability to deny black men's claims to a "manhood" comparable to their own. When they had been slaves, black men had enhanced the power and extent of white "manhood" and therefore contributed to the white man's ability to "protect" white women. After emancipation, the possibility of an independent black manhood worked to the opposite end.

The "deficiency" of postbellum white manhood was therefore engendered by the fact that in the wake of emancipation black men were no longer in their "proper" place on the plantation. "When I recollect that the crime of rape on white women was almost unknown among negro slaves before the war," Felton contended, "I ask myself, why has the crime assumed such proportions in the years following the war?" The answer to this question was not in the first instance, as might be imagined, a question of the uncontrolled sexuality of black men. For although Felton, like so many other white racists, fulminated about the "beastiality" of the black man, what she really feared was not the *myth* of the black man as beast, but rather the *reality* of the black man, empowered like any other.[26]

In fact, Felton was less exercised by the dangers of black male sexuality than she was by the fact that during Reconstruction, black men had been granted that ultimate hallmark of "free manhood," the right to vote. Indeed, Felton drew a direct connection between the supposed rape of white women and the exercise of the franchise by black men. "As long as politicians take the colored man into your embraces on election day to control his vote," she wrote, "and . . . make him think that he is a man and a brother . . . so long will lynching prevail because the causes of it grow and increase."[27] Voting, according to Felton, promoted "social equality" and "familiarity" at the polls. In this context, she actually made it sound as though the problem was that black men were meeting white women at the ballot box. Of course, this was hardly the case as voting was an exclusively male endeavor. Nevertheless, Felton was not entirely wrong in seeing the black male franchise as the root of her dilemma. For in the act of voting, the black man was empowered like the white man, empowered, among other things, to relate to white women as white men did—or so Felton feared.[28]

According to Felton, the better educated, the more economically independent, the more politically empowered the black man became, the more likely he was to commit the "rape" of white women. In other speeches on the subject, she even went so far as to contend that there was a direct relationship between increases in the postwar budget for the common school education of black children and rising crime rates.[29] Indeed, the same reforms that Felton advocated to empower white women—improved access to higher education, expanded employment opportunities, and by the early twentieth century, even the vote—she advocated taking away from black people, especially black men. Indeed, it was no accident that Felton, who went on to become one of Georgia's most prominent advocates of the vote for white women, was also one of the state's most outspoken racists. No more than that, as C. Vann Woodward put it in *Origins of the New South*, Progressivism emerged in the region "for whites only."[30]

Of course, one could argue that Felton's racist gender politics were simply her own idiosyncratic problem, or that they constituted a displacement of the oppression of white male domination onto the category of race. Either way, one could thereby avoid the conclusion that there was anything inherently or necessarily racist about white women's efforts for gender reform in the late-nineteenth-century South. In the same fashion, late-nineteenth-century farmers might have argued that there was nothing essentially gendered about their class politics. Of course it was Felton herself who so brilliantly deconstructed the male farmer's claim to the pristine autonomy of class in her advocacy of the "Wife's Farm." At least in retrospect, we should perhaps also recognize that just as white male class privilege was inextricably fused to gender in the late-nineteenth-century South, so too was white female gender privilege inextricably fused to race.

CHAPTER 11

LOVE, HATE, RAPE, LYNCHING: REBECCA LATIMER FELTON AND THE GENDER POLITICS OF RACIAL VIOLENCE

In the long, hot summer of 1897, the headlines of the southern press screamed out the news of seemingly ever escalating incidents of violence, mayhem, and race hatred. Front-page headlines of the *Atlanta Constitution* read, "In Hot Pursuit. Clayton County Men Will Lynch. The Negro Is Caught." The *Atlanta Journal* added, "Hunting Him to Death. Several Counties Are Up in Arms to Avenge the Crime of the Negro Oscar Smith." And only days later, the headlines read, "This Black Brute Will Be Burned. Anthony Williams, Who Murdered Miss Williams at West Point, Tenn. Caught in Alabama. Will Be Taken to the Scene." Wrapped around this lurid reportage was a running commentary on the innocence and vulnerability of white women, the looming threat posed by black men, and the apparently uncontrollable mob violence of white men.[1]

The actual reportage always began with the white man—white men in hot pursuit, white men lynching black men, white men worrying about the safety of white women, white men discussing the mob behavior of other white men. The actions of those in the lead roles, however, the roles of the virginal "victim" and the black "beast," always preceded the actual newspaper coverage and were left to the assumptions and the imagination of the reader. While the question of the morality of mob violence by white men was discussed, the southern press never questioned the innocent virginity of the woman victim or the violent passion of the black man. When and if the stories of the black men and white women actually involved were told, the account was secondhand, after the fact, shaped by rumor and innuendo. After all, at the point that many of these stories were told, the key participants were not able to testify. The black man was maimed, burned, dead; the white woman was shamed, humiliated, mute.

The way these stories were told in the press reflected the social location of their white male writers or the white male participants they chose to interview. There were virtually no white women reporters in the southern press in the summer of 1897, and it was unusual for any coverage of women's accounts of events to appear as front-page news. In the case of the lynching controversy, newspaper editors almost never solicited black men's opinions. At best they found deferential ministers willing to confirm the white man's story, apologizing for the apparent immorality of some members of the Negro race and pledging their support for swift punishment. As a result, we will probably never know what actually transpired between Oscar Smith and Jewel Campbell or Anthony Williams and Rene Williams in the summer of 1897. At least we will never know how they would freely and openly tell us their story if they were with us today.

It stands as a testament to how much race and gender relations have changed in the last 100 years that today, even without Oscar Smith's or Rene Williams's testimony, we can read much of this 1897 news coverage and imagine a very different scenario from that which was envisioned by many readers at the time. Take, for example, the story that appeared in the *Atlanta Constitution* on July 25, 1897. The headline read, "Negro Finds Safety in Jail. Insulted a Lady and Her Neighbors Were Aroused." The story was reported as follows. The "Negro" (who remained nameless) went to his employer's house to ask his employer's wife, Mrs. W. Anderson (who has only her husband's name), for a lock of her hair to make a watch charm. "Fortunately," as this account put it, the husband came upon the two, and the "Negro" beat a hasty retreat. When the "incident" became known to the neighbors, they were so infuriated by the "impudence" of the black man that by nightfall some 50 men were searching for him. Had they found him they would have lynched him on the spot.[2]

We read this story today and we wonder how the simple request for a lock of a white woman's hair by a black man could enrage 50 white male neighbors to the brink of lynching. We wonder whether Mrs. Anderson really thought the request was "impertinent," as the press recounted, or whether her husband decided it was, and she simply stood by, in her "proper" place as his wife: shamed, humiliated, and mute. Perhaps, we could conjecture, it was really Mr. Anderson who was the brute, or at least the neglectful and unappreciative husband, and perhaps the unnamed black man was actually an engaging and admiring companion of Mrs. Anderson. We will never know. What we do know is that something very intense was going on between black men and white women in the summer of 1897. It may have been violence, or it may have been love, or perhaps it was both. Whatever it was, it was so intense that it disrupted the white male–dominated southern social order, and the white male–dominated press. It put the story of the relationships between black men and white women, however distorted, however filtered through dominant racial and gendered lenses, on the front page of the daily news.

While the discussion of lynching in the southern press was dominated by white male writers, and the actual actors were never able to tell their own story directly, the very violence of white men's response opened the way for at least some black men and some white women to be heard in public. The result was explosive when the position of one white woman—Rebecca Latimer Felton, a well-known advocate of white women's issues—and one black man—Alex Manly, a prominent black newspaper editor and officeholder in Wilmington, North Carolina—were picked up and widely circulated on the front pages of the major newspapers of the South, serving to further inflame white male supremacist sentiment and leading ultimately to the Wilmington racial massacre in the fall of 1898. Historians of white racial violence, whether that violence be lynchings or massacres, have been inclined to emphasize the economic and political motivations behind white men's behavior. Feeling threatened by the political and economic accomplishments of black men and the black community more generally, southern white men increasingly resorted to violence in order to perpetuate the white supremacist social order of the South in the 1890s. From this perspective, lynchings for the alleged reason of rape of white women played an obfuscatory role, serving to legitimate white men's repression of black men for the "real" reasons of economic and political competition. In tracing out the connection, however twisted and distorted, between sexual relations between black men and white women and the Wilmington racial massacre, this essay attempts to contribute to our understanding of the role that sexuality, particularly efforts to regulate white women's sexuality, played in the racial violence of the 1890s and in the consolidation of white supremacy in the South of Jim Crow.

Not surprisingly, the black voice that was first taken up by the white press of the South in the discussion of racial violence in the summer of 1897 at least tacitly accepted the description of sex across the color line as being the "rape" of white women. On July 28, the *Atlanta Constitution* reported on a series of resolutions adopted by the Bannister Baptist Association. The headlines read, "Negro Preachers Condemn the Crime. Assaults upon Defenseless Women Are Severely Censured. Lynching Is Made a Side Issue. The Offense and Not the Work of the Mobs the Great Wrong." This group of ministers committed themselves to "cooperate with the whites to bring to justice any and all who may be guilty, and to use their influence in the larger community to create sentiment against the crime." They commended the governor for affirming the power of the law to "mete out full justice and punishment to those who have or may attempt to outrage it."[3]

In their resolutions, these ministers took a stance against rape, describing it as "the most dastardly, cowardly and infamous crime known to humanity." They pledged their resources to cooperate in hunting down the alleged perpetrators of such crimes. They did not directly condemn lynching, but instead tried to wrap their own position in the authority of the governor, who opposed lynching on the grounds that the regular workings of the legal system were sufficient to bring rapists to justice. They apparently hoped that they could reduce the incidence of the lynching of black men by conceding the possibility that some black men might have perpetrated violent crimes against some white women, thus reassuring whites that the black community would support the effective working of the rule of law. The closest any black man came to actually being able to condemn violence against black men in the white-dominated southern press was a sermon by an Atlanta minister, the Reverend Proctor. He pointed out that there was a natural tendency to look to the faults of others rather than to seriously consider one's own. He argued that both lynching and rape were crimes, and that the white community should take care of their problem and the black community would take care of theirs.[4]

While, by August of 1897, a few black men did gain at least some space for their perspective on white mob violence, however hedged about, white women were still mute. Indeed, southern newspapers actively reinforced the appropriateness of their silence, particularly on "political" matters. In July, for instance, the press covered the story of the Atlanta Woman's Christian Temperance Union (WCTU), which had just been kicked out of its long-standing meeting place in the basement of the Trinity Methodist Church for advocating woman suffrage. The church's minister charged the membership of the group with turning the church into a "town hall" by speaking to a Sunday school class on the Anti-Barroom Bill that was currently pending in Atlanta. "Men," according to the minister, "lose respect for women who dabble in politics." Women, he went on to assert, were not suited to public political activities because their brains were "smaller than men's, lighter and finer in structure."[5]

On August 3, however, in the face of the relentless press coverage of lynchings for the alleged crime of rape, Bill Arp, who wrote a regular column for the *Atlanta Constitution*, actually went so far as to call directly for the opinion of white women on mob violence. In a lengthy commentary, Arp indicated that he had very little confidence in the seemingly endless discussion in the daily press from clergy, judges, lawyers, and, as he put it, "young unmarried men who lived in rock built cities." None of these men, Arp claimed, had any real-life experience in the "dangers" of isolated country living. For himself, he recounted how he had moved his family out of the countryside some years earlier and into the "rock built" city in order to "protect" his wife. According to Arp, lynching for what he termed the "nameless crime" had nothing to do with the ineffectiveness of the legal system, as some lawyers, ministers, and politicians had been claiming. Instead, he argued that mob violence by white men constituted a "spontaneous outburst of emotions long felt and long smothered and those emotions are based on love—love for the home and wife and children, love and respect for wives and daughters of neighbors."[6]

Arp called upon white women to step forward and take a public stand on the question, a question that he had framed as a matter of white men's love for white women. This was presumably an issue on which white women were well qualified to speak. From the vantage point of 100 years later, we might choose to frame the question in a more open way, and rather than simply asking white women to affirm white men's loving behavior toward them, we might think that the more appropriate question to ask would be, who is really loving whom here? Was rape really the act of hate, while lynching was the act of love, as Bill Arp and the white press more generally asserted? Or, was the alleged "rape" really the act of love, and lynching the act of hate, as the story of Mrs. Anderson, the lock of hair, and the unnamed black farmhand might suggest?

Bill Arp did not have to wait long to receive an answer from white women, or at least from one white woman. On August 12, at the annual meeting of the Georgia State Agricultural Society, Rebecca Latimer Felton gave a speech entitled, innocuously enough, "Woman on the Farm." This was not the first time she had given this speech. It was not even the first time she had given it before the Georgia State Agricultural Society. Indeed, by the summer of 1897, Rebecca Latimer Felton was already one of the most publicly outspoken members of her sex in the American South. She began her political career over 20 years earlier, as the campaign manager for her husband, William Harrell Felton, in his two successful bids for a seat in the U.S. Congress. At that time it was rumored that not only did she manage his campaign but she also wrote many of his speeches. Whatever the truth or falsity of that rumor, she certainly did write biting editorials in his defense, which she sent to the local press, never actually signing with her own name, but instead employing pseudonyms, such as "Bartow" (the name of her upcountry county) or "Plowboy" (a reference to the Felton's political alliance with the white yeomanry of the region). It was not until Rebecca Felton joined the WCTU in 1886 that she actually entered the political arena in her own right. Already well known for her powerful editorial style, she became even better known for her oratorical talents, as she stumped the state in defense of what she understood to be women's interests, especially temperance reform.[7]

Felton gave her speeches over and over again, revising them somewhat to suit her particular audience or changing social conditions. Amid the lengthy discussion of rural violence and lynching that occurred in the daily press in the summer of 1897, Felton added two new issues to her "Woman on the Farm" speech. She added a call for improved educational opportunities for white women, including their admission to the University of Georgia, and she advocated the lynching of black men if it would "protect" white women from rape. Not surprisingly, it was her advocacy of lynching that dominated the front pages of the state's newspapers the next day. The first line of the *Atlanta Constitution* headline simply read, " 'Lynch,' Says Mrs. Felton," followed by, "She Makes a Sensational Speech Before the Agricultural Society at Tybee." In the speech's most widely quoted passage, Felton was reported as taking to task the churches, the courthouse, and the very "manhood" of the white South for failing to "put a sheltering arm about innocence and virtue." If, she concluded, "it needs lynching to protect woman's dearest possession from the ravening human beasts— then I say lynch, a thousand times a week, if necessary."[8]

The one sentence—"if it will save one white woman, I say lynch a thousand black men"—would be repeated endlessly in the press commentary, and by Rebecca Latimer Felton herself in the months and years that followed. She claimed to have been driven to this position after reading the news coverage of five lynchings of black men (sometimes she claimed it was six, other times seven) for the rape of white women in the week preceding her August 12 lecture. And exactly how did she read these press accounts? At first consideration, it would appear that she read them with the same underlying assumptions as the white men who wrote them. That is, the victimization of the white woman is a given, the guilt of the black man is assumed, and the question is apparently simply whether the retaliatory actions of the white male mob were justified. Here Felton would appear to be much more a tool of the white male–dominated press, at least of that faction, exemplified by Bill Arp, which advocated white mob behavior, than the black ministers, some of whom at least attempted to deconstruct the white male telling of the story by suggesting that lynching was as much of a crime as was rape, or at least by suggesting that the law would suffice to mete out retribution for criminal acts.[9]

Indeed, when Felton was moved in her speech to discuss the "crimes" on both sides, she focused not on lynching in conjunction with rape, but rather on what might initially appear to be an unlikely parallel: the "crime" of lynching and the "crime" of election fraud. She argued that lynching belonged in the same category of lawlessness as encouraging crimes against the electoral process, such as registration fraud, ballot box stuffing, and false counting. According to Felton, white men's crime was in having "initiated" black men as voters into these "mysteries" by bribing and otherwise corrupting the black man's vote in order to ensure their own political party's victory at the polls. In her speech at Tybee Island, she argued that it was not surprising that once black men came to understand that they could break the election laws with impunity, they would also come to assume that they could engage in "theft, rape and murder" without fear of legal retribution.[10]

While Bill Arp claimed that the "crime" of lynching was the result of the "frustrated love" that white men felt for white women, Felton made it sound as though lynching was a result of a misplaced "embrace" between black and while men at the polls. As she put it, "as long as your politicians take the colored man into their embrace on election day and make him think that he is a man and brother, so long will lynching prevail, for familiarity breeds contempt." In one of the most critical responses to Felton's speech, the *Boston Transcript* severely criticized this condemnation of brotherhood on her part. In an editorial, the paper charged that rather than being a problem of misplaced love, the problem was one of misplaced hate on the part of white southerners for black southerners. "If," the *Transcript* editorial queried, "the colored man is made to feel that he is not a man and a brother, how can he be blamed for acting the part assigned him in some times being a brute?" Perhaps, the editorial suggested, what was notable about the southern black man's behavior was that in the midst of such "fiendish sentiment," he should continue to "adhere to progressive human standards."[11]

With the front-page publication of Felton's speech, it appeared that a new stage in racial violence had opened in Georgia. According to the *Transcript* editorial, while mob violence had already reached the point of casting "reproach and blight upon the state," the entry of white women into the debate as its militant advocates could only intensify the levels of already horrific behavior. Indeed, the *Transcript* even went so far as to charge that the real hatemongers in the South were in fact white women like Felton. As the editor put it, "When it comes to declaring who are the wild beasts of Georgia society, the black man would not get all the votes."[12]

Felton read this criticism of her speech by the *Transcript* as a particularly clear manifestation of northerners' general attitude of "hatred" for all things southern—and by "southern" she obviously meant the white South. According to Felton, the North felt such deep animosity for the white South, and for southern white women in particular, that northern editors actually lined up with the "perpetrator of the crime." Felton argued that the northern press was so antagonistic toward southern white women that it did not even consider these assaults upon "defenseless" white women to be criminal acts, not, that is, when they were committed by what she termed the North's "pet political favorite," the black man. Here Felton reiterated her underlying position regarding who was doing the loving and who was doing the hating in the summer of 1897. There was too much "love" for the black man by the white man, on the one hand, according to Felton, and not enough love for the white woman by the white man, on the other. Northern white men were clearly the most guilty in this regard, southern white men were at least complicitious, as could be seen by their fraternization with black men at the polls.[13]

While Felton clearly took offense at this manifestation of "brotherhood" between black and white men, she was actually more concerned about what she assumed was a fairly direct connection between this political "embrace" and a social embrace between black men and white women, a social embrace that she refused to understand as anything other than rape. This was a concern that she assumed the "abolitionist" northern press, like the *Boston Transcript*, did not share. To the contrary, as she pointed out in her response to the *Transcript* editorial, northern laws actually "appear to encourage and promote the mixture of the white and black races—because these laws authorize and permit marriage between the two races." She went on to suggest, undoubtedly somewhat tongue in cheek, that perhaps this was the reason the editor of the *Transcript* did not understand why such miscegenation was forbidden by the laws of Georgia. While she graciously "declined to comment" on the question of northern law and custom with regard to mixed-race marriage, she felt fully empowered to speak for the South. "Let the editor of the Boston *Transcript* remember," she threatened, "that the irrevocable edict has gone forth from every farm house in Georgia and from every true man's heart, that the black fiend who lays unholy and lustful hands on a white woman in the state of Georgia shall surely die!"[14]

Here was the core of the social illness that led to mob violence in the summer of 1897. Felton could not understand an embrace between a black man and a white woman as being anything other than rape. As a result, she frequently conflated the rape of white women by black men with marriage between white women and black men, as she did in this response to the *Transcript* editorial. The fact that the love of some black men for some white women had to be hate in the minds of many white southerners, stood at the center of the radical distortions of who was loving whom, who was hating whom, and what was the "real" meaning of "rape" and "lynching" in the summer of 1897. It helps to explain why a loving request for the lock of a white woman's hair could be read by many white southerners as essentially a "rape" of the white woman, a "rape" that then called for a lynching.

The whole question of who was doing the loving and who was doing the hating became a quagmire in the late-nineteenth-century South because love for the white supremacist social order as a whole required turning the individual love of some black men for some white women into an act of hate, into rape, as surely as it required that brotherhood between black men and white men be understood as a veritable "crime." It had to be hate because, as Felton was inclined to put it, white women were the "coming mothers of the white race." As such, they were more than simply individual women who loved individual men, they were literally the carriers of white supremacy. Even if some individual black men genuinely loved some individual white women, such a love was at the same time an act of hate against the larger white supremacist social order of the South as a whole.[15]

There was, however, more than one way to maintain white supremacy. At least this was Felton's response to what she perceived as the crisis of the racial order in the summer of 1897. If white men were going to fall down on the job, and black men were going to aspire to social as well as political equality, southern white women could still be expected to hold the line. They, after all, had it within their power never to understand the social advances of a black man as anything besides an act of hatred. They could single-handedly transform love into hate in the way that the white supremacist social order required in order to perpetuate itself. The problem that Felton faced, however, was that her shock troops in the battle for white supremacy, white women themselves, also appeared to be in some danger of giving way. So while Bill Arp and the white male press in general referred to the "nameless crime" and meant to indicate rape, it was the actual or potential "falling down" of white women that constituted the truly "nameless crime" for Felton. A "crime" that she could never actually bring herself to name but which nonetheless stood at the center of her proposals for the reform of white rural women's condition.[16]

The intensity of the debate that surrounded Felton's advocacy of racial violence in the white male press tends to obscure the fact that she actually added two new points, not just one, to her speech on farm women. Along with advocating the lynching of black men, she also advocated improved educational opportunities for white women. She demanded improved access to a common school education for white farm women, and, for more privileged white women of the middle and upper classes, like herself, she asked for admission to the University of Georgia. In the case of the

poorest of white rural women, Felton assumed that a common school education would allow them to pull themselves up faster in class terms than
any black man could possibly rise up to meet them. She liked to tell a story
in her speeches to illustrate this point. She would tell her audience about a
train ride she had recently taken. While walking through the cars to the
smoker, she tells of passing a neatly dresed black woman who was busy
reading a book in Greek. She asked the woman why she was reading the
book, and the woman answered that she was on her way to teach summer
school and was refreshing her mastery of the subject she would teach.
Arriving at her own seat in the rear coach, Felton happened to gaze out the
window at a nearby cotton field, only to see four young white women
hoeing cotton, "shabbily dressed—in the same field with negro men and
boys." For Felton, it was a moving scene: "I have never been so heart
sick ... These are unwholesome conditions. ... These are the coming
mothers of our race."[17]

In earlier versions of her "Woman on the Farm" speech—for instance,
the version that she gave at the 1891 meeting of the Georgia State
Agricultural Society—Felton held white men solely responsible for the
deplorable conditions of white women on the family farm. Who, after all,
was responsible for these young white women being "reduced" to working
in the fields beside black men, if not their white male relations? In her earlier
versions of the speech, she castigated the white men in her audiences for
failing to appreciate properly the contributions of white women on the
family farm. Men who went to town on Saturdays to hold forth about the
state of "my crop," "my house," and "my farm" with their fellow farmers,
elicited Felton's particular wrath. According to Felton, gender relations on
the family farm provided at least one case in which the old adage, "the man
and his wife are made one," was realized, and, in the realization, "that one
is the man." White men needed to recognize, Felton repeatedly argued,
that the most important "crop" they would ever raise was their children
and that in this business their wives were their best asset.[18]

From Felton's perspective in 1891, white men had it within their power
to mend whatever ailed the family farm and the position of white women
on it. They had it within their power to love their women as they should,
or at least as Felton thought they should. They could acknowledge their
partnership with their wives by coming to understand that they would
"never raise a more important crop than their children." In this way, they
could put their women, and domesticity more generally, at the center of
what should properly be referred to as "our farm" and "our house." In 1891,
Felton suggested to her farm audience that they could manifest concretely
their advocacy of a gender reformed farm family by setting aside a portion
of their crop as the "Wife's Farm," the idea being that just as the wife made
the husband's breakfast in the morning, so should the husband work in the
wife's fields. Felton must have been pleased when, at the 1891 meeting of
the Georgia State Agricultural Society, her proposal was adopted and she
was made state president of the "Before Breakfast Clubs."[19]

By 1897, however, Felton no longer considered reforms internal to the family farm and white gender relations sufficient to ameliorate the condition of white farm women. Now she added external "threats" and external "solutions"—the external "threat" of violence by the black man and the external "solution" of the lynch mob. At the same time, however, she also called for another external solution, the expanded education of white women. By empowering women in their own right, Felton hoped to put white women in a position to protect themselves against the potential abuse of both black and white men. As long as women could be educated to do what Felton considered to be right on their own, the dangers that the shortcomings of men of both races posed to the maintenance of a "constructive" social order could be reduced.[20]

All this is not to say that Felton envisioned no role for white men in the reform of white women's condition. After all, it was white men whom she continued to petition for support, in this case for improved educational opportunities for their women. Felton also assumed that improved educational opportunities, and the increased autonomy for white women that accompanied them, created another "new" role for white men. For as white women became more integrated into public life, they also became more "vulnerable" to the designs of strange men. White men's "new" role, then, was to "clear the path" of other men who blocked white women's way to the schoolhouse, the university, and ultimately even the voting booth. The most extreme form of this new kind of "protection" that white men were now being called upon to provide was that of lynching black men for the alleged rape of white women. From this perspective, however, Felton's call to "lynch a thousand black men if it would save one white woman" appears to be only the tip of the iceberg. Felton was in fact grappling with a far larger structural problem: how to empower white women to "protect" themselves without at the same time granting them the power to make choices that would undercut the white racial hierarchy.

Historians have long wondered why Rebecca Latimer Felton, one of the leading advocates for women's rights in the South, should also have been one of the region's most outspoken racists—why the "protection" of one group, white women, became fused in her thinking with the advocacy of the violent repression of another, black men. The key to this question is not to be found in an examination of either Felton's race or gender politics alone, but rather in the way that her increasingly reactionary race politics were created by, and in turn nourished, her increasingly progressive gender politics, through the medium of sexual relations, itself perhaps the ultimate form of fusion. It was the horror of this fusion that drove Felton on, that propelled her ever more militant advocacy of racial violence and gender "protection" in order to secure a segregated domestic integrity, where both black and white women would be properly recognized and empowered as the "coming mothers" of their respective races.[21]

For this reason, the greatest threat to Felton's project was sexual relations across the color line, and it is the primacy of her opposition to miscegenation that provides the key to her race politics and her gender politics. Indeed, her initial motivation for entering the political arena in her own right had little to do with either white women or black men. It did, however, have everything to do with miscegenation. It was during William Felton's second term in office that Rebecca Felton came upon a report concerning the convict lease system in Georgia. The Feltons were horrified at the extent to which the lease appeared to recapitulate the system of slavery, with the vast majority of the prisoners assigned to the lease being black, and the lessees being white. What particularly appalled Rebecca Felton was the way in which criminals were thrown together on the chain gang, regardless of their age or sex, or the seriousness of their crime. The presence of mixed-race children on the chain gang, fathered by the white guards and black women prisoners, was, in Felton's estimation, the bitterest fruit of this obscene system.[22]

This issue galvanized Rebecca Felton. As she explained it, when she looked around Georgia in the mid-1880s for organized women's groups who might be concerned about the treatment of women and children on the convict lease, she found only one statewide organization outside the churches, the Woman's Christian Temperance Union. In 1886 she joined the WCTU in order to organize support for a petition to the state legislature opposing the lease. With her heart pounding in her chest at her own temerity, as she related later, she gave her first public address before the WCTU, urging the organization to sponsor her petition against the conditions of the lease. The WCTU adopted her petition, and in 1887 she presented it to the state legislature. Even for simply presenting the petition—she did not actually address the state legislature—she was nonetheless thoroughly excoriated. The state's elected leaders roundly denounced her as the "political She" of Georgia.[23]

It is perhaps hard to understand how a woman who got her own independent start in politics by trying to improve the conditions of black women and children, and who withstood considerable social opprobrium for her inappropriate behavior in doing so, could, a short ten years later, advocate the lynching of black men. What is critical to realize, however, is that in her mind, the problem posed by black women on the lease and white women in rural areas was the same. They were both examples of the basic wrong of miscegenation. The difference, however, was that when it came to black women, Felton was more than capable of naming the "nameless crime." It was here, then, that she could begin a crusade directly against miscegenation. Indeed, Felton had a long-standing opposition to white men's sexual abuse of black women for the way that it undercut the position of white women as their wives and as the mothers of their children. She railed against the way that white men, in the days of slavery, had "kept two households under one roof." She charged that the "crime that made slavery a curse lies in the fact that unbridled lust placed the children of bad white men in slave pens, on auction blocks." For this "crime" against their "parental responsibility," "the retribution of wrath

188   Gender Matters

was hanging over this country and the South paid penance in four years of bloody war."[24]

The defeat of the Confederacy and the emancipation of the slaves, thus, held forth the possibility that white women could finally command the first attention of their men, an attention that had always been threatened under slavery. The real horror of the convict lease system in Felton's mind was that it represented the return of the worst of the slave-owning South, where, as Felton put it, "mulattos were as common as blackberries." In the 1880s, Felton took up the reform of white men by organized white women with a vengeance. Under the auspices of the WCTU, she went after a whole complex of white men's "sins," including drinking, gambling, and prostitution. In 1891, when she gave her first farm speech, she was hopeful that white men could be induced or, at worst, forced—through prohibition, as well as through the reform of the convict lease—to commit to a new form of segregated domesticity. Then, white women would finally be at the center of white men's lives and would finally be loved and appreciated as they never had been under the old slaveholding, staple crop system of the antebellum South of her birth.[25]

Instead, just as white women and the "white life for two"—as the WCTU dubbed the single sexual standard—appeared to be gaining some public and political advocacy, the bottom of the white supremacist social order seemed to be sliding out in the other direction. Sexual relations between black men and white women were considerably more threatening to Felton than those between white men and black women. As painful as white men's philandering might be to white women, it was still within the power of the white race to control. Granted, some white men seemed entirely unwilling to control their behavior, but by the 1890s, some white women seemed at last to be acquiring enough public power to force or convince white men to straighten up. Black men were, however, outside of Felton's control, and most frightening of all was the possibility that white women themselves would, with their newfound empowerment, choose black men rather than choosing white men as their "partners" in a "white life for two."

Racial violence and gender mutilation: these were Felton's answers to the possibility of love between white women and black men in the summer of 1897. Black men would have to be exterminated, and white women who had been with them would have to be seen as "ruined," as Felton put it, a fate that any respectable woman would regard as worse than death itself. And yet, even in the face of this mounting racial and gender violence, some black men and some white women refused to keep their place in the southern social order. Indeed, Felton's own outspoken discussion of the need to lynch black men in order to protect white women opened the door for a more militant public statement on sexual relations across the color line. It was not until August of 1898, almost a year after the initial publication of Felton's speech, that Alexander Manly, the editor of the *Wilmington Record*, a popular black-owned daily in the South, decided to respond to Felton's allegations against black men in her "Woman on the Farm" speech.

Unfettered by the constraints placed upon black men in the white male press, Manly published a reply that finally named the nameless, an act that was like throwing gasoline on the smoldering embers of the previous summer's mayhem of lynching and mob violence.[26]

Manly began his editorial by agreeing with many of Felton's positions on white women, though he was inclined to include black women as well. He thought that lower-class women of both races were sorely in need of moral upliftment and that improved educational opportunities would indeed "protect" them on the farm. Not only did Manly concur with Felton's suggested reforms for white women, he also agreed with her assessment of the shortcomings of white men. "We suggest that the white men guard their women more closely," he wrote, "thus giving no opportunity for the human fiend, be he white or black." He suggested that poor white men were "careless" about their women: "You leave your goods out of doors and then complain because they are taken away." It was at this point that Manly parted company with Felton, however, for while Felton was only too willing to detail the various ways that white men abused their position of power— whether that was in their failure to respect and empower their women sufficiently or in their fatal "embrace" of black men at the polls—she was unable to grant white women any agency in their own predicament. Manly had no such compunctions. He suggested that poor white men were so careless toward their women that "their women were not any more particular in the matter of clandestine meetings with colored men, than are the white men with colored women." He asserted that "meetings of this kind go on for some time, until the woman's infatuation or the man's boldness bring attention to them and the man is lynched for rape."[27]

As if it were not enough to suggest in cold, hard print that the whole matter was a result of white women's "infatuation" with black men, Manly went on—well past the point of endurance for most southern whites—to point out that while every black man who was lynched for the alleged crime of rape was described in the white press as a "big, burly, black brute," many were actually the sons of white fathers. They not only were not "black" and "burly," but they were also "sufficiently attractive for white girls of culture and refinement to fall in love with them, as is well known to all." Alexander Manly was himself the acknowledged offspring of Charles Manly, governor of North Carolina from 1849 to 1851, and one of his slave women. From Felton's perspective, Alexander Manly represented all the errors of the white man, beginning with his mixed-race background, extending to the Fusion politics in North Carolina that had put him into public office as the register of deeds, and ending with his position as editor of an independent black newspaper. The initial ill-founded "embrace" of the white man had in this case borne fruit in the form of a mixed-race man, now in a position not only to embrace the white woman, but also to write about it for all the world to read.[28]

In Alexander Manly, Rebecca Latimer Felton had indeed met her match. For if Felton was the white woman who gained the most public space to speak in the race crisis of the 1890s, Manly was the black man who found himself most empowered to represent the experience of black men. If Felton emerged as one of the leading New White women of the turn-of-the-century South, Manly epitomized the New Black man. If Felton was the "political She" of Georgia—notorious for her outspoken criticism of white men and white gender relations—Manly, as an editor and office-holder, was an equally outspoken advocate of the interests of his race. From their common condition as members of groups subordinate to the power of the white man, they could and did concur on many aspects of what they saw as his abusive behavior. In his editorial, for instance, Manly suggested that Felton should "begin at the fountainhead if she wishes to purify the stream." He pointed out that white men needed to be taught "purity" by their women. This was one of Felton's main arguments for admitting white women to the University of Georgia in her Tybee Island speech. She assumed that the presence of young women would improve the moral environment for the young men there. But, as with Manly's discussion of poor white women, he once again carried the matter one step further than Felton, across the color line. "Tell your men," he advised Felton, "that it is no worse for a black man to be intimate with a white woman than for a white man to be intimate with a colored woman." Manly's argument was once again color-blind. All men should live by the single sexual standard advocated by Felton and the WCTU. Moreover, Felton should realize, and white people more generally should acknowledge, that the "sin" cut both ways. White men were clearly in no position to be passing judgment on black men, much less lynching them, for "sins" that they so frequently committed themselves.[29]

Not surprisingly, Manly's speech set the state of North Carolina on fire. In the summer and fall of 1898, the white supremacist Democratic press used the speech as a centerpiece of the campaign to organize popular opposition to the Fusion coalition of the Republicans and Populists, which had put black men into public offices and had thereby contributed to giving them the power to name the unnameable. After successfully using racial intimidation and appeals to white solidarity to capture the elections in the fall of 1898, mob sentiment moved beyond the lynching of one man to the massacre of the race. Manly's press was burned as the starting point of a conflagration that left at least 11 blacks dead, and promoted a general exodus of the black population, led by Manly himself, who had fled to New Jersey sometime before the racial massacre.

Felton wrote a reply to Manly's editorial and to the massacre that followed it. She read both as a graphic confirmation of the truth of the stance that she had taken on mob violence in her Tybee Island speech the previous summer. In her reply to Manly's editorial, she claimed that since the delivery of her Tybee speech the incidence of lynchings in the state of Georgia had decreased by half. In North Carolina, however, what she described as "corruption in politics and undue familiarity with North Carolina negroes at the polls" had instead created the conditions for a general racial massacre. In what was for her a typical slide from politics to social life, she charged that "the black race will be destroyed by the whites in self-defense unless law and order prevail in regard to the crime of rape and lynching that follows." She revealed the real bottom line of her politics by arguing that when "the negro Manly attributed the crime of rape to intimacy between negro men and white women of the South, the slanderer should be made to fear a lyncher's rope rather than occupy a place in New York newspapers."[30]

As much as Felton's speech gave Manly the ground to stand on, Manly's speech forced Felton to reveal that the real problem was not violence against white women, but rather the possibility of intimacy between black men and white women. The real threat to the social order was not hatred but love. And as Felton opened the door to Manly, so Manly opened the door for a white woman to acknowledge that love. But it could not happen—not, at least, within the geographical confines of the South. The Wilmington massacre made the whole question of southern race relations front-page news across the nation. In the North, African Americans held meetings to protest the massacre. At one such meeting, at the Cooper Union in New York City, a white woman, Mrs. Elizabeth Grannis, "set the audience wild" when she claimed, "I am only here tonight to represent womanhood. Now we all know that white women and white girls of the South are full of colored blood." Infuriated, Rebecca Felton penned a reply charging Elizabeth Grannis with "telling a willful and venomous untruth." According to Felton, Grannis was purposefully playing on the "basest passions of that ignorant audience." The North, according to Felton, could keep Elizabeth Grannis. Not even "colored citizens" of Georgia would tolerate her presence with such "base falsehood on her lips."[31]

There was no place in the South for white women who openly affirmed their relationships with black men. Indeed, by the next year, after the vehement reaction of southerners to her remarks, Elizabeth Grannis had decided to leave the country altogether and set sail for Europe. There was no place for black men either, at least if Alexander Manly's experience was any indicator. He decided to resettle permanently in the North. Felton, however, remained in the South. The events of the late 1890s, her exchanges with Manly and Grannis, and her proposed "solutions" to the threat of the likes of Oscar Smith and Rene Williams propelled her ever further into public prominence and political power. In 1901, she became the first woman to address the state legislature in Georgia. Clark Howell, the state senator who introduced her, noted that while there is a "great deal of discussion and contention as to who is the smartest man in Georgia, it is universally conceded that the woman who is to address you today is the brightest and the smartest woman in the state." Felton had come a long way since 1887, scarcely more than a decade earlier, when simply for presenting a petition in the very same statehouse, she had been roundly condemned as the "political She" of Georgia.[32]

By the end of her long life, Rebecca Latimer Felton would see many of the reforms she advocated in the summer of 1897 made into law: disenfranchisement of the black population, the admission of white women to the University of Georgia, the passage of prohibition and compulsory education legislation, the abolition of the convict lease, and the establishment of a separate system of juvenile correction. As her politics of racially segregated domesticity became law throughout the South, so too did she continue to ride the political wave, becoming the first U.S. woman senator in 1923. Years later, she reveled in the changes in the status of southern white women that her appointment to the U.S. Senate indicated. "It meant that a woman reared in the sheltered security of an antebellum plantation was to be the first of her sex to sit in the U.S. Senate. It was hard to realize. Who in that day would have had the hardihood to predict that the time would come when Georgia women would hold public office?" she wondered. Perhaps only the unnamed, the silenced, the mute men and women, whose lives and deaths nonetheless drove her story, as surely as she was empowered by theirs, could have answered her question.[33]

Notes

Introduction

1. At this point studies of the role of gender are wide ranging, from the origins of slavery, to the making of the first industrial working class, the role of citizens in democratic societies, the transmigration of peoples, the preservation of the family farm under corporate capitalism to the very writing of history itself. See, e.g., Gerda Lerner, *The Creation of Patriarchy* (New York, Oxford University Press, 1986); Anna Clark, *Struggle for the Breeches: The Making of the British Working Class* (Berkeley, University of California Press, 1995); Linda Kerber, *No Constitutional Right to Be Ladies* (New York, Hill and Wang, 1998); Linda Reeder, *Widows in White: Migration and the Transformation of Rural Women, Sicily, 1880–1920* (Toronto, Toronto University Press, 2003); Mary Neth, *Preserving the Family Farm: Women, Community and the Foundations of Agribusiness in the Midwest, 1900–1940* (Baltimore, Johns Hopkins Press, 1995); Bonnie Smith, *The Gender of History: Men, Women and Historical Practice* (Cambridge, MA., Harvard University Press, 1998); and Joan Wallach Scott, *Gender and the Politics of History* (New York, Columbia University Press, 1988).
2. Barbara Jeanne Fields, "Ideology and Race in American History," in *Region, Race and Reconstruction: Essays in Honor of C. Vann Woodward*, J. Morgan Kousser and James McPherson, eds. (New York, Oxford University Press, 1982), 143–178.
3. Stephen Hahn, *The Roots of Southern Populism: Yeomen Farmers and the Transformation of Georgia's Upper Piedmont, 1850–1890* (New York, Oxford University Press, 1983). Wayne Durrill, *War of Another Kind: A Southern Community in the Great Rebellion* (New York, Oxford University Press, 1990). Eric Foner, *Reconstruction: America's Unfinished Revolution, 1863–1877* (New York, Harper & Row, 1988).
4. Elizabeth Fox-Genovese, *Within the Plantation Household: Black and White Women of the Old South* (Chapel Hill, University of North Carolina Press, 1988).
5. David Roediger, *The Wages of Whiteness: Race and the Making of the American Working Class* (London and New York, Verso, 1991).
6. Stephanie McCurry, *Masters of Small Worlds: Yeoman Households, Gender Relations and the Political Culture of the Antebellum South Carolina Low Culture* (New York, Oxford University Press, 1995).
7. By seeing men, both white and black, as having gender, historians have been able to address other pivotal issues in nineteenth-century southern political culture, such as the Civil War, Reconstruction, and progressive era reform movements. For example, see Nancy Bercaw, *Gendered Freedoms: Race, Rights and the Politics of the Household in the Delta, 1861–1875* (Gainesville, University

of Florida Press, 2003); Laura Edwards, *Gendered Strife and Confusion: The Political Culture of Reconstruction* (Urbana, University of Illinois, 1987); Glenda Gilmore, *Gender and Jim Crow: Women and the Politics of White Supremacy in North Carolina, 1896–1920* (Chapel Hill, University of North Carolina Press, 1996); Nancy MacLean, *Behind the Mask of Chivalry: The Making of the Second Ku Klux Klan* (New York, Oxford University Press, 1994); Rebecca Montgomery, *The Politics of Education in the New South: Women and Reform in Georgia, 1890–1930* (Baton Rouge, Louisiana State University Press, 2005); and LeeAnn Whites, *The Civil War as a Crisis in Gender: Augusta, Georgia, 1860–1890* (Athens, Georgia, University of Georgia Press, 1995).

8. Michael Johnson, *Toward a Patriarchal Republic: The Secession of Georgia* (Baton Rouge, Louisiana University Press, 1977).

Chapter 1   The Civil War as a Crisis in Gender

1. Harriet Beecher Stowe read this eyewitness account by the man who helped the escaping slave woman and her child ashore in an antislavery magazine. It formed the basis for an early incident in her novel. Harriet Beecher Stowe, *Uncle Tom's Cabin; or Life Among the Lowly* (New York, 1892 [1853]), xiii.

2. Catharine Beecher, *A Treatise on Domestic Economy* (Boston, Thomas H. Webb & Co, 1843). See also Kathryn Kish Sklar, *Catharine Beecher: A Study in American Domesticity* (New Haven, Yale University Press, 1973), and Jeanne Boydston et al., *The Limits of Sisterhood: The Beecher Sisters on Women's Rights and Women's Sphere* (Chapel Hill, University of North Carolina Press, 1988). The political and social implications of the expansion of women's domestic authority in the North during this period have been discussed by many scholars. See, e.g., Barbara Welter, "The Cult of True Womanhood, 1820–1860," *American Quarterly* (Summer 1966): 151–174; Nancy Cott, *The Bonds of Womanhood: "Woman's Sphere" in New England, 1780–1835* (New Haven, Yale University Press, 1977); Mary Ryan, *Cradle of the Middle Class: The Family in Oneida County, New York, 1790–1865* (New York, Cambridge University Press, 1981); and Ann Douglas, *The Feminization of American Culture* (New York, Knopf, 1977).

3. Jane Tomkins, in her work *Sensational Designs: The Cultural Work of American Fiction* (New York, Oxford Unversity Press, 1985), argues that the emergence of this critical domestic voice actually constituted the most "politically subversive dimension of Stowe's novel, more disruptive and far reaching in its potential consequences than even the starting of a war or the freeing of slaves," 142.

4. In the first year of its publication, the novel sold 300,000 copies and within a decade it had sold more than 2 million copies. James M. McPherson, *Battle Cry of Freedom: The Civil War Era* (New York, Oxford University Press, 1988), 88–89.

5. As cited in McPherson, *Battle Cry of Freedom*, 90. According to McPherson, Lincoln consulted Stowe's work, *A Key to Uncle Tom's Cabin*, when he was confronting the problem of slavery in the summer of 1862, 89.

6. Chesnut discusses Stowe's work on 20 separate occasions in her diary. Mary Boykin Chesnut, *Mary Chesnut's Civil War*, C. Vann Woodward, ed. (New Haven, CT, Yale University Press, 1981), 880.

7. Of course the middle-class northern household was supported by the labor of domestic servants and so it was hardly innocent of class tensions. However, Catharine Beecher's treatise on domestic economy was in part dedicated to rationalizing domestic labor so that the household could function as close to servantless as possible. See Catharine Beecher and Harriet Beecher Stowe, *The American Woman's Home: or, Principles of Domestic Science; Being a Guide to the Formation and Maintenance of Economical, Healthful, Beautiful and Christian Homes* (New York and Boston, J.B. Ford and Company, 1869).

8. Chesnut, *Mary Chesnut's Civil War*, 245.

9. Nell Irvin Painter identifies a similar "maternal" attitude among the planter-class women in "The Journal of Ella Gertrude Clanton Thomas: An Educated White Woman in War and Reconstruction," in *The Secret Eye*, Virginia I. Burr, ed. (Chapel Hill, University of North Carolina Press, 1990).

10. Chesnut, *Mary Chesnut's Civil War*, 169.

11. Ella Gertrude Clanton Thomas, "Journal" (Special Collections, Perkins Library, Duke University, Durham, North Carolina), January 2, 1858.

12. In her biography of the best known of all southern women abolitionists, the Grimké sisters, Gerda Lerner argues that the root of their abolitionist sentiment lay in their resentment of their treatment when compared with their brother's. It was, according to Lerner, Sarah Grimké's squelched desire to have the same educational and professional opportunities as her brother that led her to identify with the position of her family's slaves. Of course perhaps no other southern women went to the lengths that the Grimkés did in actually leaving the South in order to carry out their commitment to a different social order. Gerda Lerner, *The Grimké Sisters from South Carolina: Rebels Against Slavery* (Boston, Houghton Mifflin, 1967).

13. Rebecca Latimer Felton, *Country Life in the Days of My Youth* (Atlanta, Index Press, 1919), 93.

14. Ibid., 86–87, 101.

15. Chesnut, *Mary Chesnut's Civil War*, 169; Elizabeth Fox-Genovese, *Within the Plantation Household* (Chapel Hill, University of North Carolina Press, 1988), and Nell Irvin Painter, "The Journal of Ella Gertrude Clanton Thomas," have both discussed at greater length the ways in which planter-class women's gender interests were subordinated to their race and class privilege.

16. Mounting tension over the patriarchal powers of southern planter-class men in the decade before the outbreak of war has been discussed elsewhere at some length. See William M. Taylor, *Cavalier and Yankee: The Old South and American National Character* (New York, G. Braziller, 1961), Anne Firor Scott, *The Southern Lady: From Pedestal to Politics, 1830–1930* (Chicago, University of Chicago, 1970), and "Women's Perspective on the Patriarchy in the 1850's," *Journal of American History* LXI (1974): 52–64; and Michael P. Johnson, "Planters and Patriarchy: Charleston, 1800–1860," *Journal of Southern History* XLVI (1980): 45–72. Suzanne Lebsock makes the case for a veritable gender backlash in the town of Petersburg in the 1850s. See *The Free Women of Petersburg: Status and Culture in a Southern Town, 1784–1860* (New York, Norton, 1984), 225–236.

17. Joseph Jones to Caroline Davis Jones (Joseph Jones Papers, Tulane University, New Orleans), February 12, 1859.

18. Ibid., March 6, 1859.

19. As Fredrika Bremer wrote to Harriet Beecher Stowe upon the original publication of the novel, "I wondered that the woman, the mother, could look at these things and be silent—that no cry of noble indignation and anger would escape her breast, and rend the air, and pierce to the ear of humanity. I wondered, and God be praised! It has come [in the form of Stowe's novel] . . . the woman, the mother, has raised her voice out of the very soil of the new world in behalf of the wronged ones, and her voice vibrates still through two great continents, opening all hearts and minds to the light of truth." Harriet Beecher Stowe, *Uncle Tom's Cabin*, xxvii–xxviii.

20. For a further discussion of the development of northern women's feminist and abolitionist politics see Barbara Berg, *The Remembered Gate: Origins of American Feminism* (New York, Oxford University Press, 1978); Ellen Carol Dubois, *Feminism and Suffrage: The Emergence of an Independent Women's Movement in America, 1848–1869* (Ithaca: Cornell University Press, 1978); Blanche Hersh, *The Slavery of Sex: Feminist Abolitionists in America* (Urbana, University of Illinois Press, 1978); and Caroll Smith-Rosenberg, *Disorderly Conduct: Visions of Gender in Victorian America* (New York, A.A. Knopf, 1985).

21. Augusta *Chronicle and Sentinel*, April 18, 1861.

22. Chesnut, *Mary Chesnut's Civil War*, 86. The question of war as an assertion of masculine identity has received considerable recent attention. See Nancy Hartsock, "Masculinity, Heroism and the Making of War," in *Rocking the Ship of State*, Adrienne Harris and Ynestra King, eds. (Boulder, CO, Westview Press, 1989), 133–152. Sandra Gilbert, "Soldier's Heart: Literary Men, Literary Women and the Great War," *Signs* 8, no. 3 (1983): 422–450; Carol Cohn, "Sex and Death in the Rational World of Defense Intellectuals," *Signs* 12, no. 4 (1987): 687–718; and Jean Bethke Eltshain, "Women as Mirror and Other," *Humanities in Society* 5, nos. 1–2 (1982).

23. Here Wyatt-Brown means to refer to white southern men who saw the challenge to their right to own slaves from the North as a denial of their liberty, of their prerogatives as free men. Bertram Wyatt-Brown, *Southern Honor: Ethics and Behavior in the Old South* (New York, Oxford, 1982), 35. See also Gerald Linderman, *Embattled Courage: The Experience of Combat in the American Civil War* (New York, Free Press, 1987), 8–16.

24. For a further discussion of the manner in which black men perceived participation in the war as "masculinizing," see James McPherson, *The Negro's Civil War: How American Negroes Felt and Acted During the War for the Union* (New York, Vintage, 1965) and *The Struggle for Equality: Abolitionists and the Negro in the Civil War and Reconstruction* (Princeton, Princeton University Press, 1964), as well as Joseph T. Glatthaar, *Forged in Battle: The Civil War Alliance of Black Soldiers and White Officers* (New York, Free Press, 1990).

25. As cited in Steven A. Channing, *Crisis of Fear: Secession in South Carolina* (New York, Simon and Schuster, 1974), 287.

26. Discussion of the cause of the Civil War was intense for many generations afterward; see Thomas J. Pressly, *Americans Interpret Their Civil War* (New York, Collier Books, 1962), for a treatment of this discourse. Despite this lengthy tradition, the possibility that the war might have a gendered face has received scant attention until recently. See Jean Bethke Eltshain, *Women and*

War (New York, 1987), 94101; and LeeAnn Whites, "The Civil War as a Crisis in Gender: Augusta Georgia, 1860–1890" (Athens, Georgia, 1995).

27. As cited in David W. Blight, *Frederick Douglass' Civil War: Keeping Faith in Jubilee* (Baton Rouge, Louisiana State University Press, 1989), 13.

28. McPherson, *Negro's Civil War*, 131.

29. See Blight, *Frederick Douglass' Civil War* for a more extended discussion of this point.

30. McPherson asserts that Northern blacks met this response "everywhere they turned," *Negro's Civil War*, 22.

31. Ibid., 162.

32. Eric Foster, *Free Soil, Free Labor, Free Men: The Ideology of the Republican Party before the Civil War* (New York, Oxford University Press, 1970) discusses how Republican hostility toward the "slavepower" was in part a displacement of northern men's fears of the erosion of their status as economically independent, and therefore "free men," in the face of Northern economic development.

33. This collapse of the southern social order from within is discussed by James L. Roark, *Masters without Slaves: Southern Planters and the Civil War and Reconstruction* (New York, Norton, 1977). Berlin et al., *Freedom: A Documentary History of Emancipation: 1861–1867* (Cambridge, Cambridge University Press, 1990); and by Clarence Mohr, *Masters and Slaves in Civil War Georgia* (Athens, University of Georgia Press, 1986).

34. See, e.g., J. L. Underwood, *The Women of the Confederacy* (New York, The Neale Pub. Co., 1906); Matthew Page Andrews, *The Women of the South in Wartimes* (Baltimore, Norman, Remington, Co., 1920); Francis Butler Simkins and James Welch Patton, *The Women of the Confederacy* (Richmond, Garrett and Massey, 1936); H. E. Sterkx, *Partners in Rebellion: Alabama Women in the Civil War* (Rutherford, Fairleigh Dickinson University Press, 1970); and Bell Wiley, *Confederate Women* (Westport, CT, Greenwood Press, 1975); and George C. Rable, *Civil Wars: Women and the Crisis of Southern Nationalism* (Urbana, University of Illinois, 1988).

35. As originally cited in H. E. Sterkx, *Partners in Rebellion*, 5, and then later by Bell Wiley, in *Confederate Women*. In a break with this line of argument, Drew Gilpin Faust has suggested that the war may have been lost because its "paternalist" assumptions appeared increasingly meaningless to Confederate women as the war progressed and the loss of life and disruption of domestic life in general mounted. See Drew Gilpin Faust, "Confederate Women and the Narratives of War," in *Divided Houses: Gender and the Civil War*, Catherine Clinton and Nina Silver, eds. (New York, Oxford University Press, 1992), 171–199.

36. Julia Cumming, who saw all four of her sons enlist in the first six months of the war, confessed privately to her daughter of how the loss weighed on her, casting a "very peculiar shade of gloom on my spirits," but even then she immediately went on to berate herself for her lack of faith, saying that she knew she should have "more confidence and serenity than I now feel." Julia Bryan Cumming to Emily Cumming Hammond (Hammond, Bryan, Cumming Collection, Carolina Library, University of South Carolina, Columbia), May 24, 1861.

37. Joseph Jones to Caroline Davis Jones, October 8, 1861.

38. Caroline Davis Jones to Joseph Jones, November 12, 1861.

39. Simkins and Patton, *The Women of the Confederacy*, 8–9.

40. Sterkx, *Partners in Rebellion*, 42.

41. Augusta *Chronicle and Sentinel*, April 25, 1861.

42. Ibid.

43. Mary Elizabeth Massey makes this point in *Bonnet Brigades* (New York, 1966), 367.

44. Augusta *Chronicle and Sentinel*, September 22, 1862.

45. Ibid., May 7, 1861. Julia Bryan Cumming wrote to her daughter of the humiliation her son did in fact feel at his failure to enlist at the time. "Poor Jule, the Guards have gone without him and how immensely more painful is his state, than that of any of them, who have gone to face the horrors of honorable warfare." Julia Bryan Cumming to Emily Cumming Hammond, May 24, 1861.

46. This propensity to sacrifice for the cause led some women to strip their own households virtually bare. According to Mary Elizabeth Massey, this was an important reason why the domestic population suffered from serious shortages. Mary Elizabeth Massey. *Ersatz in the Confederacy* (Columbia, University of South Carolina Press, 1952), 31. See also Simkins and Patton, *The Women of the Confederacy*, 27.

47. Augusta *Chronicle and Sentinel*, June 7, 1861.

48. Ibid., August 13, 1861.

49. Rebecca Latimer Felton, "Temperance," n.d., Felton Papers (Special Collections, University of Georgia, Athens). Looking back many years after the war, Felton claimed that it was the root of southern women's emergence as public figures. "The change stirred something in them—perhaps a murmur of the independence that was to echo down the corridors of future decades." Felton, *The Romantic Story of Georgia's Women* (Atlanta, Atlanta Georgian and Sunday American, 1930), 23. A position most forcefully argued by Scott, *The Southern Lady;* as well as by Massey, *Bonnet Brigades*, and Wiley, *Confederate Women.*

50. Augusta *Chronicle and Sentinel*, January 9, 1863. Amy Clark fought on until she was wounded twice and taken prisoner. Her sex finally discovered, she was required to "don female garb" in federal prison.

51. Ibid., June 10, 1862.

52. Sarah Morgan Dawson, *A Confederate Girl's Diary*, James I. Robertson, ed. (Bloomington, University of Indiana Press, 1960), May 9, 1862.

53. William G. Deloney to Rosa Deloney (William Gaston Deloney Papers, (Special Collections, University of Georgia. Athens), March 13, 1862.

54. Ibid., March 16, 1862.

55. M. D. D. to Rosa Deloney, November 6, 1863.

56. Anne Scott has argued that the Civil War "opened every door" to women, giving women entree into wage labor and public organizations in the postbellum period, but Suzanne Lebsock has subsequently argued that the war opened those doors only in the context of poverty and personal loss and no white southern women felt that load more heavily in the postwar period than women widowed by the war. Anne Scott, *The Southern Lady*, 106–133; and Lebsock, *Free Women of Petersburg*, 237–249.

57. By the last year of the war, Frank Coker was urging his wife to borrow money rather than suffer for enough to eat and wear. He counted on his

ability to make money after the war was over to bail them out of debt. Frank Coker to Sarah Coker, February 1, 1865. Two weeks later she wrote to tell him that she was hiring out more of their slaves because she lacked the resources to support them. Sarah Coker to Frank Coker, February 15, 1865.

58. Jacqueline Jones, *Labor of Love, Labor of Sorrow: Black Women, Work and the Family, from Slavery to the Present* (New York, Basic Books, 1985), 44–78; Susan Archer Mann, "Social Change and Sexual Inequality: The Impact of the Transition from Slavery to Sharecropping on Black Women," *Signs* 14, no. 4 (Summer 1989), pp. 133–157.

59. Augusta *Chronicle and Sentinel*, April 4, 1865.

60. Susan Cornwall, "Journal" (Southern Historical Collection, University of North Carolina, Chapel Hill), May 29, 1866. For a more extended discussion of the way in which the family closed around both white men and women after the war, see Jean Friedman, *The Enclosed Garden: Women and Community in the Evangelical South, 1830–1900* (Chapel Hill, University of North Carolina, 1985), 92–109.

61. There are many first-hand accounts of widespread depression among white men of the South after defeat. See, e.g., John T. Trowbridge, *The Desolate South: 1865–1866*, Gordon Carroll, ed. (New York, Duell, Slozn, and Pearce, 1956); John Richard Dennett, *The South As It Is, 1865–1866*, Henry M. Christman, ed. (Athens, University of Georgia Press, 1986); Whitelaw Reid, *After the War: A Tour of the Southern States, 1865–1866*, C. Vann Woodward, ed. (New York, Harper & Row, 1965). Contemporary historians have discussed it as well. See Dan Carter, *When the War Was over: The Failure of Self Reconstruction in the South* (Baton Rouge, Louisiana State University Press, 1985), and James Roark, *Masters without Slaves*. For a discussion of this depression as a more explicitly gendered expression of the loss of the war as a failure of their manhood, see Gaines M. Foster, *Ghosts of the Confederacy: Defeat, the Lost Cause and the Emergence of the New South* (New York, Oxford University Press, 1987).

62. Susan Cornwall, "Journal," August 22, 1865. This sentiment was intensified by the widespread ridicule of southern white manhood in defeat in the northern press. See Nina Silber, "Intemperate Men, Spiteful Women, and Jefferson Davis," in *Divided Houses: Gender and the Civil War*, Catherine Clinton and Nina Silver, eds. (New York, Oxford University Press, 1992), 283–305.

63. "Burial Services for John Francis Shaffner, M.D.," Fries and Shaffner Papers (Southern Historical Collection, University of North Carolina), September 20, 1908. Charles Reagan Wilson discusses the importance of religion as a source of consolation for defeated ex-Confederate men in *Baptized in Blood: The Religion of the Lost Cause* (Athens, University of Georgia, 1980).

64. Stowe, *Uncle Tom's Cabin*, 467.

Chapter 2 Strong Minds and Strong Hearts: The Ladies National League and the Civil War as an Intragender War

1. For a more extended discussion of the "fire in the rear," see, James McPherson, *Battle Cry of Freedom: The Civil War Era* (New York, Oxford University Press, 1988), 591–526.

2. Loyal Publication of New York, "The Great Mass Meeting of Loyal Citizens" (New York, s.n., 1863; Loyal Reprints no. 3), 5. On the crisis of

loyalty and the formation of Loyal Leagues, see George M. Fredrickson, *The Inner Civil War: Northern Intellectuals and the Crisis of the Union* (New York, Harper & Row, 1965), 130–150; Jorg Nagler, "Loyalty and Dissent: The Home Front and the American Civil War," in *On the Road to Total War and the German Wars of Unification, 1861–1871*, Stig Forster and Jorg Nagler, eds. (Washington, D.C. and Cambridge, German Historical Institute 1997), 329–356; Guy James Gibson, "Lincoln's League: The Union War Movement during the Civil War," Ph.D. Diss., University of Illinois, 1957; and Silvestro Clement Mario, "None but Patriots: The Union Leagues in Civil War and Reconstruction," Ph.D. Diss., University of Wisconsin, 1959.

3. "The Great Mass Meeting of Loyal Citizens," 5. The contribution that Confederate women's demoralization played in the defeat of the Confederacy has been discussed at some length. See Drew Faust, "Altars of Sacrifice: Confederate Women and the Narratives of War," *Journal of American History* 76 (March 1990): 1200–1228 and Gary Gallagher, *Confederate War* (Cambridge, MA, Harvard University Press, 1997). Perhaps because the North won, little attention has focused upon the significance that flagging support from northern women played in the Union war effort. Instead, northern women have generally been presented as supportive of the war effort. Early positive accounts include Frank Moore, *Women at War: Their Heroism and Self Sacrifice* (Hartford, CT, National Publishing Co, 1866) and L. P. Brockett and Mary Vaughn, *Woman's Work in the Civil War: A Record of Heroism, Patriotism and Patience* (Philadelphia, Zeigler, McCurdy & Co, 1867). More recent histories in this patriotic vein include, Elizabeth Leonard, *Yankee Women: Gender Battles in the Civil War* (New York, W.W. Norton, 1994); Jeanie Attie, *Patriotic Toil: Northern Women and the American Civil War* (Ithaca, Cornell University Press, 1998); Judith Ann Giesberg, *Civil War Sisterhood: The U.S. Sanitary Commission and Women's Politics in Transition* (Boston, Northeastern University Press, 2000).

4. On the role of women in antebellum women to partisan politics see, Elizabeth Varon, *"We Mean to Be Counted": White Women and Politics and Antebellum Virginia* (Chapter Hill, University of North Carolina Press, 1998) and Michael D. Pierson, *Free Hearts and Free Homes: Gender and American Antislavery Politics* (Chapel Hill, University of North Carolina, 1991). Discussion of Ladies Loyal Leagues has focused primarily upon their relationship to the women's rights movement. See Faye Dudden, "New York Strategy and the New York Women's Movement in the Civil War," in *Votes for Women: The Struggle for the Suffrage Revisited*, Jean H. Baker, ed. (New York, Oxford University Press, 2002), 56–76; Wendy Hamand Venet, *Neither Ballots nor Bullets: Women Abolitionists and the Civil War* (Charlottesville, University of Virginia Press, 1991); and Mary Elizabeth Massey, *Bonnet Brigades* (New York, Knopf, 1966), 163–166.

5. Many historians have discussed the early and intense militancy of Confederate women see, e.g., George Rable, *Civil Wars: Women and the Crisis of Southern Nationalism* (Urbana, University of Illinois Press, 1989); H. E. Sterkx, *Partners in Rebellion: Alabama Women in the Civil War* (Rutherford, Fairleigh Dickenson University Press, 1970); and Bell Wiley, *Confederate Women* (Westport, CT, Greenwood Press, 1975). On Confederate women's response to invasion and occupation by Union troops, see Jacqueline Glass Campbell, *When Sherman Marched North from the*

Sea: Resistance on the Confederate Home Front (Chapel Hill, University of North Carolina, 2003); Lisa Tendrich Frank, "To 'Cure Her of Pride and Boasting': The Gendered Implications of Sherman's March," Ph.D. Diss., University of Florida, 2001 and Kirsten Lenore Streater, "She-Rebels on the Border: Gender and Politics in Civil War Kentucky," Ph.D. Diss., University of Kentucky, 2001.

6. On the political significance of the transformation of northern women's domestic work into public labor during the war, see Attie, *Patriotic Toil* and Melinda Lawson, *Patriot Fires: Forging a New American Nationalism in the Civil War North* (Lawrence, University of Kansas, 2002), 14–40.

7. For a further discussion of the singularly radical gender potential of the Women's Loyal Leagues, Venet, *Neither Ballots nor Bullets*, 94–122.

8. "Women of the Republic," *New York Tribune*, March 30, 1863.

9. "Proceedings of the Meeting of the Loyal Women of the Republic," (New York, Phair & Co., 1863), 4–5.

10. Ibid., 49.

11. Ibid., 27.

12. Venet, *Neither Ballots nor Bullets*, 120–122.

13. Ibid.

14. "Proceedings of the Meeting of the Loyal Women of the Republic," 19–27.

15. St. Louis *Daily Missouri Democrat*, March 24, 1863. See also, April 19, 1863; April 22, 1863; April 28, 1863; May 4, 1863; and April 20, 1862; and St. Louis *Daily Missouri Republican*, April 6, 1863 and April 29, 1863. On southern sympathizing women as "She Devils," see also Reid Mitchell, *Vacant Chair: The Northern Soldier Leaves Home* (New York, Oxford University Press, 1993), 89–114.

16. *Missouri Democrat*, March 24, 1863.

17. *Missouri Republican*, April 6, 1863.

18. *Reminiscences of the Women of Missouri during the Sixties* (n.p., n.d.), 44–49; 69–73; 78–84. Hannah Stagg, "Local Incidents in the Civil War," *Missouri Historical Society Collections, vol. 5,* January 1910, 69–72.

19. Paula Coalier, "Beyond Sympathy: The St. Louis Ladies' Union Aid Society and the Civil War," *Gateway Heritage* 11, no. 1 (Summer 1970): 38–51; "Ladies National League," St. Louis *Daily Missouri Democrat*, May 4, 1863; and *In Her Place: A Guide to St. Louis Women's History*, Katherine C. Corbett, ed. (St. Louis, Missouri Historical Society Press, 1999), 85–88.

20. Laura Staley, "Suffrage Movement in St. Louis during the 1870's," *Gateway Heritage* 3, no. 4 (Spring 1983): 34–41.

21. *Report of the Organization of the Ladies National League, of St. Louis, their constitution and pledge* (St. Louis, Printed at the Missouri Democrat Office, 1863), 16.

22. Ibid., 9.

23. Ibid., 8–19.

24. Caroline Kirkland, "A Few Words on Behalf of the Loyal Women of the United States by One of Themselves" (New York, W.C. Bryant & Co., Printers, 1863), 1.

25. Ibid., 5.

26. Ibid., 11. As unlikely as these charges against Confederate women may appear, they were reported as fact in serious postwar histories. See, Brockett, *Woman's Work in the Civil War*, 781.

27. Ibid., 9.

28. On the ideological usefulness of the "slavepower" to the Republican Party, see, Eric Foner, *Free Soil, Free Labor, Free Men: The Ideology of the Republican Party before the Civil War* (New York, Oxford University Press, 1970), 73–102.

29. Gerda Lerner, *The Grimké Sisters from South Carolina: Pioneers for Women's Rights and Abolition* (New York, Schocken Books, 1971); see also, Jean Fagin Yellin, *Women and Sisters: The Antislavery Feminists in American Culture* (New Haven, Yale University Press, 1989) and Ronald Walters, *The Antislavery Appeal: American Abolitionism after 1830* (Baltimore, Johns Hopkins University Press, 1976).

30. "A Few Words on Behalf of the Loyal Women of the United States," 10–11

31. Walters, *The Antislavery Appeal*, 91–110.

32. "A Few Words on Behalf of the Loyal Women of the United States," 11.

33. Discussion of Butler's General Order #28 has generally considered it as a serious attack on southern men's masculinity, rather than as a seriously needed defense of northern men. See, e.g., Silber, *The Romance of Reunion: Northerners and the South*, 26–27 and Mary Ryan, *Women in Public: Between Banners and Ballots, 1825–1880* (Baltimore, Johns Hopkins Press, 1990), 143–146.

34. "A Call to My Countrywomen," *Atlantic Monthly*, vol. 11, March 1863, 347.

35. "The Ladies Loyal League," *Continental Monthly*, vol. 3, March 1863, 53–54.

36. "A Call to My Countrywomen," 345–346.

37. Ibid., 347.

38. *Missouri Republican*, April 20, 1863; *Missouri Democrat*, April 22, 1863; *Missouri Democrat*, May 4, 1863.

39. *Missouri Democrat*, April 28, 1863.

40. *Missouri Democrat*, April 28, 1863; April 29, 1863. On General Order #28, see also *Missouri Democrat*, May 4, 1863.

41. *Missouri Democrat*, April 6, 1863; June 25, 1863; Organization of the Ladies National League of St. Louis, St. Louis Missouri, *Missouri Democrat*, 1863, 14.

42. *Missouri Democrat*, April 9, 1863.

43. *Missouri Republican*, May 14, 1863.

Chapter 3 "A Rebel Though She Be": Gender and Missouri's War of the Households

1. Anne Ewing Lane to Sarah Lane Glasgow (Box 9, William Carr Lane Papers, Missouri Historical Society, St. Louis, Missouri), June 28, 1863.

2. This war between the women has gone largely unnoted by historians although the picture of southern as "she devils" and the intense loyalty of women on both sides has been discussed at some length. Reid Mitchell, *The Vacant Chair: The Northern Soldier Leaves Home* (New York, Oxford University Press, 1993), 89–114; Nina Silber, *The Romance of Reunion, Northerners and the South* (Chapel Hill, University of North Carolina Press, 1993), 13–38; Charles Royster, *The Destructive War: William Tecumseh Sherman, Stonewall Jackson, and the Americans* (New York, Vintage Press, 1993), 86–87; L. P. Brockett, *Woman's Work in the Civil War: A Record of Heroism, Patriotism and Patience* (Philadelphia, Zeiger, McCurdy & Co., 1867), 781. On the early and intense Union sympathies of some women in St. Louis, see Hannah Stagg, "Local Incidents of the Civil War," in *Missouri Historical Society Collections*, vol. 4, 1912–1913, 63–72 and Paula Coalier,

"Beyond Sympathy: The St. Louis Ladies Aid Society and the Civil War," *Gateway Heritage* 11, no. 1 (Summer 1990): 39–51.

3. Mrs. Samuel McRee, Files of Individual Citizens, U.S. Provost Marshal Records, Reel #1371, Missouri State Archives, Jefferson City, Missouri.

4. William Glasgow Bruce Carson, "Anne Ewing Lane," *Missouri Historical Bulletin* 21, no. 2 (January 1965): 87–99 and "Secesh," *Missouri Historical Bulletin* 23, no. 2 (January 1967): 119–145.

5. The Civil War as unexpectedly and frequently wrenchingly transformative of women's peacetime roles regardless of region, class, or race is a long-standing and central theme in the study of women and the Civil War. See, e.g., Judith Ann Giesberg, *Civil War Sisterhood*; Elizabeth D. Leonard, *Yankee Women: Gender Battles in the Civil War* (New York, W.W. Norton, 1994); Mary Elizabeth Massey, *Bonnet Brigades* (New York, Knopf, 1966) in the North. For the South, see, Nancy Bercaw, *Gendered Freedoms: Race, Rights and the Politics of the Delta, 1861–1875* (Gainesville, FL., University of Florida Press, 2003) 19–50; Victoria Bynum, *Unruly Women: The Politics of Social Control in the Old South* (Chapel Hill, University of North Carolina Press,1992), 111–150; Drew Gilpin Faust, *Mothers of Invention: War of the Slaveholding South in the Civil War* (Chapel Hill, University of North Carolina Press, 1995); Anne Scott, *The Southern Lady: From Pedestal to Politics* (Chicago, 1970), 81–102; LeeAnn Whites, *The Civil War as a Crisis in Gender: Augusta, Georgia, 1860–1890* (Athens, University of Georgia Press, 1995).

6. William Carr Lane to John Law (William Carr Lane Papers), July 24, 1861.

7. Anne Ewing Lane to Sarah Lane Glasgow (Box 8, William Carr Lane Papers), undated fragment, probably 1862.

8. Juliette B. Garesche, Files of Individual Citizens, U.S. Provost Marshal Records, Reel #1189, Missouri State Archives, Jefferson City, Missouri.

9. Anne Ewing Lane to Sarah Lane Glasgow (Box 9, William Carr Lane Papers), February 23, 1863.

10. Anne Lane to Sarah Lane Glasgow (Box 8, William Carr Lane Papers), January 12, 1862.

11. Juliette B. Garesche File, U.S. Provost Marshal Records, Reel #1189.

12. Ibid.

13. Anne Ewing Lane to Sarah Lane Glasgow (Box 8, William Carr Lane Papers), January 12, 1862.

14. St. Louis *Missouri Democrat*, December 12, 1861. See also December 14, 1862 and December 21, 1861.

15. St. Louis *Missouri Democrat*, February 11, 1862. See also February 4, 1862. On guerilla warfare in the state, see Michael Fellman, *Inside War: The Guerilla Conflict in Missouri during the Civil War* and on the particular experience of southern sympathizers in St. Louis, see Louis S. Gerteis, *Civil War St. Louis* (Lawrence, KA, University of Kansas Press, 2001), 169–201.

16. St. Louis *Missouri Republican*, December 3, 1861 and December 5, 1861.

17. St. Louis *Missouri Democrat*, February 11, 1862.

18. "Protest to Major General Halleck," Box 1, William McPheeters's Papers, Missouri Historical Society, St. Louis, Missouri.

19. Ibid.

20. Ibid.

21. Scrapbook Clippings, Box 1, William McPheeters's Papers.

22. St. Louis *Missouri Democrat*, February 4, 1862.

23. Scrapbook Clippings, Box I, William McPheeters's Papers.

24. "Reasons for Joining the Southern Army," July 24, 1865, Box 1, William McPheeters's Papers.

25. Ibid.

26. Ibid.

27. Ibid., "Banishment of My Wife," July 27, 1865, Box 1, William McPheeters's Papers.

28. Ibid

29. Sallie McPheeters, Files of Individual Citizens, U.S. Provost Marshal Records, Reel #1371.

30. Ibid.

31. Mrs. Samuel McRee, Files of Individual Citizens, U.S. Provost Marshal Records, Reel #1371.

32. Ibid.

33. Ibid.

34. Anne Ewing Lane to Sarah Lane Glasgow (Box 8, William Carr Lane Papers), September 1862.

35. Anne Ewing Lane to Nannie (Box 9, William Carr Lane Papers), March 9, 1864.

36. Mrs. William R. McLure, Files of Individual Citizens, U.S. Provost Marshal Records, Reel #1370. For McClure's own recollection of these events see, *Reminiscences of the Women of Missouri during the Sixties*, Missouri Division, United Daughters of the Confederacy, Compiler (Jefferson City, Missouri, 1912), 78–84.

37. Mrs. William R. McLure, U.S. Provost Marshal Records.

Chapter 4 Home Guards and Home Traitors: Loyalty and Prostitution in Civil War St. Louis

1. Jennie Atwood File, f. 1220, Individual Citizen Files, U.S. Provost Marshal Records, Missouri State Archives, Jefferson City, Missouri.

2. Anonymous to McKinstry, August 29, 1861; McKinstry to General (illegible), September 23, 1861, Letters and Orders sent by the Provost Marshal, e. 1732, Record Group 393 (hereinafter RG 393), Part IV, National Archives, Washington D.C. (hereinafter NARA).

3. Social histories of Civil War soldiers have focused primarily upon the field and camp experience of soldiers, as in the now classic work of Bell Irvin Wiley, *The Common Soldier in the Civil War* (New York, Grosset & Dunlap, 1952) and more recently such works as Reid Mitchell, *Civil War Soldiers* (New York, Viking Press, 1988) and Gerald F. Linderman, *Embattled Courage: The Experience of Combat in the Civil War* (New York, Free Press, 1987). More recently Civil War historians have begin to consider the relationship between soldiers and female civilians, as in Michael Fellman, *Inside War: The Guerilla Conflict in Missouri during the Civil War* (New York, Oxford University Press, 1989), 193–230 and Reid Mitchell, *The Vacant Chair: The Northern Soldier Leaves Home* (New York, Oxford University Press, 1993). New work promises to further expand our understanding of the military experience from the perspective of the female citizen, see Victoria Bynum, *Unruly Women: Sexual and Social Control in the Old South* (University of North Carolina Press, 1992); Jacqueline Glass Campbell, *When Sherman Marched*

North from the Sea: Resistance on the Confederate Home Front (Chapel Hill, University of North Carolina Press, 2003); Lisa Tendrich Frank, "To Cure her of Pride and Boasting': The Gendered Implications of Sherman's March," Ph.D. Diss., University of Florida, 2001; and Kirsten Lenore Streater, "She-Rebels on the Border: Gender and Politics in Civil War Kentucky," Ph.D. Diss., University of Kentucky, 2001. On the question of prostitution and the Civil War, see E. Susan Barber, "Depraved and Abandoned Women: Prostitution in Richmond, Virginia, across the Civil War," in *Neither Lady Nor Slave: Working Women of the Old South*, Susanna Delfino and Michele Gillespie, eds. (Chapel Hill, University of North Carolina Press, 2002), 155–173; Catherine Clinton, *Public Women and the Confederacy* (Milwaukee, Marquette University Press, 1999); and Thomas P. Lowry, *The Story the Soldiers Wouldn't Tell: Sex and the Civil War* (Mechanicsburg, Pennsylvania, Stackpole Books, 1994).

4. S. T. Glover to Col. B. G. Farrar (Letters Received, St. Louis Post, e. 1146, RG 393, Part IV, NARA), January 2, 1862.
5. Ibid. In a similar vein, Fellman also observes the significance of sexual practices to the perception of honorable personal and military conduct among Missouri guerillas in *Inside War*, 205–214.
6. On prostitution in antebellum St. Louis, see, Jeffrey S. Adler, "Streetwalkers, Degraded Outcasts, and Good for Nothing Hussies: Women and the Dangerous Class in Antebellum St. Louis" *Journal of Social History* 25, no. 4, 737–756, 1992. For antebellum attitudes toward prostitution more generally, see, Timothy J. Gilfoyle, *City of Eros: New York City, Prostitution and the Commercialization of Sex, 1790–1920* (New York, W.W. Norton, 1992); Helen Leftkowitz, *Rereading Sex: Battles over Sexual Knowledge and Suppression in Nineteenth Century America* (New York, Knopf, 2002); Carroll Smith-Rosenberg, *Disorderly Conduct: Visions of Gender in Victorian America* (New York: A.A. Knopf, 1985); Nancy Isenberg, *Sex and Citizenship in Antebellum America* (Chapel Hill, University of North Carolina Press, 1998).
7. *Missouri Republican*, July 31, 1861.
8. Ibid.
9. *Missouri Democrat*, February 2, 1863.
10. For a discussion of the general circumstances of St. Louis during the War, see Louis Gerteis, *Civil War St. Louis* (Lawrence, KS, University Press of Kansas, 2001) and James Neal Primm, *Lion of the Valley: St. Louis, Missouri, 1764–1980* (St. Louis, Missouri Historical Society Press, 1998, 3rd ed.), 227–271. On the Civil War hospitals of St. Louis, see William E. Parrish, "*The Western Sanitary Commission*," Civil War History, March 1990, vol. 36, 17–35. While the problem of disorder was a serious one, given the number of soldiers stationed in the city or passing through, it is difficult to assess the typical behavior of the enlisted man. The first annual report of the soldier's reported that 12,000 soldiers went through the home and while it noted that "many" of those men "proved themselves unworthy of the assistance and hospitality," and "some" became "intoxicated and made beasts of themselves" nonetheless it concluded that "nearly all" "evidenced . . . true manhood." *Missouri Republican*, March 21, 1863.
11. *Missouri Republican*, August 1, 1861.
12. *Missouri Republican*, August 3, 1861.

13. *Missouri Republican Triweekly*, May 12, 1861.

14. George Julius Engelmann, "Journal," August 30, 1861, Missouri Historical Society, St. Louis, Missouri.

15. *Missouri Republican*, August 14, 1861. See also, *Missouri Republican Triweekly*, August 16, 1861, November 26, 1861 and *Missouri Democrat*, September 16, 1861, June 10, 1863.

16. Letters and Orders Sent by the Provost Marshal, Orders 1–21.

17. Ibid., Orders 36, 41. The first Police Board, created on April 10, 1861 when southern sympathizers still controlled much of the formal political apparatus of the city and the state, increased the size of the police force to 320 men in order to watch the acts of the United States troops stationed in the city. When martial law was established and a new Police Commissioner was appointed by the Provost Martial, he purged the police force of disloyal members, reducing the size of the force to 175 men. Despite repeated requests from the now loyal police force for a return to their original number, the force never numbered more than 225 men throughout the war. *Mayor's Message with Accompanying Documents submitted to the Common Council of the City of St. Louis*, St. Louis Police Library, St. Louis, April 29, 1862: May 11, 1863.

18. Letters and Orders Sent by the Provost Marshal, September 1, 1861; August 25, 1861; August 28, 1861, e. 1732. For a list of more banned newspapers, See Special Orders, e. 1738, May 10, 1863, RG 393, Part IV, NARA.

19. While historians have discussed the violation of citizen's civil liberties during the war at some length, they have given little consideration to this sort of domestic discipline as an integral part of military policy. See Mark Grimsley, *The Hard Hand of War: Union Military Policy Toward Southern Civilians* (New York, Cambridge University Press, 1995); Mark Neely, *The Fate of Liberty: Abraham Lincoln and Civil Liberties* (New York, Oxford University Press, 1991); and Phillip Paludin, *Victims: A True Story of the Civil War* (Knoxville, University of Tennessee Press, 1981).

20. Engelmann, "Journal," August 30, 1861.

21. *Missouri Republican Triweekly*, August 27, 1861.

22. For a statement of the basic policy, see Special Orders, September 24, 1862, e. 1738. Here the initial order is no liquor and no soldiers in any drinking saloon on punishment of arrest and being permanently shut down. However, the Order of October, 12, 1863, that only soldiers found in low saloons, dance houses of "other disreputable places" would be arrested appears more likely to have been the policy actually enforced. James E. Yeatman, one of the Western Sanitary Commissioners, put the situation bluntly in a letter to the Provost Marshal in September of 1864. "There is no controlling liquor consumption among the troops. 8–12 cases of Dts in hospital in the last week. Can't you do something?" Letters Received, St. Louis Post, e. 1146, September 12, 1864, RG 393, Part IV, NARA. See also *Missouri Republican*, September 14, 1861; September 10, 1861; September 29, 1861; January 17, 1862 on military liquor policy.

23. R. J. Howard to Gen. McKinistry ("Citizen File," e. 2636, Box 1, RG 393, Part I, NARA), September 6, 1861; Engelmann, *Journal*, September 23, 1861.

24. Letters and Orders Sent by the Provost Marshal, August 29, 1861, e. 1732, RG 393, Part IV, NARA.

25. The Provost Marshal's orders reflect this pattern of constant arrest, release, and sometimes rearrest of the same saloonkeepers. See Orders 281, 394, 32,

83, 79, 313. While allowed to reopen, it was frequently upon the condition of "no lewd women" or dance halls, see Orders 71, 160, 162. The newspapers followed these openings and closing, see *Missouri Republican*, January 27, 1862; March 28, 1862; September 2, 1863; September 8, 1863; December 9, 1863; November 30, 1864; December 14, 1864; April 17, 1864.

26. On the extent of soldier resistance to Union military policy on alcohol consumption, see Special Orders, e. 1738, October 12, 1863. The Provost Marshal in St. Louis even went so far as to order that anyone purchasing Union officer uniforms must immediately cut off the buttons and dye them another color. Anyone caught wearing any portion of recognizable Union officer uniforms would be arrested and any uniforms known to be sold for such purposes were to be confiscated. Special Orders, e. 1738, October 12, 1863. See also, March 4, 1864 and March 22, 1864.

27. e. 2953, Box 11, October 17, 1863.

28. Guard reports of orderly officers and prostitutes. "Navy officers are in the habit of visiting low dance houses in this city in full uniform. A public prostitute was found above the public dance houses in the uniform of a naval officer." Capt. A. J. Edgerton, Commanding, Prov. Guard to Major OD Greene, AA General.

29. *Mayor's Message with Accompanying Documents Submitted to the Common Council of the City of St. Louis*, April 29, 1862 and June 16, 1864.

30. E. W. Prewitt to Maj. Gen. Rosencrans, "Citizen File," e. 1146, Part IV, RG 393.

31. *Missouri Republican*, February 26, 1864: E. W. Prewitt to Maj. Gen. Rosencrans.

32. E. W. Prewitt to Maj. Gen. Rosencrans. Some saloonkeepers were sent to prison for serving liquor to men they thought could drink because on furlough. See, *Missouri Democrat*, March 16, 1864.

33. Frustrated citizens took matters into their own hands, as with the neighborhood riot where Moll Whitney's establishment was sacked. The citizens were fined $25 for rioting and Moll Whitney continued on in business. The press could only note in response to the judgment: "The law in regard to such houses as the one kept by this woman is so worded that while it fixes a heavy penalty, it is almost impossible to obtain a conviction. Our legislators are 'too squeamish' to pass legislation and thus they remain a pest to the community and a curse to society. Until they have the 'courage' to deal with it, we shall not be rid of this great social evil." *Missouri Republican*, December 9, 1864.

34. Name illegible to CC Allen, Captain and Provost Marshal, November 23, 1863, "Citizen File," e. 2636.

35. Ibid.

36. Amos P. Foster, Capt., April 16, 1863, "Citizen File," e. 2636.

37. R. R. Livingston, Col. Comdg. Cavalry to Provost Marshal, November 16, 1863, e. 2593, Box 10. As the war continues reports of victimized soldiers increases. See *Missouri Republican*, November 30, 1863; January 15, 1864, October 14, 1864 and *Missouri Democrat*, December 24, 1861; September 2, 1863; October 14, 1864; October 30, 1863; and October 28, 1864. Finally, the Provost Marshall orders the prostitutes from Almond Street, the lowest street in town to be evicted and replaces them with 30 homeless Union refugee families.

38. Letters and Orders Sent by the Provost Marshal, September 23, 1861, e. 1732.

39. Kate Graham, f. 1330, Individual Citizen Files, U.S. Provost Marshal Records, Missouri State Archives, Jefferson City, Missouri.
40. John Gallagher, f. 1330, Individual Citizen Files, U.S. Provost Marshal Records, Missouri State Archives, Jefferson City, Missouri.

Chapter 5 "Stand By Your Man": The Ladies Memorial Association and the Reconstruction of Southern White Manhood

1. Augusta *Chronicle and Sentinel*, April 14, 1865.
2. Anne Firor Scott, *The Southern Lady: From Pedestal to Politics, 1830–1930* (Chicago, University of Chicago Press, 1971). For a different view on this issue, see, Jean Friedman, *The Enclosed Garden: Women and Community in the Evangelical South, 1830–1900* (Chapel Hill, University of North Carolina Press, 1985); Jean Bethe Eltshain, *Women and War* (New York, Basic Books, 1987); and George Rable, *Civil Wars: Women and the Crisis of Southern Nationalism* (Urbana, University of Illinois Press, 1989).
3. One notable exception is Suzanne Lebsock, whose *Free Women of Petersburg: Status and Culture in a Southern Town, 1784–1860* (New York, Norton, 1984) points to the way white women gained power indirectly, through the economic difficulties of their husbands, which led to the establishment of separate estates for their wives.
4. Historians of gender roles have now begun to consider how the war affected southern white men. See, e.g., Nina Silber, "Intemperate Men, Spiteful Women, and Jefferson Davis," and Victoria Bynum, "Reshaping the Bonds of Womanhood: Divorce in Reconstruction North Carolina," in *Divided Houses: Gender and the Civil War*, Clinton and Silber, eds. (New York, Oxford University Press, 1992), 283–305, 320–334; and LeeAnn Whites, *The Civil War as a Crisis in Gender: Augusta, Georgia, 1860–1890* (Athens, GA, University of Georgia Press, 1995).
5. For an extensive discussion of the history of Confederate monuments, see Gaines Foster, *Ghosts of the Confederacy: Defeat, the Lost Cause and the Emergence of the New South* (New York, Oxford University Press, 1987).
6. Augusta Ladies Memorial Association Minutes, April 5, 1873, Richmond County Historical Society Collection, Augusta, GA, Augusta *Chronicle and Sentinel*, November 1, 1878. According to this account, 10,000 gathered for the cornerstone laying for the monument on April 26, 1875, and 20,000 three years later for the unveiling. The city's population was under 30,000.
7. Among historians of southern women, Jean Friedman contends that in the postwar period white women's wartime organizations disappeared entirely. Historians of the Confederate memorial tradition are similarly inclined to ignore the very existence of the Ladies Memorial Association. See Gerald Linderman, *Embattled Courage: The Experience of Combat in the American Civil War* (New York, Free Press, 1987), 266–297; and Charles Reagan Wilson, *Baptized in Blood: Religion of the Lost Cause, 1865–1920* (Athens, GA, University of Georgia Press, 1980). Foster's, *Ghosts of the Confederacy*, an exception to this pattern, includes a chapter on the organization; however, he concludes that because the Ladies Memorial Association was "within the realm of sentiment," it had few "ideological or political implications" and

"did not offer a coherent historical interpretation of the war and therefore did little to define the Confederate Tradition," 46.

8. See, e.g., "A History of the Origin of Memorial Day as Adopted by the Ladies Memorial Association of Columbus, Georgia" (Columbus, 1898); Marielou Armstrong Cory, "The Ladies Memorial Association of Montgomery, Alabama: Its Origin and Organization, 1860–1870" (Montgomery, AL, 1902), 57–58.

9. Augusta *Chronicle and Sentinel*, June 7, 1861.

10. Anne Firor Scott notes the connection between the soldiers' aid societies and the Ladies Memorial Associations in *Natural Allies: Women's Associations in American History* (Chicago, University of Chicago Press, 1991). The Augusta, GA, Columbus, GA, Charleston, SC, Montgomery, AL, and Raleigh, NC associations all follow this pattern. For a further discussion of these cases, see Charles Colcock Jones and Salem Dutcher, *Memorial History of Augusta, Georgia* (Syracuse, NY, D. Mason, 1890), 181; Marielou Armstrong Cory, *The Ladies Memorial Association of Montgomery, Alabama, 1860–1870* (Montgomery, Alabama printers Co., 1902); P. F. Pescud, *A Sketch of the Ladies Memorial Association of Raleigh, NC: Its Origin and History* (Raleigh, NC, s.n. 1882); James G. Holmes, ed., *Memorials to the Memory of Mrs. Mary Amarintha Snowden* (Charleston, SC, s.n. 1898); and United Daughters of the Confederacy, corp. author, *History of the Origin of Memorial Day* (Columbus, Georgia, T. Gilbert, 1898).

11. For a graphic discussion of the difficulties of disinterring and burying decaying bodies in leaky, hastily constructed coffins, see Pescud, *Sketch of the Ladies Memorial Association*. For a discussion of the difficulties of returning the soldiers to their place of origin, see *Confederate Memorial Day at Charleston, SC: Reinterment of the Carolina Dead from Gettysburg* (Charleston, SC, 1871). In the Charleston case, it was not until six years after the war that the bodies were reclaimed from Gettysburg.

12. Not only did women assert this politicized view of their domestic labors as a result of the demise of the Confederacy, the local press and prominent spokesmen for the Confederate memorial tradition did as well. See, e.g., the speeches of Charles Colcock Jones, "Annual Addresses Delivered before the Confederate Survivors Association in Augusta, Georgia" (Augusta, 1879–1891). Jones was the lifetime president and founder of the Augusta Confederate Survivors Association.

13. *History of the Origin of Memorial Day*, 24–25.

14. Ibid., 6.

15. For a further discussion of the relationship between southern white men's position as heads of household and their "liberties" in the antebellum South, see Elizabeth Fox-Genovese, *Within the Plantation Household: Black and White Women of the Old South* (Chapel Hill, University of North Carolina Press, 1988), 37–99; and Stephanie McCurry, *Masters of Small Worlds: Yeoman Households, Gender Relations, and the Political Culture of the South Carolina Low Country* (New York, Oxford University Press, 1995), 37–91. For a discussion of the way the Civil War and Reconstruction transformed that relationship, see Whites, *Civil War as a Crisis in Gender*, esp. chap. 5.

16. Whites, *Civil War*, 30, 25.

17. Augusta *Chronicle and Sentinel*, April 2, 1873.

18. The association between the Confederate dead and the war's survivors was a frequent topic of memorializing speeches. See, e.g., the speeches of one prominent Georgia Confederate Memorial Day speaker, Joseph B. Cumming, in Occasional Addresses (Augusta, Ga., n.d.).

19. Holmes, "Memorials to the Memory of Mrs. Mary Amarintha Snowden," 22–25. Mrs. Snowden's career is archetypal. Wife of a prominent Charleston doctor, she took up hospital work during the war. Widowed and impoverished after the war with a family to support, she mortgaged her only asset, her home, to finance the establishment of a home for Confederate widows and orphans, simultaneously employing herself and her sister.

20. For example, see Rebecca Latimer Felton, *Country Life in the Days of My Youth* (Atlanta, Index Printing Company, 1919), 95–107, 270–272.

21. A study of the officers of the Ladies Memorial Association of Augusta indicated that of the 25 officers of the organization who could be identified, more than half held positions as officers in other organizations, the most common being the widows' home, but other organizations included the King's Daughters, the Women's Exchange, the United Daughters of the Confederacy and the Woman's Christian Temperance Union. The organizational work of some of these women over their lifetimes is truly staggering. Take, for instance, the case of Catherine Rowland, who was the wife of a cotton commission merchant in the town and a young matron at the time of the Civil War. In the war's aftermath, she held the position of president of the Ladies Memorial Association, director of the Widows' Home, member of the executive committee of the Women's Exchange, president of the King's Daughters, and vice president of the United Daughters of the Confederacy, although not all at the same time. Ella Gertrude Clanton Thomas, young wife of a substantial planter, followed a similarly prodigious postwar organizational career: vice president of the Ladies Memorial Association, officer of the WCTU, recording secretary of the UDC, and finally president of the Atlanta woman's suffrage association.

22. Susan Lawrence Davis, *Authentic History of the Ku Klux Klan, 1865–1877* (New York, American Library Service, 1924), 8. The story of the origins of the KKK has been told repeatedly. See also John C. Lester and Daniel L. Wilson, *Ku Klux Klan: Its Origin, Growth and Disbandment* (New York, The Neale Publishing Company, 1905); Stanley F. Horn, *Invisible Empire* (Boston, Houghton Mifflin Company, 1939); Walter L. Fleming, *The Sequel of Appomattox* (New Haven, Yale University Press, 1919); and more recently, William Randall, *The Ku Klux Klan: A Century of Infamy* (Philadelphia, Chilton Books, 1965); and Allen Trelease, *White Terror: The Ku Klux Klan Conspiracy and Southern Reconstruction* (New York, Harper & Row, 1971).

23. H. Grady McWhiney and Francis B. Simkins make a strong case, using interviews with Klan victims from the U.S. congressional investigation conducted in 1871, that the black population was not taken in by this "ghostly" attire but rather feared the violence employed by the Klan against them. See McWhiney and Simkins, "The Ghostly Legend of the KKK," *Negro History Bulletin* 16 (1950–1951): 109–111. See also Gladys-Marie Fry, *Night Riders in Black Folk History* (Knoxville, University of Tennessee Press, 1975).

24. Davis, *Authentic History of the Ku Klux Klan*, 88.

25. Lester and Wilson, *Ku Klux Klan: Its Origin, Growth and Disbandment* and John C. Reed, *The Brothers' War* (Boston, Little, Brown and Company, 1905)

were both participant accounts. Mr. and Mrs. W. B. Romine, *History of the Original Ku Klux Klan* (Pulaski, TN, Pulaski Citizen, 1934) and Davis, *Authentic History of the Ku Klux Klan* were written by descendants of Klan members. They all present the organization as grounded in domestic defense.

26. Romine and Romine, *History of the Original KKK*, 15.
27. Davis, *Authentic History of the KKK*, 310.
28. Ibid., 90. As in the "White Life for Two" advocated by the WCTU. Ted Ownby, *Subduing Satan: Religion, Recreation and Manhood in the Rural South, 1865–1920* (Chapel Hill, University of North Carolina Press, 1990), discusses this postwar "domestication" of southern white men.
29. Randall, *The Ku Klux Klan*, 14. See also Trelease, *White Terror*, xii.
30. For a further discussion of this theory, see Charlotte Perkins Gilman, *Women and Economics* (Boston, Small, Maynard & Company, 1898), esp. 99–145.

Chapter 6 "You Can't Change History By Moving a Rock": Gender, Race, and the Cultural Politics of Confederate Memorialization

1. The use of such stone markers was commonplace in mid-Missouri at the time. The UDC erected almost identical commemorative stones at the Confederate Soldiers's Home at Higgensville and also at the state capitol in Jefferson City. While official UDC records do not discuss the reason for their use of granite boulders, the placement of the picture of the unveiling of the stone in Columbia next to a large picture of the Rock of Gibraltar in the Columbia Chapter's scrapbook is suggestive. While the Rock of Gibraltar had stood unconquerable since ancient times, speculation in 1935 was that it would fall to the modern technology of German warfare, much as the Confederacy was alleged by the UDC to have fallen because of the superior industrial might of the North, despite its stalwart and "rock like" defense. John S. Marmaduke Scrapbook, 1931–1935, Belle Troxell Collection, Western Historical Manuscripts, University of Missouri, Columbia Missouri. For a further discussion of Confederate monuments in the state see, "Monuments and Memorials in Missouri," *Missouri Historical Review* 19, no. 4 (July 1925): 555–603; and "Civil War Monuments and Battle Sites," Vertical File, Missouri State Historical Society, Columbia, Missouri.
2. On the history of the United Daughters of the Confederacy, see Karen L. Cox, *Dixie's Daughters: The United Daughters of the Confederacy and the Preservation of Confederate Culture* (Gainesville, Florida, University Press of Florida, 2003) and Mary B. Poppenheim et al., *The History of the United Daughters of the Confederacy* (Raleigh, NC, Edwards Broughton Company, 1925). See also, Fred Bailey, "Mildred Lewis Rutherford and the Patrician Cult of the Old South," *Georgia Historical Quarterly* (Summer 1994): 509–535 and "The Textbooks of the 'Lost Cause' Censorship and the Creation of Southern State Histories' " *Georgia Historical Quarterly* (Summer 1991): 507–533; "A Monument to Southern Womanhood: The Founding Generation of the Confederate Museum," in *A Woman's War: Southern Women, Civil War, and the Confederate Legacy*, Edward D. C. Campbell, Jr. and Kym S. Rice, eds. (Charlottesville,

University of Virginia Press, 1996), 131–163; Angie Parrott, "Love Makes Memory Eternal?: The United Daughters of the Confederacy in Richmond, Virginia, 1897–1920," in *The Edge of the South: Life in Nineteenth Century Virginia*, Edward Ayers and John Willis, eds. (Charlottesville, University of Virginia Press, 1991), 219–238.

3. On the role of monuments and memorialization more generally in mediating contemporary social conflicts see, David W. Blight, *Race and Reunion: The Civil War in American Memory* (New York, Belknap Press, 2001); John Bodnar, *Remaking America: Public Memory, Commemoration and Patriotism in the Twentieth Century* (Princeton, Princeton University Press, 1992) and *Bonds of Affection: Americans Define Their Patriotism*, John Bodnar, ed. (Princeton, Princeton University Press, 1996) and *Where These Memories Grow: History, Memory and Southern Identity*, W. Fitzhugh Brundage, ed. (Chapel Hill, Chapel Hill University Press, 2000).

4. Mrs. Foster Martin to Mrs. SC (Margaret Blight) Hunt, March 12, 1925, Hunt Family Papers, Western Historical Manuscripts Collection, University of Missouri-Columbia, Columbia, Missouri.

5. On the Ladies Memorial Association, see Gaines M. Foster, *Ghosts of the Confederacy: Defeat, the Lost Cause and the Emergence of the New South, 1865–1913* (New York, Oxford University Press, 1987), 36–46. LeeAnn Whites, *The Civil War as a Crisis in Gender* (Athens, Georgia, University of Georgia, 1995), 160–198; and Catherine Bishir, "A Strong Force of Ladies: Women, Politics and Confederate Memorial Associations in Nineteenth Century Raleigh," *North Carolina Historical Review*, 77, no. 4 (October 2000): 455–491.

6. Mary Tucker Clipping, Scrapbook #1, United Daughters of the Confederacy Collection, John S. Marmaduke Chapter. On guerilla warfare in Columbia, see *History of Boone County, Missouri*, William Switzler, comp. (St. Louis, 1882), 43–53; and Thomas Prather, "Unconditional Surrender: The Civil War at the University of Missouri-Columbia, 1860–1865," April 10, 1989, paper in the possession of the Missouri State Historical Society, Columbia, Missouri. On guerilla war in Missouri see, Gerald Fellman, *Inside War: The Guerrilla Conflict in Missouri during the American Civil War* (New York, Oxford University Press), 1989; Richard S. Brownlee, *Gray Ghosts of the Confederacy: Guerilla Warfare in the West, 1861–1865* (Baton Rouge, Louisiana State University, 1958); and Albert E. Castel and Thomas Goodrich, *Bloody Bill Anderson, The Short, Savage Life of a Civil War Guerila* (Mechanicsburg, PA, Stackpole Books, 1998).

7. *Reminiscences of the Women of Missouri during the Sixties*, Missouri Division, United Daughters of the Confederacy, comp. (Jefferson City, 1912). Benedict Clipping, Scrapbook #1, United Daughters of the Confederacy Collection, John S. Marmaduke Chapter.

8. Ann Hickam Clipping, Scrapbook #1, John S. Marmaduke Chapter, United Daughters of the Confederacy, Western Historical Manuscript Collection, University of Missouri, Columbia, Missouri.

9. *The Confederated Memorial Association* (New Orleans, Graham Press, 1904), 215–226.

10. Minutes of the Third Annual Meeting of the Missouri Division of the United Daughters of the Confederacy (Fayette, Mo, 1900), 1–6.

R. B. Rosenberg, *Living Monuments: Confederate Soldiers' Homes in the New South* (Chapel Hill, University of North Carolina Press, 1993). Although monuments to many Union generals, including Ulysses S. Grant, Nathaniel Lyon, and Frank Blair were erected in the state as early as 1873, there were no major Confederate monuments until the first decade of the twentieth century. Vertical File, Civil War Monument and Battle Sites.

11. John S. Marmaduke Chapter Scrapbook, 1931–1935, Belle Alexander Troxell Collection.

12. Minutes of the Marmaduke Chapter, April 1924, United Daughters of the Confederacy Collection.

13. Floyd C. Shoemaker, "Missouri—Heir of Southern Tradition and Individuality," *Missouri Historical Review* (July 1942): 438–446.

14. Delia Crutchfield Cook, "Shadow across the Columns: The Bittersweet Legacy of African Americans at the University of Missouri," Ph.D. Diss., University of Missouri-Columbia, 1996. Uncle Jack Clipping, Scrapbook #1, United Daughters of the Confederacy Collection, John S. Marmaduke Chapter.

15. On the African American experience in Missouri, see Lorenzo Greene, Gary R. Kremer, Antonio Holland, *Missouri's Black Heritage* (Columbia, University of Missouri Press, 1993).

16. On the wartime experience of African Americans in the state see Ira Berlin et al., *Slaves No More: Three Essays on Emancipation and the Civil War* (Cambridge, 1992), 60–76; Green et al., *Missouri's Black Heritage*, 62–87; Michael Fellman, "Emancipation in Missouri," *Missouri Historical Review* 83 (October, 1988): 36–56; John W. Blassingame, "The Recruitment of Negro Troops in Missouri during the Civil War," Missouri *Historical Review* 68 (April 1964): 326–338; and Suzanna Maria Grenz, "The Black Community in Boone County, 1850–1900," Ph.D. Diss., University of Missouri-Columbia, 1979.

17. Switzler, *History of Boone County*, 433; John W. Blassingame, "The Recruitment of Negro Troops in Missouri During the Civil War."

18. Grenz, "The Black Community in Boone County," 27, 172.

19. For a further discussion of the particular experience of black slave women in the Civil War, see Jacqueline Jones, *Labor of Love, Labor of Sorrow: Black Women, Work and the Family From Slavery to the Present* (New York, Basic Books, 1985); Leslie Schwalm, *"A Hard Fight For We": Women's Transition of From Slavery to Freedom in South Carolina* (Urbana, University of Illinois Press, 1997); and Thavolia Glymph, "This Species of Property: Female Slave Contrabands in the Civil War," in *A Woman's War: Southern Women, Civil War and the Confederate Legacy*, 55–71.

20. *Missouri Statesman*, July 22, 1864, 3.

21. *Missouri Statesman*, November 25, 1864, 3

22. As cited in Greene et al., *Missouri's Black Heritage*, 91.

23. In the 1868 registration of voters, only 411 of the county's 3,411 white men were allowed to vote, the other 3,000 were disqualified for their wartime southern sympathies. Switzler, *History of Boone County*, 495–496. They would not regain the vote until 1871, and by that time the regional orientation of the state had been fundamentally altered. See Fellman, *Inside War*, 231–266.

24. Grenz, "The Black Community in Boone County," 30–37. The historical work that perhaps best reflects this white cultural hegemony is the only monograph on slavery in the state, Harrison A. Trexler, *Slavery in Missouri, 1804–1865* (Baltimore, Johns Hopkins Press, 1914). Based in large part on the recollections of slaveowners or their descendants in the state, it argues that close and harmonious relations between master and slave that persisted into the postwar era particularly characterized Missouri, as a small slaveholding state.

25. Greene et al., *Missouri's Black Heritage*, 140–157.

26. Vertical File, "Student Activism," University of Missouri Archives, University of Missouri-Columbia, Columbia, Missouri.

27. *Black Out*, Legion of Black Collegians Collection, UM-C College Ephemera, Collection #3628, Western Historical Manuscript Collection, University of Missouri, Columbia, Missouri. Interviews with Tommy Mendenholl, August 3, 1999, and William Berry, October 8, 1999, Columbia, Missouri.

28. *Black Out*, Legion of Black Collegians Collection.

29. Ibid.

30. Columbia *Daily Tribune*, October 5, 1971.

31. Ibid.

32. *Black Out*, Legion of Black Collegians Collection.

33. Columbia *Daily Tribune*, October 12, 1971.

34. Columbia *Missourian*, April 5, 1974; April 26, 1974; Columbia *Daily Tribune*, April 26, 1974; April 30, 1974; August 16, 1974; Columbia *Missourian*, August 17, 1974.

35. Columbia *Daily Tribune*, October 29, 1974; November 5, 1974; December 4, 1974; Columbia *Missourian* , December 6, 1974.

36. Columbia *Daily Tribune*, March 30, 1988.

37. Columbia *Daily Tribune*, October 21, 1995. See also October 29, 1995.

38. Columbia *Daily Tribune*, October 21, 2001. See also, October 16, 2001; October 29, 2001; November 6, 2001; November 8, 2001; November 10, 2001; November 13, 2001; November 20, 2001; and December 7, 2001.

39. Columbia *Missourian*, October 15, 1971.

40. Columbia *Daily Tribune*, October 8, 2001. See also April 6, 2001.

41. According to the local NAACP, the flying of the Confederate Flag from the student's dorm room window continues to be a kind of litmus test of local race relations. "The atmosphere at the University that makes a student comfortable flying a rebel flag, brings again the question of how the University of Missouri is actually doing in the area of race relations? Not very good in my opinion." Columbia *Daily Tribune*, December 7, 2001. On the other hand, there was no publicly expressed opposition to the flying of Confederate flags at the dedication of the new Civil War memorial in the town, perhaps partly because the Monument Committee, made largely of members of the local Sons of Confederate Veterans, made a point of collecting the names of the county's black as well as the white Civil War dead. The monument itself was designed to accommodate the addition of more names, pointing to the very real possibility of an even blacker memorial tradition to come in Boone County. Interview with William Berry, Chairman, Boone County Civil War Monument Committee, January 23, 2002, Columbia, Missouri.

Chapter 7 Paternalism and Protest in Augusta's Cotton Mills: What's Gender Got to Do with It?

1. For a later expansion of Mitchell's argument, see Wilbur J. Cash, *Mind of the South* (New York, Vintage, 1941).

2. Melton MuLaurin takes this position in *Paternalism and Protest; Southern Cotton Mill Workers and Organized Labor, 1875–1905* (Westport, CT, Greenwood Press, 1971). As does Bess Beatty, "Textile Labor in the North Carolina Piedmont: Mill Owners Images and Mill Worker Responses, 1830–1900," *Labor History* 25, no. 4 (Fall, 1984).

3. The story of these strikes has been told in several places. See McLaurin, *Paternalism and Protest;* Marl E. Reed, "Augusta Textile Mills and the Strike of 1886," *Labor History* 14, no. 2 (Spring, 1973): 228–246; Richard German, "Augusta Strike of 1898–1899," *Richmond County History* 4, no. 6 (Winter, 1972): 35–48.

4. Two studies of Augusta's hinterlands, source for most of the town's operatives, describe yeoman farmers in these terms; see J. William Harris, *Plain Folk and Gentry in a Slave Society: White Liberty and Black Slavery in Augusta's Hinterland* (Middletown, CT, Wesleyan University Press, 1985) and Orville Vernon Burton, *In My Father's House Are Many Mansions: Family and Community in Edgefield, South Carolina* (Chapel Hill, University of North Carolina Press, 1985). In fact, Augusta's hinterlands provided the most concentrated support for the Populist Party in Georgia in the 1890s, as Barton C. Shaw, *Wool-Hat Boys: Georgia's Populist Party* (Baton Rouge: Louisiana State University Press, 1984) has demonstrated. Augusta's textile workers were also militant supporters of the movement and of Tom Watson in particular; C. Vann Woodward, *Tom Watson: Agrarian Rebel* (New York, Oxford University Press, 1963).

5. Jacquelyn Dowd Hall, James Leloudis, Robert Korstad, Mary Murphy, LuAnn Jones, and Christopher Daly, *Like A Family: The Making of a Southern Cotton Mill World* (Chapel Hill, University of North Carolina Press, 1987) and Jacquelyn Dowd Hall, Robert Korstad, and James Leloudis, "Cotton Mill People: Work, Community, and Protest in the Textile South, 1880–1940," *American Historical Review* 91, no. 2 (April 1986): 245–286.

6. See, e.g., John W. Blassingame, *Slave Community: Plantation Life in the Plantation South* (New York, Oxford University Press, 1972). Herbert Gutman, *Black Family in Slavery and Freedom 1750–1925* (New York, Pantheon Press, 1976); and Eugene D. Genovese, *Roll, Jordan, Roll: The World the Slaves Made* (New York, Vintage, 1976).

7. McLaurin, *Paternalism and Protest,* 41–61.

8. These findings are based on a study of all households that included at least one millworker in the Augusta manuscript census. For a more extended discussion of the analysis, see LeeAnn Whites, "Southern Ladies and Millhands: The Domestic Economy and Class Politics, Augusta, Georgia, 1870–1890," PhD. Diss., University of California at Irvine, 1982, ch. 4.

9. For a further discussion of historians' treatment of black manhood, see Deboran Gray White, *Ar'n't I a Woman? Female Slaves in the Plantation South* (New York, Norton Press, 1985). Elizabeth Fox-Genovese has perhaps carried this assumption that white gender roles are the only gender roles further than any other historian, arguing that under slavery black women had

no gender; see Elizabeth Fox-Genovese *Within the Plantation Household: Black and White Women of the Old South* (Chapel Hill, University of North Carolina Press, 1988).

10. For a further discussion of changes that were occurring in the social construction of male gender roles, see Ted Ownby, *Subduing Satan: Religion, Recreation and Manhood in the Rural South, 1865–1920* (Chapel Hill, University of North Carolina Press, 1990). Anthony Rotundo, *American Manhood: Transformations in Masculinity from the Revolution to the Modern Era* (New York, Basic Books, 1993). Gail Bederman, *Manliness and Civilization: Multicultural History of Gender and Race in the United States, 1880–1917* (Chicago, University of Chicago Press, 1995).

11. For a further discussion of the limited occupational options for women in the town, see "Occupations of Women" *Augusta Daily Constitutionalist*, August 26, 1860. Although the relationship among the situation of widowed rural women, gendered migration to urban centers, and pressure for the development of new forms of industry to employ these women in towns where they congregated has received scant attention in the case of the South, Alice Kessler-Harris discusses the situation in rural New England in similar terms in *Out to Work: A History of Wage Earning Women* (New York, Oxford University Press, 1982), 17–23.

12. Catherine Barnes Rowland, Diary; entry for November 4, 1863, Georgia State Archives, Atlanta.

13. For a further discussion of the factors behind the establishment of this mill, see Griffen, "Augusta Manufacturing Company," and "Origins of the Industrial Revolution." Also, see Detreville, "Little New South."

14. The reference to the mill as a "gold mine" during the war was made by its president, John Phinizy, while he was being interviewed about the mill years later; U.S. Senate, *Capital and Labor*, 4:697. For a discussion of the benevolence and patriotism of the mill during the war itself, see *Augusta Chronicle*, April 24, 1863, October 28, 1863, October 29, 1863, November 3, 1863.

15. U.S. Senate, *Capital and Labor*, 5:697.

16. Ibid., 741.

17. Ibid.

18. Ibid., 699.

19. One Augusta capitalist, Hamilton Hickman, described this annual migration out of the countryside: "Every fall, especially when there have been poor crops, we have a number of country people who have been broken up on their farms and who come into Graniteville with their families to put them in the mill, and in many cases the children have to support the parents"; U.S. Senate, *Capital and Labor*, 5:740. In his study of Augusta's hinterlands, J. William Harris found that in 1860, 14–24% of all farm operators were renters. Conditions had deteriorated by 1880, and renters had increased to 26–30% of all farms in the counties he studied; J. Harris, *Plain Folk and Gentry*. The next step was to give up altogether and move to the mill, a process that Gavin Wright describes as a "sorting mechanism, in which families with the fewest resources and poorest prospects in agriculture found that the family unit could do better in the mill village"; Gavin Wright, *Old South, New South: Revolutions in the Southern Economy since the Civil War* (New York, Basic Books, 1986), 138. The process was similar to the one described earlier for the antebellum period, except that male-headed

households were being squeezed out to a much greater extent as the countryside was increasingly subordinated to the dictates of urban market forces.

20. Here, I rely upon officially compiled statistics for the Augusta mill workforce rather than my own research, which is based on the manuscript census in order to be consistent with the 1890 returns, available only in this form. U.S. Census Office, *Tenth Censuses*, 2:383, 379, 19(2):163; *Eleventh Censuses*, 6(2):44–49; *Twelfth Census*, 8(2):992–993, 9(3):32.

21. Wright, *Old South, New South*, 138–139, gives general figures for the shifting gender and age composition of the southern textile workforce that reflect the same pattern as that of Augusta, although at a somewhat later date. He finds a decline from 57.2% female in 1880 to 44.3% female in 1900 to 36.7% female in 1920. Wright is inclined to dismiss the role of gender in structuring the mill workforce, especially the role of Civil War widows, as he finds the predominance of females in the 1880 mill workforce to be concentrated in the age bracket between 16 and 24. In the Augusta case, however, the majority of those single females were daughters of widowed women who were of an age to have been widowed during the war.

22. U.S. Senate, *Capital and Labor*, 795.

23. Although the relationship between the influx of women into previously male-dominated areas of the workforce and the development of labor militancy in an effort to preserve laboring conditions has been discussed in several places for this period, perhaps most notably in the case of the turn-of-the-century garment industry, scant attention has been paid to the reverse case, where men entered a previously female-dominated industry. On women entering male domains, see Joan Jenson and Sue Davidson, eds., *A Needle, A Bobbin, A Strike: Women Needleworkers in America* (Philadelphia, Temple University Press, 1984); Ruth Milkman, ed., *Women, Work and Protest: A Century of U.S. Labor History* (Boston, Routledge, 1985); Ava Baron, ed., *Work Engendered: Toward a New History of American Labor* (Ithaca, NY, Cornell University Press, 1991).

24. For a further discussion of the Knights, see Kim Voss, *The Making of American Exceptionalism: The Knights of Labor and Class Formation in the Nineteenth Century* (Ithaca, Cornell University Press, 1993); Leon Fink, *Working Men's Democracy: The Knights of Labor and American Politics* (Urbana, University of Illinois Press, 1983); Gerald Grob, *Workers and Utopia: A Study of Ideological Conflict in the American Labor Movement, 1845–1900* (Evanston, IL, Northwestern University Press, 1961); Melton McLaurin, *Knights of Labor in the South* (Westport, CT., Greenwood Press, 1978).

25. Along with the demand for the abolition of the pass system and a general wage increase, the Knights also demanded an increase in machinists' wages, an end to "overworking," May 1 as a holiday, the understanding that no Knight would be required to replace a discharged Knight without investigation, and agreement that the employer would discuss hirings with the Knights; *Augusta Chronicle*, January 7, 1886. This local was also responsible for the first petition for child labor legislation that was presented to the Georgia legislature. The politics of promoting the position of male heads of household is particularly apparent here, as the Knights hoped to improve male wages by eliminating competition from children. McLaurin, *Paternalism and Protest*, discusses the Augusta Knights' role in promoting child labor legislation.

26. McLaurin, *Paternalism and Protest*, 105.
27. *Augusta Chronicle*, August 10, 1886.
28. McLaurin, *Paternalism and Protest*, 106.

Chapter 8   The De Graffenried Controversy: Class, Race, and Gender in the New South

1. Clare de Graffenried, "The Georgia Cracker in the Cotton Mills," *Century Magazine* XLI (February 1891): 483–498. This was only 1 of some 20 articles that De Graffenried wrote on similar topics; it alone focused on the South. See Lala Carr Steelman, "Mary Clare de Graffenried: The Saga of a Crusader for Social Reform," in *Studies in the History of the South, 1875–1922*, Joseph F. Steelman et al., eds. (Greenville, NC, Department of History, East Carolina College, 1966), 53–83, for a more general discussion.
2. See the *Manufacturers' Record* XIX, February 7, 1891, May 23, 1891, June 13, 1891, as well as the *Wool Hat*, July 20, 1892. Various Georgia dailies covered the story, among them the *Augusta Chronicle* and the *Atlanta Constitution*, as well as other southern mill areas outside the state, for instance the Greenville (SC) *Daily News* and the Montgomery *Advertiser*.
3. De Graffenried, "Georgia Cracker in the Cotton Mills," 483.
4. Ibid., 491 (fourth quotation), 493 (first, second, and third quotations).
5. Ibid., 497 (first quotation), 483, 497 (second quotation), 493 (third quotation), 486 (fourth quotation), 484–485 (fifth quotation).
6. Ibid., 493.
7. Ibid., 486 (first and second quotations), 496 (third quotation).
8. Ibid., 495 (first quotation), 496 (second quotation), 493 (third quotation), 484 (fourth quotation), 488 (fifth quotation).
9. Ibid., 488.
10. Ibid., 493.
11. Ibid., 486 (first, second, and third quotations), 493 (fourth quotation).
12. Ibid., 498.
13. Clare de Graffenried, " 'The Georgia Cracker in the Cotton Mills': Miss De Graffenried Explains the Motive of Her Much Discussed Article," *Manufacturers' Record* XIX (June 13, 1891).
14. Clare de Graffenried, "Child-Labor," *Publications of the American Economic Association* V (March 1890), 196.
15. Although the Woman's Christian Temperance Union, under the influence of Frances Willard, had by this date become increasingly committed to promoting social reform from a gender perspective, the development of reform specific to the problems of labor had to await the work of settlement-house reformers of the mid-1890s. See Ruth Bordin, *Women and Temperance: The Quest For Power and Liberty* (Philadelphia, Temple University Press, 1981); Jane Addams, *Twenty Years at Hull-House* (New York, New American Library, 1960); Allen F. Davis, *Spearheads for Reform: The Social Settlements and the Progressive Movement, 1890–1914* (New York, Oxford University Press, 1967). In the South, with the notable exception of De Graffenried's article, similar agitation for the improvement of living and working conditions of millworkers did not develop until the early twentieth century. See David L. Carlton, *Mill and Town in South Carolina, 1880–1920* (Baton Rouge, Louisiana State University Press, 1982). Although De Graffenried continued to produce a

spate of articles in the 1890s on subjects bearing on the status of wage-earning women and children, she never ventured to write another article focused entirely on southern conditions.

16. *Manufacturers' Record* XIX (February 7, 1891), 1.
17. Ibid.
18. See Josephine Bone Floyd, "Rebecca Latimer Felton, Political Independent," *Georgia Historical Quarterly* XXX (March 1946): 14–34; and Floyd, "Rebecca Latimer Felton, Champion of Women's Rights," *Historical Quarterly* XXX (June 1946): 81–104.
19. J. F. Hanson to R. L. Felton, March 3, 1891, Rebecca Latimer Felton Papers (Special Collections, University of Georgia Library, Athens, Georgia). Other relevant correspondence in this collection includes letters from D. H. Speer, president of the Exposition Cotton Mills, Atlanta; a letter from the president of the Roswell Manufactory Company, Roswell. Georgia; and a letter from the editor of the *Manufacturers' Record*, which later endorsed De Graffenried's position. They all offer their encouragement and support for her defense of the southern textile mill industry.
20. J. F. Hanson to R. L. Felton. April 14, 1891, Felton Papers.
21. J. F. Hanson to R. L. Felton, March 3, 1891, Felton Papers.
22. Ibid.
23. Rebecca Latimer Felton. "Address to Mill workers at Roswell, Georgia." manuscript speech, n.d., Felton Papers.
24. J. F. Hanson to R. L. Felton, March 3, 1891, Felton Papers.
25. Rebecca Latimer Felton, "Address to Mill Workers at Roswell, Georgia."
26. *Augusta Chronicle*, May 10, 1891.
27. *Atlanta Constitution*, newspaper clipping, n.d., Felton Papers.
28. *Augusta Chronicle*, May 10, 1891.
29. Ibid.
30. Ibid.
31. Ibid.
32. Manuscript Census Returns. Tenth Census of the United States, 1880, Richmond County, Georgia. Schedule I—Population. For a fuller discussion of the relationship between the structure of the family and the workplace among Augusta millworkers see LeeAnn Whites. "Southern Ladies and Millhands: The Domestic Economy and Class Politics; Augusta, Georgia, 1870–1890" (unpublished Ph.D. diss. University of California, Irvine, 1982), chaps. 5 and 6.
33. Tenth Census, 1880, Richmond County. Schedule I. Hall, Korstad, and Leloudis arrive at similar conclusions concerning the persistence and even increased significance of family and community among millworkers during this period. Jacquelyn Dowd Hall, Robert Korstad, and James Leloudis, "Cotton Mill People: Work, Community, and Protest in the Textile South, 1880–1940," *American Historical Review* XCI (April 1986): 245–286.
34. There was only one male household head listed as unemployed out of 199 male household heads, nine listed themselves as disabled, and seven of these were over 50. Whites, "Southern Ladies and Millhands," 207. The poverty of the community was not so much the result of slackard men but rather the absence of adult male wage earners in an economy that failed to pay women a living wage on the assumption that every woman was, in one way or another, supported by a male wage earner.

35. De Graffenried. "Georgia Cracker in the Cotton Mill," 496 (first quotation), 486 (second and third quotations); Felton, "Address to Mill Workers at Roswell. Georgia." Felton's emphasis on the situation of female-headed households is intended not only to demonstrate the way in which the mills offered a better life for such women and children but also to defuse fears of the impact of integrating women into wage labor. If the mill owners acted as substitute fathers and husbands, then despite the fact that these women were not contained within a paternalistic family structure, they continued to be protected and dominated by some male figure. It was, after all, Felton herself who chose to focus on the question of morality among millworkers. This reflects a typical nineteenth-century attitude toward the probable impact of integrating women into wage labor and thereby freeing them, if only in part, from their subordinate domestic status. See Alice Kessler-Harris, *Out to Work: A History of Wage-Earning Women in the United States* (New York, Oxford University Press, 1982), for a more general discussion of this question. To integrate women into wage labor was tantamount to freeing them from sexual restraints and would lead to immorality and the decline of good domestic order. The assumption that an autonomous woman was by definition an immoral woman was still a common prejudice and one that Felton tried to rebut in her reply to De Graffenried.

36. In interviews conducted by a U.S. Senate investigative committee on the status of labor and capital in 1883, Augusta mill owners claimed that female factory workers could actually make twice as much money working in cotton factories as they could in any other occupation. "You take a girl and put her into a sewing-house here and she has got to work very hard to make 50 cents a day, and many cannot do that. . . . Now, these girls (in the factory), when they understand the business, will make from $1 to $1.25 a day, and you cannot put an ordinary woman at any work outside a factory at which she can make that much." Senate Committee on Education and Labor, 49 Cong., 2 Sess., *Report . . . Upon the Relations Between Labor and Capital* (5 vols.; Washington, G.P.O. 1885), IV, 741 (quotation), 754. A millworker wrote to the *Augusta Daily Chronicle and Constitutionalist* to point out the advantages of millwork when compared with rural wage labor for women. "It is not surprising that girls refuse to become scrubs in the country, when it is a well known fact that even farmers' wives are worked to a shoe string and die young. No, sir; for one, I'll take my chances in the city, where I am regarded as an equal of all with whom I work and associate." *Augusta Daily Chronicle and Constitutionalist*, July 26, 1882.

37. Fetton, "Address to Mill Workers at Roswell, Georgia."

38. Tenth Census, 1880, Richmond County, Schedule I. Female-headed households also played a larger role in the mill workforce than their numbers alone would indicate because a larger percentage of their members were employed by the mills than in male-headed households. Whereas 59% of all members of female-headed households were employed by the mills, only 46% of members of male-headed households were so employed. Whites, "Southern Ladies and Millhands," chap. 5. These differences reflect the wider opportunities for men in the workforce than for women and the greater dependence, therefore, of female-headed households upon mill employment. These households also tended to concentrate in the heart of the mill district, while male-headed households tended to be more

dispersed, another factor contributing to their significance in the community as a whole.

39. De Graffenried made passing reference to the economic difficulties that forced her to leave the state in her rebuttal to Felton's critique of her work. "If there is one Georgian whom necessity has forced into exile who has never rooted either home or affections elsewhere, who clings to her vicarious citizenship, who is held in proven and precious loyalty in the hearts of numberless friends, it is I," *Augusta Chronicle*, May 24, 1891.

40. Felton, "Cotton Mill Labor in Georgia," manuscript speech, n.d., Felton Papers.

41. Here Rebecca Felton's racial politics, as in the case of her class politics, were subsumed by gender categories. She was primarily concerned about maintaining what appeared to be the material prerequisites for a proper gender division of labor. Not only had the economic devastation and death of men exposed white women to market forces in a new way, but the emancipation of the slaves had also exposed them to a fundamental challenge to the racial hierarchy, a fact symbolized in Felton's mind by the image of white women reduced to field labor. As economic conditions continued to deteriorate in the 1890s, Felton held on to this gendered perspective—that the failure of white men to "protect" their women resulted in the "exposure" of white women. Ultimately this broke forth as a virulent racism on Felton's part; the whole gender problem was displaced upon black men who were accused of raping white women. See Rebecca Latimer Felton, "Racial Problems," manuscript speech, n.d., Felton Papers; Joel Williamson, *The Crucible of Race: Black-White Relations in the American South Since Emancipation* (New York, Oxford University Press, 1984); Jacquelyn Dowd Hall, " 'The Mind That Burns in Each Body': Women, Rape and Racial Violence," in *Powers of Desire: The Politics of Sexuality*, Ann Snitow, Christine Stansell, and Sharon Thompson, eds. (New York, Monthly Review Press, 1983), 328–349.

42. *Augusta Chronicle*, May 26, 1891.

43. Clare de Graffenried, "Child-Labor," *Publications of the American Economic Association* V (March 1890): 196.

44. *Manufacturers' Record* XIX (June 13, 1891), 5.

45. *Augusta Chronicle*, May 29, 1991.

46. Ibid., May 24, 1891.

47. Ibid.

48. Ibid., May 29, 1891.

49. Ibid.

50. Ibid.

51. Clare de Graffenried to Rebecca Latimer Felton, May 22, 1891, Felton Papers.

52. Ibid. De Graffenried did, in fact, write several articles for the working-girls' newspaper, *Far and Near*, published by the National League of women workers in New York. Titles include "An Active Club Eighteen Years Old" 1, no. 4 (February 1891); "Co-operation in Maryland," 1, no. 10 (August 1891); "London Siftings—What English Workers Do" 1, no. 3 (January 1891); and "Trades-Unions for Women" III, no. 27 (January 1893).

53. For a further discussion of Rebecca Felton's background, her own recollections are invaluable. See Rebecca Latimer Felton, *Country Life in Georgia in*

the Days of My Youth (Atlanta, Index Printing Company, 1919). There is also an engaging biography by John E. Talmadge, *Rebecca Latimer Felton: Nine Stormy Decades* (Athens, University of Georgia Press, 1960). Aside from Lala Carr Steelman's article "Mary Clare de Graffenried" see Anne Floor Scott, *The Southern Lady: From Pedestal to Politics, 1830–1930* (Chicago, University of Chicago Press, 1970), 121–133. There is some genealogical material in the De Graffenried Papers. Southern Historical Collection (University of North Carolina, Chapel Hill). See in particular Thomas P. de Graffenried, "Miss Mary Clare de Graffenried" typescript, n.d. Unfortunately the interviews with workers upon which her articles were based have apparently been destroyed, per correspondence with Jerry N. Hess of the Scientific, Economic and Natural Resources Branch, Civil Archives Division, National Archives, Washington, D. C. Hess to Whites, February 14, 1986, in author's possession.

54. Although Mary Clare de Graffenried was her given name, De Graffenried published under the name of Clare de Graffenried. She acquired her initial government position as a copyist in the Patent Office in May 1886 through the influence of L. Q. C. Lamar, Secretary of the Interior and a friend of her father. Two months later she became an investigator for the newly founded Bureau of Labor, where she remained until she retired in July 1906. Steelman, "Mary Clare de Graffenried," 54–55.

55. Clare de Graffenried, "The 'New woman' and Her Debts," *Appletons' Popular Science Monthly* XLIX (May–October 1896): 666–667. This article was originally delivered to the graduating class of the Pratt Institute in Brooklyn, a new school of industrial education for women. For further discussion of the New Woman's role in gender politics according to De Graffenried see "The Needs of Self Supporting Women," *Journal of the Tenth Biennial Meeting of the International Conference of Women's Christian Associations*, October 24, 1889; "The Condition of Wage-Earning Women," *Forum* XV (March–August 1893): 68; and "Some Social and Economic Problems," *American Journal of Sociology* 11 (September 1896): 190–201.

56. De Graffenried, "The 'New Woman,' " 667.

57. *Manufacturers' Record* XIX (June 13, 1891), 5.

58. Rebecca Latimer Felton, "Education of Veterans' Daughters," typescript, n.d., Felton Papers.

59. Ibid.

60. Ibid.

61. Rebecca Latimer Felton, "Books and Education" typescript, n.d., Felton Papers.

62. Felton, "Education of Veterans' Daughters."

63. Felton, "Address to Mill Workers at Roswell, Georgia."

64. Ibid.

65. Ibid.

66. Ibid.

67. Ibid.

68. Ibid.

69. Ibid.

70. Felton, "Education of Veterans Daughters."

71. Rebecca Latimer Felton, "Temperance," manuscript speech, 1892, Felton Papers. There are many temperance speeches in Felton's papers, but they all

tend to be very similar. This particular version was delivered at the Lithia Springs (Georgia) Chautauqua in 1892.

72. Felton, "Education of Veterans Daughters."
73. *Augusta Chronicle*, May 24, 1891.
74. Ibid., May 26, 1891.
75. De Graffenried, "Child-Labor," 196.
76. See Jonathan M. Wiener, *Social Origins of the New South: Alabama, 1860–1885* (Baton Rouge, Louisiana State University Press, 1978), especially chap. 7 for a fuller discussion of this position.
77. For further discussion of southern labor's attempts to organize during this period see Melton Alonza McLaurin, *Paternalism and Protest: Southern Cotton Mill Workers and Organized Labor, 1875–1905* (Westport, CT, Greenwood Publishing Corp, 1971). McLaurin stresses the difficulty of organizing in the textile industry when many mills were located in isolated rural settings. For this reason, he argues, the most militant organizational efforts in the industry occurred in Augusta, Georgia, where there was a concentration of urban mills. Even in Augusta, however, efforts to organize were met by mill management with lockouts and recruitment from rural areas to break the Unions. For a specific discussion of strike-breaking efforts see Merl E. Reed, "The Augusta Textile Mills and the Strike of 1886," *Labor History* XIV (Spring 1973): 228–246; and Richard H. L. German, "The Augusta Textile Strike of 1898–1899," *Richmond County Historical Journal* IV (Winter 1972): 37–49.
78. See, e.g., the response to one Union organizing effort in the Augusta mitts in the winter of 1896. *Augusta Chronicle*, December 10, 1896, December 20, 1896, and December 24, 1896.
79. German, "The Augusta Textile Strike of 1898–1899," discusses the ready availability of white rural labor used to break the strike. The letter book of one of the Augusta mill superintendents offers an informative correspondence between the superintendent and potential rural recruits during the strike. The correspondence is largely to card grinders, one of the more skilled positions in the mills, who were undoubtedly difficult to replace in a way that unskilled workers were not. See Joe Smith Correspondence, January 16, 1899, January 18, 1899, and January 19, 1899, King Mills (King Mill Vault, Augusta, GA). Gavin Wright discusses the generally depressing impact of the condition of black labor upon white labor in the south during this period in *Old South, New South: Revolutions in the Southern Economy Since the Civil War* (New York, Basic Books, 1986), chap. 6.
80. By the late 1890s the growth of the southern textile industry served further to threaten southern labor organization. Owners of older southern mills found that they were being undercut by newer, "cheaper" labor in the Piedmont. The response of the older southern mill owners was to cut the wage rates. "The Officers of the different mills were contemplating calling a meeting of the Manufacturers' Association to take into consideration the advisability of reducing wages to as near as basis possible as that paid by competitors in the Piedmont Section. The feeling was general that now was the most opportune time to do so. The difference between pay here and the Piedmont section was known to be 20 to 25% lower than ours and the impression seemed to be that the officers of the different Mills should get together and adopt a schedule of wages at about 15% from the present rate paid." Minutes of the Board of Directors, June 8, 1897, Sibley Mills

(Graniteville Mill Vault, Graniteville, SC). Workers unsuccessfully attempted to resist this wage cut when they went on strike in 1898.

81. *Augusta Chronicle*, May 24, 1891.

82. De Graffenried, "Georgia Cracker in the Cotton Mills," 497. Not only did the hierarchical racial division of labor set limits on the possibilities for labor reform, but it also affected the possibilities for domestic reform. In discussing how millworking women might save money by doing their own laundry, De Graffenried recorded a revealing conversation. "The traditional prejudice against the washtub ruled the mind of a limp, tattered creature who earned scarcely enough to keep body and soul together. 'You do your own washing?' was innocently demanded. 'Is I a nigger?' quoth she, witheringly," 490.

83. When child labor legislation did come to the South, and to Georgia in particular, the legislation came late and was weak. Nevertheless, its very passage speaks to the relative strength of labor as opposed to women's organizations in the region. Although labor made repeated efforts to get child labor legislation passed in Georgia, usually during the periods of labor militancy, it met with little success. The eventual passage of the legislation was the result of the combined efforts of women's organizations in the state, especially the General Federation of Women's Clubs, and sympathetic ministers. As such it reflects the massive explosion of women's domestic organizations and influence in the 1890s. See Elizabeth H. Davidson, *Child Labor Legislation in the Southern Textile States* (Chapel Hill, University of North Carolina Press, 1939).

Chapter 9 Rebecca Latimer Felton and the Problem of Protection in the New South

1. Rebecca Latimer Felton, *The Romantic Story of Georgia's Women* (Atlanta, Atlanta Georgian and Sunday American, 1930), 44.

2. Ibid., 45.

3. See A. Elizabeth Taylor, "Development of the Woman's Suffrage Movement in Georgia," *Georgia Historical Quarterly* 62 (December 1958): 339–354, and "The Last Phase of the Women's Suffrage Movement in Georgia," *Georgia Historical Quarterly* 63 (March 1959): 11–28.

4. For a discussion of the centrality of protection to antebellum white gender relations, see Bertram Wyatt-Brown, *Southern Honor: Ethics and Behavior in the Old South* (New York, Oxford University Press, 1982). For the ways in which the Civil War stressed the quid pro quo of white southern gender relations, see Victoria E. Bynum, "War within a War: Women's Participation in the Revolt of the North Carolina Piedmont, 1863–1865," *Frontiers* 4, no. 3 (1987): 43–49; Drew Faust, "Altars of Sacrifice: Confederate Women and Narratives of War," *Journal of American History* 76, no. 4 (1990): 1200–1228; Donna D. Krug, "The Folks Back Home: The Confederate Homefront during the Civil War," Ph.D. Diss., University of California, Irvine, 1990; and LeeAnn Whites, "The Civil War as a Crisis in Gender: Augusta, Georgia, 1860–1890" (Athens, Georgia, 1995).

5. The outcome of this wartime rupturing of antebellum gender roles is contested. In her pathbreaking study, *The Southern Lady: From Pedestal to Politics, 1830–1930* (Chicago, University of Chicago Press, 1970), Anne Scott argued

that the Civil War "opened every door" for elite white southern women. More recently, historians have argued in a more pessimistic vein. Suzanne Lebsock, *The Five Women of Petersburg: Status and Culture in a Southern Town, 1784–1860* (New York, W.W. Norton, 1984), suggests that impoverished and defeated white men were not inclined to tolerate increased gender equity with any more equanimity than they greeted the prospect of racial equity. Jean Friedman, *The Enclosed Garden: Women and Community in the Evangelical South, 1830–1900* (Chapel Hill, University of North Carolina Press, 1985), and George Rable, *Civil Wars: Women and the Crisis of Southern Nationalism* (Urbana, University of Illinois Press, 1989), have carried this line of argument further and suggested that the autonomous roles women took up in the context of war had little lasting impact on postwar gender relations. More attention to the experience of individual women whose experience spanned the period may help sort out the nature of the relationship between persistence and change in women's roles and gender relations as well. See Kathleen Berkeley, "Elizabeth Avery Merriwether, 'An Advocate for Her Sex': Feminism and Conservatism in the Post Civil War South," *Tennessee Historical Quarterly* 43 (Winter 1984): 390–407; Joan Cashin, "Varina Howell Davis," in *Portraits of American Women: From Settlement to Present*, C. J. Barker-Benfield and Catherine Clinton, eds. (New York, St. Martin's, 1991), 259–275; and Nell Irvin Painter, "The Journal of Ella Gertrude Clanton Thomas: An Educated White Woman in the Eras of Slavery, War and Reconstruction," in *The Secret Eye: The Journal of Ella Gertrude Clanton Thomas, 1848–1889*, Virginia lngraham Burr, ed. (Chapel Hill, University of North Carolina Press, 1990), 1–67.

6. Treatments of Rebecca Latimer Felton's political career focus almost exclusively on her work in the male political arena. See John E. Talmadge, *Rebecca Latimer Felton: Nine Stormy Decades* (Athens, University of Georgia Press, 1960). See also Josephine Bone Floyd, "Rebecca Latimer Felton, Political Independent," *Georgia Historical Quarterly* 30 (March 1946): 14–84, and "Rebecca Latimer Felton, Champion of Women's Rights," *Georgia Historical Quarterly* 30 (June 1946): 81–104. This focus ignores both the domestic impetus for Felton's participation in the formally constituted male political arena and the interrelated emergence of a whole world of female political activity on Felton's part in the Ladies Aid Societies, Ladies Memorial Association, the United Daughters of the Confederacy, the Woman's Christian Temperance Union, the General Federation of Women's Clubs, as well as the Georgia Woman's Suffrage Association. Anne Scott first outlined this move from "pedestal to politics" among elite white southern women in *The Southern Lady*. See also Friedman, *The Enclosed Garden*, 110–130; Kathleen Berkeley, " 'The Ladies Want to Bring Reform to the Public School?: Public Education and Women's Rights in the Post Civil War South," *History of Education Quarterly* 44 (Spring 1984): 45–58; LeeAnn Whites, "The Charitable and the Poor: The Emergence of Domestic Politics in Augusta, Georgia, 1860–1880," *Journal of Social History* 17 (Summer 1984): 601–615; and Anastatia Sims, "Feminism and Femininity in the New South: White Women's Organizations in North Carolina, 1888–1980," Ph.D. Diss., University of North Carolina at Chapel Hill, 1985.

7. Rebecca Latimer Felton, *Country Life in Georgia in the Days of My Youth* (Atlanta, Index Printing, 1919), 29.

8. Rebecca Latimer Felton, "Impact of the Civil War on Women," May 20, 1892, Felton Papers, Special Collections, University of Georgia, Athens, GA.

9. Scott, *The Southern Lady*, 3–22. See also Catherine Clinton, *Plantation Mistress: Woman's World in the Old South* (New York, Pantheon Books, 1982).

10. Felton, *Country Life*, 25. See also Felton, "Impact of the Civil War on Women." For a more general discussion of the ways race and class position tended to override gender identification, see Jacqueline Jones, *Labor of Love, Labor of Sorrow: Black Women, Work and the Family, from Slavery to the Present* (New York, Basic Books, 1985); and Elizabeth Fox-Genovese, *Within the Plantation Household: Black and White Women of the Old South* (Chapel Hill, University of North Carolina Press, 1989).

11. George Fitzhugh, *Sociology for the South or the Failure of Free Society* (New York, L. 8. Franklin, 1966), 218–214.

12. Felton, *Country Life*, 79–94.

13. Ibid., 104.

14. In her recollections Felton gives a graphic description of the state in which she found her plantation upon returning home: "I never saw the home any more until August, 1865. When I reached the gate I picked up the springs that had been a part of my dead child's fine baby carriage, also the arm of a large parlor mahogany chair that had also burned. Desolation and destruction everywhere, bitter, grinding poverty—slaves all gone, money also." Felton, *Country Life*, 89.

15. Rebecca Latimer Felton, "Education of Veteran's Daughters," 1893, Felton Papers. The fact that Felton came to identify with lower-class white women in the context of her own class fall does not mean that the sentiment was reciprocated. For a discussion of the difference class location could make in the political commitments of Southern women, see Jacquelyn Dowd Hall, "O. Delight Smith's Progressive Era: Labor, Feminism, and Reform in the Urban South"; Dolores Janiewski, *Sisterhood Denied. Race, Gender, and Class in a New South Community* (Philadelphia, Temple University Press, 1985); and Stephanie McCurry, "Their Ways Were Not Our Ways" (Paper delivered at the Southern Historical Association Meeting, Houston, TX, 1985).

16. Felton, "Impact of the Civil War on Women." See also Rebecca Latimer Felton, "Southern Womanhood in Wartimes," n.d., Felton Papers.

17. For a further discussion of this dilemma in the particular context of the nineteenth-century South, see Suzanne Lebsock's analysis of the position of free black women in antebellum Petersburg in *The Free Women of Petersburg*, 87–111. For a similar discussion in a different time and place, see Judith Bennett, "History that Stands Still: Women's Work in the European Past," *Feminist Studies* 14 (Summer 1988): 269–283.

18. Felton, *Country Life*, 88.

19. Felton was inclined to use the same incidents from her life over and over again to illustrate her arguments. In the case of displacing responsibility for the decline of the planter-class onto black men, her favorite example was a story of crop theft. Felton, *Country Life*, 57–59.

20. Talmadge, *Rebecca Latimer Felton*, chap. 5.

21. Felton, *Romantic Story*, 227.

22. Talmadge, *Rebecca Latimer Felton*, 83.

23. Frances Willard, *Woman and Temperance or the Work and Workers of the WCTU* (Hartford, CT, Park Publishing, 1883), 570.

24. Lula Barnes Ansley, *History of the Georgia Woman's Christian Temperance Union from Its Organization, 1883–1907* (Columbus, GA, Gilbert, 1914), 58. For a further discussion of the Georgia Woman's Christian Temperance Union in the nineteenth century, see Henry Anseim Scamp, *King Alcohol in the Realm of King Cotton* (Chicago, Blakely, 1888), 677–678; and, more generally, Ruth Bordin, *Woman and Temperance: The Quest for Power and Liberty, 1873–1900* (Philadelphia: Temple University Press, 1981).

25. Rebecca Latimer Felton, "Temperance," 1892, Felton Papers.

26. Ibid. For a discussion of the centrality of drink to southern male culture, see Ted Ownby, *Subduing Satan: Religion, Recreation, and Manhood in the Rural South, 1865–1920* (Chapel Hill, University of North Carolina Press, 1990).

27. Felton, "Temperance."

28. Ibid.

29. Rebecca Latimer Felton, "Southern Women and Farm Life," n.d., Felton Papers.

30. Rebecca Latimer Felton, "The Before Breakfast Club," 1891, Felton Papers.

31. Felton, "Southern Women and Farm Life." Joel Williamson, *The Crucible of Race: Black White Relations in the American South since Emancipation* (New York, Oxford University Press, 1984), discusses this incident. For a further discussion of race, gender, and the lynching of black men, see Jacquelyn Dowd Hall, *Revolt against Chivalry: Jessie Daniel Ames and the Women's Campaign against Lynching* (New York, Columbia University Press, 1979).

32. Felton, 'The Education of Veteran's Daughters." See also "The Duty and Obligation that Lies on Southern Women," n.d., Felton Papers.

33. Rebecca Latimer Felton, "Rescue Work," n.d., Felton Papers. See also "The Problems that Interest Motherhood," in Felton, *Country Life*, 279–283.

34. Felton, "Rescue Work."

35. Ibid.

36. See, e.g., Rebecca Latimer Felton, "Votes for Women," n.d., Felton Papers, and "Why Am I a Suffragist? The Subjection of Women and the Enfranchisement of Women," in Felton, *Country Life*, 246–260.

37. Felton, "Votes for Women," In retrospect, clear parallels can be drawn between southern black women's efforts to organize to protect themselves against abusive white men or against debilitating stereotypes in their own communities and the organizing efforts of southern white women like Felton, even though white women rarely recognized the similarities between them at the time. See Darlene Clark Hine, " 'We Specialize in the Wholly Impossible': The Philanthropic Work of Black Women," in *Lady Bountiful Revisited: Women, Philanthropy and Power*, Kathleen McCarthy, ed. (New Brunswick, NJ, Rutgers University Press, 1990), 70–93; and Anne Firor Scott, "Most Invisible of All; Black Women's Voluntary Organizations," *Journal of Southern History* 61 (February 1990): 3–22.

38. Felton, "Votes For Women."

39. Ibid.

40. Rebecca Latimer Felton, "Southern Congressman Opposing Equal Suffrage," n.d., Felton Papers. For a further discussion of the relationship

between the woman suffrage movement and the politics of white supremacy in the South, see Marjorie Spruill Wheeler, *New Women of the New South: The Leaders of the Woman Suffrage Movement in the Southern States* (Oxford, Oxford University Press, 1993).

41. Felton, "Southern Congressman Opposing Equal Suffrage."

42. Corinne Stecker Smith to Rebecca Latimer Felton, October 7, 1922, Felton Papers.

43. Henrietta Grossman to Rebecca Latimer Felton, October 3, 1922, Felton Papers.

44. Alice Paul to Rebecca Latimer Felton, October 27, 1922, Felton Papers.

45. F. A. Powell to Rebecca Latimer Felton, October 7, 1922, Felton Papers. For a further discussion of the ways in which political expediency would momentarily elevate white women's political status in the South, see Judith McArthur, "Democrats Divided: Why the Texas Legislature Gave Women Primary Suffrage in 1918" (Paper delivered at the Southern Historical Meeting, Fort Worth, Tex., 1991).

46. As one correspondent described the situation, "Woman is not what she once was, pure and good, and bless her, the fault is not hers that she has changed. Time was when man was her sword and her provider and she, per-force, was above the ten commandments, but man failed, and she was com-pelled to become her own sword and provider so man and woman instead of being one, became competitors.... Alas! The race of Toombs, of Webster and of Calhoun has run out. That is the reason that Women feel impelled to go into politics. Why don't you say it?" H. L. Trisler to Rebecca Latimer Felton, October 27, 1922, Felton Papers.

Chapter 10   Rebecca Latimer Felton and the Wife's Farm: The Class and Racial Politics of Gender Reform

1. The literature on Felton's political career is fairly extensive, no doubt partly because she eventually became the first woman to be appointed to the U.S. Senate. See, for instance, John E. Talmadge, *Rebecca Latimer Felton: Nine Stormy Decades* (Athens, Ga., University of Georgia Press, 1960); Josephine Bone Floyd, "Rebecca Latimer Felton, Political Independent," *Georgia Historical Quarterly* 30 (March 1946): 14–34, and "Rebecca Latimer Felton, Champion of Women's Rights," *Georgia Historical Quarterly* 30 (June 1946): 81–104. She also left a memoir and collection of her speeches, *Country Life in the Days of My Youth* (Atlanta, Index Printing Company, 1919).

2. Lula Barnes Ansley discusses Felton's role in the Woman's Christian Temperance Union in *History of the Georgia Woman's Christian Temperence Union From Its Organization, 1883–1907* (Columbus, GA, 1914). Marjorie Spruill Wheeler discusses her role as a leading southern suffragist in *New Women of the New South: The Leaders of the Woman Suffrage Movement in the Southern States* (New York, Oxford University Press, 1993).

3. Rebecca Latimer Felton, undated newspaper clipping, scrapbook, Rebecca Latimer Felton Papers, Special Collections, University of Georgia libraries (hereinafter cited as "Woman on the Farm"). Although Felton's papers

contain many versions of the speech that she made at Tybee Island, I have only been able to locate this particular version of the speech as it was printed in the local press. After giving the speech at Tybee, she gave it around the state for farmer audiences through the auspices of the Farmer's Institute. See, e.g., "Southern Women and Farm Life," n.d., Felton Papers.

4. This argument for agricultural diversification was undoubtedly a familiar one to her farmer audience. It had received new vigor as market prices for staple crops declined precipitously in the 1880s. For a discussion of organized farmer efforts to promote crop diversification and other agricultural reforms, see Robert McMath, *Populist Vanguard: A History of Southern Farmers' Alliance* (Chapel Hill, University of North Carolina Press, 1975), and Lawrence Goodwyn, *The Populist Moment: A Short History of the Agrarian Revolt in America* (New York, Oxford University Press, 1978); Gavin Wright, *The Political Economy of the Cotton South: Households, Markets, and Wealth in the Nineteenth Century* (New York, Norton, 1978); and Steven Hahn, *The Roots of Southern Populism: Yeoman Partners and the Transformation of the Georgia Upcountry, 1850–1890* (New York, Oxford University Press, 1983) concur with Felton's advocacy of self-sufficiency as one of the few possible alternatives to increasing market indebtedness for the yeoman farmers in the late-nineteenth-century South.

5. It was in making this connection between the position of women on the farm and the plight of southern farms in relation to market forces that Felton made an original contribution to the discussion of agricultural reform. The role of women and gender issues in the development of southern agricultural politics has received scant attention from southern historians as well. See Julie Roy Jeffrey, "Women in the Southern Farmers' Alliance: A Reconsideration of the Role and Status of Women in the Late Nineteenth Century South," in *Our American Sisters: Women in American Life and Thought,* Jean Friedman and William Shade, eds. (Lexington, MA, D.C. Heath, 1982), 348–371, and Elizabeth Fox-Genovese, "Women in Nineteenth Century Agriculture," in *Agriculture and National Development: Views on the Nineteenth Century,* Lou Ferleger, ed. (Ames, Iowa, Iowa State University Press, 1990). For a more general discussion of women's roles see Joan Jensen, *With These Hands: Women Working on the Land* (Westbury, NY, Feminist Press, 1981) and Rachel Ann Rosenfeld, *Farm Women: Work, Farm and Family in the United States* (Chapel Hill, University of North Carolina Press, 1985).

6. "Woman on the Farm." Here we see that the wife herself contributes to the market focus, turning her own and her children's labor to her husband's effort to produce the market crop. She is "enslaved" to her husband, who is enslaved to the market. Felton's description of the situation of southern farm women is largely confirmed in the interviews of Margaret Jarman Hagood in *Mothers of the South: Portraiture of the White Tenant Farm Woman* (Chapel Hill, University of North Carolina Press, 1939).

7. "Woman on the Farm."

8. Ibid. The relationship between the decline of agriculture and the increased participation rate of white farmer class women in wage labor, particularly textile production, is discussed by Jacquelyn Dowd Hall et al., *Like a Family: The Making of a Southern Cotton Mill World* (Chapel Hill, University of North Carolina Press, 1987).

9. For a further discussion of ways in which the development of wage labor, for women has served to contextualize women's unpaid domestic labor, see Teresa L. Amott and Julie A. Matthaei, *Race, Gender and Work* (Boston, South End Press, 1991), 291–314; Julie Matthaei, *An Economic History of Women in America: Women's Work, The Sexual Division of Labor and the Development of Capitalism* (New York, Shocken Books, 1982); and Claudia Goldin, *Understanding the Gender Gap: An Economic History of American Women* (New York, Oxford University Press, 1990), 10–57.

10. "Woman on the Farm."

11. Ibid. (italics mine).

12. This "domestic reform" politics was not particular to Felton but was the basic approach of the leading women's reform organization of the South in the 1880s, the Woman's Christian Temperance Union. The first commitment of the Union was to work to make men more responsible to the interests of their families, not to "liberate" women from their domestic position. See Lulu Barnes Ansley, *History of the Georgia Woman's Christian Temperance Union from Its Organization, 1883–1907* (Columbus, GA, Gilbert Printing Co, 1914) and more generally, Ruth Bordin, *Women and Temperance: The Quest for Power and Liberty, 1873–1900* (Philadelphia, Temple University Press, 1981), and Barbara Leslie Epstein, *The Politics of Domesticity: Women, Evangelism and Temperance in Nineteenth Century America* (Middletown, CT, Wesleyan University Press, 1981).

13. Rebecca Latimer Felton, "Southern Chivalry: The Wife's Farm—The Husband's Pledge!" Felton Papers.

14. "Woman on the Farm."

15. At this point in her Tybee Island speech, Felton asked the farmers who had participated in the program to stand up. She claimed to have such a farm, as did her neighbors. As late as 1903, she received a letter thanking her for establishing the program. Ela James Sims to Rebecca Latimer Felton, June 14, 1903, Felton Papers.

16. Felton, *Country Life in the Days of My Youth*, 94.

17. Ibid., 86–87.

18. See Elizabeth Fox-Genovese, *Within the Plantation Household: Black and White Women of the Old South* (Chapel Hill, University of North Carolina Press, 1988) and Nell Irvin Painter, "An Educated White Woman in the Eras of Slavery: War and Reconstruction," her introduction to Virginia Ingraham Burr, ed., *The Secret Eye: The Journal of Ella Gertrude Glanton Thomas, 1848–1889* (Chapel Hill, University of North Carolina Press, 1990) for a further discussion of the manner in which white women's control of black women's domestic labor created the groundwork for their position as mistress of the plantation, both during and after slavery. Felton's own response was on the one hand to resent the way that men of the planter class were empowered in gendered terms by the institution of slavery, while using her own privileged class and race position in relation to her slaves to aggrandize her own domestic position. Thus she militantly refused to see the integrity of any family unit on the plantation, except as an extension of her own. To illustrate just how happy this "family" was, she told a story repeatedly of her mammy, who was sold in order that she might live with her husband, since his owner was unwilling to sell him to the Feltons. In Felton's account,

"mammy" returned shortly to her, with the plea that she buy her back—an indication, according to Felton, of mammy's priorities—first to Felton's family and then to her own husband, Rebecca Latimer Felton, "Southern Womanhood In Wartimes," Felton Papers.

19. Felton, *Country Life in the Days of My Youth*, 93.

20. C. Vann Woodward, ed., *Mary Chesnut's Civil War* (New Haven, CT., Yale University Press, 1981), 169.

21. Anne Firor Scott, *The Southern Lady: From Pedestal to Politics, 1830–1930* (Chicago, University of Chicago Press, 1970) traces the relationship between southern white men's defeat in the Civil War and the emergence of white women onto the public arena in the postwar era.

22. Felton went so far as to assert in this speech that poor white farm women were so debilitated by the difficulties of their situation that they had come to make up over 75% of the state's insane asylum population. In other farm speeches she simply argued that they were literally working themselves to death. "Woman on the Farm."

23. Ibid. The lynching portion of Felton's speech has been discussed by Joel Williamson, *The Crucible of Race: Black–White Relations in the American South since Emancipation* (New York, Oxford University Press, 1984), 424–430. See also Jacquelyn Dowd Hall, *Revolt against Chivalry: Jesse Daniel Ames and the Women's Campaign against Lynching* (New York, Columbia University Press, 1974) for a discussion of how lynching black men was related to the suppression of white women in the late-nineteenth-century South.

24. "Woman on the Farm." For a further discussion of this tragic fusion between the failure of "protection" for white women and race reaction in early-twentieth-century Georgia, see Nancy MacLean, "The Leo Frank Case Reconsidered: Gender and Sexual Politics in the Making of Reactionary Populism," *Journal of American History* 78 (December 1991): 917–948, and "White Women and Klan Violence in the 1920s: Agency, Complicity and the Politics of Women's History," *Gender and History* 3 (Autumn 1991): 287–303. In the case of North Carolina, see Anastatia Sims, "Protecting the 'White Goddess of Democracy': White Supremacy and the Southern Lady in North Carolina," paper delivered at the Second Southern Conference on Women's History, Chapel Hill, June 1991.

25. "Woman on the Farm." Needless to say, this speech elicited editorial response from all over the country, the analysis of which tends to break down along race and regional lines—the southern white press affirming her speech, the New England and the southern black press condemning her. By far the most famous reply came from A. L. Manly, a black newspaper editor in Wilmington, NC, who asserted that it was not a question of rape at all, but of white women preferring black men. In some ways Manly concurred with Felton's assessment of white men. He pointed out in his editorial that Felton was right, white men were notoriously careless about their women, leaving them without sufficient "protection." As a result of this editorial, Manly was forced to flee town, his press was burned and a race riot ensued. See H. Leon Prather, *We Have Taken a City: The Wilmington Racial Massacre and Coup of 1898* (Rutherford, NC, Fairleigh Dickinson University Press, 1984).

26. "Women on the Farm." Felton discusses the question of the black man and the vote repeatedly in her speeches and in her newspaper rebuttals to her critics. See "The Race Problem in the United States," "Lynching and its Causes," and "Mrs. Felton vs. Manly," Felton Papers.

27. "Woman on the Farm."

28. The fact that Felton feared the possibility of sexual relations between black men and white women was occasionally alluded to in her writings. Take for instance her rebuttal to the *Boston Transcript's* critique of her Tybee island speech. In the midst of discussing the alleged rape of white women by black men, she argued, "It is the younger class of negroes that have enjoyed the tutelage of the Boston Transcript and its admirers, and who have preached social and political equality as a 'man and brother' to the young and ignorant colored men, and whose apparent aspiration seems to be to level all distinctions between the African and the Anglo-Saxon races, not only in Massachusetts, but also in Georgia—to make this amalgamation and unity complete." Here she seems to slide from rape to interracial sex. "Mrs. Felton's Reply," Felton Papers.

29. Felton, "The Race Problem in the United States."

30. C. Vann Woodward, *Origins of the New South: 1877–1913* (Baton Rouge, Louisiana State University Press, 1951). Woodward's title for chapter 14 is "Progressivism—For Whites Only."

Chapter 11   Love, Hate, Rape, Lynching: Rebecca Latimer Felton and the Gender Politics of Racial Violence

1. *Atlanta Constitution*, July 12, 1897; *Atlanta Journal*, July 12, 1897; *Atlanta Journal*, July 14, 1897. Reports of lynching for the alleged crime of rape were frequent. See also, *Atlanta Constitution* 15, July 25; 3, August 12, 1897; and *Atlanta Journal* 16, July 22; August 4, 1897.

2. *Atlanta Constitution*, July 25, 1897.

3. Ibid., July 28, 1897.

4. Ibid., August 3, 1897.

5. Ibid., July 2, 1897.

6. Ibid., August 1, 1897. For a further discussion of the issue by Bill Arp, see ibid., July 4, 1897.

7. On Rebecca Latimer Felton, see John E. Talinadge, *Rebecca Latimer Felton: Nine Stormy Decades* (Athens: University of Georgia Press, 1960); Josephine Bone Floyd, "Rebecca Latimer Felton: Political Independent," *Georgia Historical Quarterly* 30 (March 1946): 14–34, and "Rebecca Latimer Felton, Champion of Women's Rights," *Georgia Historical Quarterly* 30 (June 1946): 81–104.

8. As published in the *Macon Telegraph*, August 18, 1897. I cite the newspaper version of this speech because the various handwritten versions of the speech in her papers do not include the notorious sentence that made the speech so incendiary. Either the versions in her papers are not the version she gave at Tybee, or, more likely, she added the call for the lynching of black men in the heat of the delivery of the speech. See her speech, "Southern Women and Farm Life," Rebecca Latimer Felton Papers, Hargrett

Library, University of Georgia, Athens (hereafter, HL), reel no. 15. Here she discusses the "fear of outrage" but does not advocate lynching as the solution.

9. In her Tybee Island speech, Felton claimed to have read of fire lynchings in the press the week before; as the debate heated up, the number increased to six, and 18 months later she claimed it was seven; see *Atlanta Constitution*, December 22, 1898.

10. Ibid.

11. As reprinted in the *Macon Telegraph*, August 20, 1897.

12. Ibid.

13. Ibid.

14. Ibid.

15. For more on the "coming mothers of the white race," see "Duty of Mothers" and "The Duty and Obligation that Lies on Southern Women," in Felton Papers, HL, box 14, and "Mrs. Dr. W. H. Felton On Heredity" and "The Problems that Interest Mothers," in *Country Life in Georgia in the Days of My Youth*, Rebecca Latimer Felton (1919; reprint, New York, Arno Press, 1980), 264–270 and 279–284.

16. For some examples of the centrality of sexuality to Felton's reform proposals for white women, see "The Education of Veterans Daughters," "The Ladies of the Home Missionary Society," and "Rescue Work," in Felton Papers, III, box 15, and "The Industrial School For Girls," in Felton, *Country Life*, 270–272.

17. "Address Before the Georgia Legislature, November, 1901," in Felton, *Country Life*, 170–192.

18. "Mrs. Felton's Addresses to Farm Institutes in the Early Nineties," Felton Papers, III, box 15.

19. "Southern Chivalry: The Wife's Farm—The Husband's Pledge," Felton Papers, HL, reel no. 13.

20. For example, see Talmadge, *Rebecca Latimer Felton*, 125.

21. "Mrs. Dr. W. II. Felton on Heredity," in Felton, *Country Life*.

22. Felton, *Country Life*, 120.

23. Ibid.

24. Ibid., 93.

25. Ibid., 79.

26. See H. Leon Prather, *We Have Taken a City: The Wilmington Racial Massacre and Coup of 1898* (Cranbury, NJ, Associated University Presses, 1984), esp. 47–80, for the most complete discussion of Manly's editorial and the racial massacre that followed.

27. Ibid., 72–73.

28. Ibid., 68–69.

29. Ibid., 73.

30. "Mrs. Felton vs. Manly," Felton Papers, HL, reel no. 13.

31. "Grannis Answered: Mrs. WH Felton Pays Her Respects to a Slanderer," Felton Papers, III, reel no. 18.

32. Felton, *Country Life*, 171.

33. Rebecca Latimer Felton, *The Romantic Story of Georgia's Women* (Atlanta, Atlanta Georgian and Sunday American, 1930), 45.

ACKNOWLEDGMENTS

A book that is so long in the making incurs many debts. Debts to the institutions and granting agencies that supported it financially; debts to the libraries, archives, and historical societies that provided the very stuff that it was made out of; and, most importantly, debts to the colleagues, friends, and family, who listened; who agreed; who disagreed; and who in the process made it so much more than it ever would have been by my efforts alone. Indeed, although my friends and colleagues may think that I should take sole responsibility for this work, at least for all the errors of judgments it may contain, I am inclined to give credit to them as well. This book is so much the product of the larger workings of the profession, the end product of so many conference papers, so many journal articles, so many symposiums, it must surely reflect the contribution of all those reviewers, all those audiences, all those private and public conversations, some friendly and some not. I thank you all.

When I entered the historical profession as a graduate student in the mid-1970s, there was no field of gender studies and there was barely a field of women's history. I went to graduate school because I wanted to emancipate myself from gender, however inchoate my understanding of it may have been at the time. I certainly did not plan to spend all these years thinking and writing about how much it matters. Now I have along with this book a daughter, a young woman who is herself just setting out in the world. I dedicate this work to her, in the sincere hope that she will in her lifetime see the day when gender truly does not matter.

INDEX

Columbia, Missouri, *see also* University of
Missouri, Columbia: Civil War
memorial in, 109, 111, 214n41
Concannon, Elizabeth, 63
Confederacy: effects of defeat of, 85–6,
88–9; influence on culture, 105–6, 110,
214n41; motives for fighting, 89–90,
92, 196n23; opposition to memorials
of, 95–6; spies in St. Louis, 43, 45, 97;
sympathizers driven to join, 57–9;
women's support for, 12, 19–21, 28–9,
32–5, 87–8, 97, 197nn35,36, 198n46
Confederate dead, 98; Ku Klux Klan as
arisen, 92–3; Ladies Memorial
Associations caring for, 86, 99;
memorials to, 86, 99–100, 109, 211n1,
214n41
Confederate flags, controversy over,
105–8, 110, 214n41
Confederate Memorial Day, 86–7, 89, 109
Confederate Rock (Columbia, MO), 105,
211n1; controversy over, 95, 100–1,
107–9; dedication of, 99–100
Confederate Soldier's Home, 99, 211n1
Confederate sympathizers, *see* southern
sympathizers
convict lease system, 187
Cornwall, Susan, 23
"Cotton Mill Labor in Georgia"
(Felton), 136
"cult of domesticity," 11–12
Curtis, General, 41–3

Davis, Angela, 108
Davis, Caroline, 14–15
Davis, Susan Lawrence, 93
De Graffenried, Clare, 127, 129;
background of, 140–1, 221n39, 222n54;
vs. Felton 135–9, 139–40; goals of, 138,
141–2, 147–9; recommendations for
reform, 130–1, 146; truthfulness
attacked, 133–4
De Graffenried, William Kirkland, 140
De Graffenried Controversy, The, 127
Deloney, William, 22
Democrats, 26, 162–63
domestic corruption, of Union soldiers,
69, 77, 80–2
domestic influence, women's, 93–4, 153,
162; of Confederate sympathizers,

61–3; as political power, 26–7, 40–1; for
war effort, 29–30, 43–4
domestic reform, 224n82, 230n12
domestic sphere, 46, *see also* households:
black, 161, 230n18; care of dead in,
87–90; of Confederate sympathizers,
46, 48, 49, 61; government
intervention in, 130–1, 145–6, 160–1;
improved by labor reform, 137–8;
planter men not protecting, 172–3;
politics and, 37, 63, 89, 145; relation to
production sphere, 131, 147, 149, 159,
168, 170–2, 185; temperance work as,
144–5, 157–8; vs. public, 57–9; war
efforts as, 33–4, 153–4; women's focus
on, 152, 170–1
Douglass, Frederick, 17–18
draft, 26, 48

economy, 148, *see also* employment:
agriculture and, 20, 168, 172, 216n19,
229n4; Civil War's effects on, 22, 50–3,
86, 142–3, 153–4, 198n57, 226n14;
collapse of plantation-based, 20, 155;
of Confederate sympathizers, 54–7;
danger of pursuit of profit, 154–5,
158–9, 162, 170–3; effects of slavery in,
173, 197n32; racial repression in, 17, 179;
textile industry and, 119–20, 136–7,
144, 223n80; women's vulnerability to,
155, 158–60
education: calls for state intervention in,
146, 161; vs. child labor 130–1, 146–7;
Felton advocating, 167, 174, 184–6;
goals of, 147, 160, 189
emancipation, 27, 29–30, 104
Emancipation Proclamation, 18, 25–6
employment, 148, 216n19, 224n82, *see also*
textile industry: for men, 129–31, 135,
219n34; wages in, 220n36, 223n80; for
women, 118–21, 135–7, 140, 198n56,
220n36, 229n8; women needing, 154,
216n11; women's contribution to family
farms, 158–9, 168–72, 185

families, *see* domestic sphere; households
Felton, Rebecca Latimer, 7–8;
advocating suffrage for white
women, 161–2; background of, 152,
226n14; on black families, 161, 230n18;